EDEXCEL
BUSINESS STUDIES
for GCSE

- IAN MARCOUSÉ
- MICHELLE BILLINGTON
- LOUISE STUBBS

DL DYNAMIC LEARNING

HODDER EDUCATION
AN HACHETTE UK COMPANY

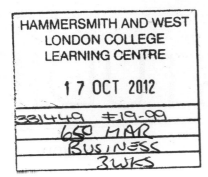
Orders: please contact Bookpoint Ltd, 130 Milton Park, Abingdon, Oxon OX14 4SB. Telephone: (44) 01235 827720. Fax: (44) 01235 400454. Lines are open 9.00 - 5.00, Monday to Saturday, with a 24-hour message answering service. You can also order through our website www.hoddereducation.co.uk.

British Library Cataloguing in Publication Data

A catalogue record for this title is available from the British Library

ISBN: 978 0 340 985830

First published 2009

Impression number   10 9 8 7 6 5 4

Year   2012 2011

Hachette UK's policy is to use papers that are natural, renewable and recyclable products and made from wood grown in sustainable forests. The logging and manufacturing processes are expected to conform to the environmental regulations of the country of origin.

Cover photo © PeskyMonkey/iStockphoto.com

Typeset by Servis Filmsetting Ltd, Stockport, Cheshire.

Illustrations by Oxford Designers and Illustrators and Barking Dog Art

Printed in Italy for Hodder Education, an Hachette UK company, 338 Euston Road, London NW1 3BH

Contents

SECTION 4

Making the Start-up Effective

SECTION 5

Understanding the Economic Context

SECTION 6

Marketing

SECTION 7

Meeting Customer Needs

SECTION 8

Effective Financial Management

SECTION 9

Effective People Management

SECTION 10

The Wider World

Using this book

Edexcel Business Studies for GCSE covers and fully supports the 'Introduction to Small Business' and 'Building a Business' units of the new Edexcel GCSE specification. It highlights why and how to show enterprise, how to turn an idea into a business reality and then the challenges that are part of developing from a small firm into a medium-sized company.

The book examines the amazing range of business start-ups, using the real stories of dozens of different companies as they make daily decisions that affect the lives of staff and customers.

It brings GCSE business to life for students, moving away from facts and jargon to cover the excitement of starting and running a small business. It focuses on enterprising people doing enterprising things. Most are in business to make money, but the book also looks at why and how people start social enterprises such as charities.

Edexcel Business Studies for GCSE looks at key issues in marketing, finance and the management of people and operations, and the way that businesses interact with their communities and the wider world. The units follow the logic of starting up and running a business, and its development and growth. Nevertheless, they are written to be self-contained, so unit 13 can be read before unit 12, if you wish.

Although the text celebrates people who have the courage and determination to take risks, it also makes clear the need to take care. Specific units highlight the importance of limited liability and the need for a serious approach to taxation and the legal framework of business. The book also emphasises the responsibilities of bosses when dealing with staff, the importance of ethics in business, and the potential effects of business practices on the environment.

The units highlight revision terms, pose questions about the text and present exam-style articles with questions. The units are organised into 10 sections:

1. Spotting a Business Opportunity

2. Showing Enterprise

3. Putting a Business Idea into Practice

4. Making the Start-up Effective

5. Understanding the Economic Context

6. Marketing

7. Meeting Customer Needs

8. Effective Financial Management

9. Effective People Management

10. The Wider World

Edexcel Business Studies for GCSE is written to match the GCSE course from Edexcel that has a strong focus on starting a small business. Most of the material, though, can be a huge help in developing skills needed for OCR and AQA exams. Nothing is more central to GCSE business than successful start-up.

Acknowledgements

Every effort has been made to trace and acknowledge ownership of copyright. The publishers will be glad to make suitable arrangements with any copyright holders whom it has not been possible to contact.

The author and publishers would like to thank the following for the use of photographs in this volume:

© Emrah Turudu/iStockphoto.com, p.1; With kind permission by Global Ethics Ltd, pgs. 3 & 5; © Janine Wiedel/Photofusion, p.19; © snappdragon / Alamy, p. 21; © mediablitzimages (uk) Limited / Alamy, p.25; With kind permission by Sam's Brasserie, p.27; © Natalya Korolevskaya – Fotolia.com, p.30; © T.M.O.Buildings / Alamy, p.39; © Murat Giray Kaya/iStockphoto.com, p.43; © PA Archive/PA Photos, p.46; © Canadian Press / Rex Features, p.48; © Jonathan Player / Rex Features, p.55; © Derek Hudson/Getty Images, p.58; © Sipa Press / Rex Features, p.58; © Michael Williams / Rex Features, p.60; With kind permission by Codemasters Software Co. Ltd, p.62; © Canadian Press / Rex Features, p.65; © Voisin/Phanie / Rex Features, p.68; © Arnold Slater / Rex Features, p.70; © UPPA/Photoshot, p.73; © AP/PA Photos, p.76; © Peter Dench/Corbis, p.78; © Skip ODonnell/IStockphoto.com, p.83; © Ronald Hudson – Fotolia.com, p.85; © UPPA/Photoshot, p.86; With kind permission by Scoop Gelato, p.88; © Andrew Bruce – Fotolia.com, p.91; © Alex Segre / Alamy, p.96; © Paul M Thompson / Alamy, p.108; © DWP – Fotolia.com, p.110; © ELEN – Fotolia.com, p.111; © Jonathan Hordle / Rex Features, p.117; © William Nicklin / Alamy, p.122; © Elnur Amikishiyev/iStockphoto.com , p.129; © Francesco Guidicini / Rex Features, p.130; © Igor Shootov – Fotolia.com, p.133; © Mike Marsland/WireImage, p.138; © Joanne Obrien / Photofusion, p.144; © Tom Jenkins/Guardian News & Media Ltd 2006, p.149; © Helene Rogers / Alamy, p.153; © Photo News / TopFoto, p.156; © Chloe Johnson / Alamy, p.159; With kind permission by Jagex Ltd., p.162; © Sipa Press / Rex Features, p.167; © iStockphoto.com, p.173; © mediablitzimages (uk) Limited / Alamy, p.182; © Action Press / Rex Features, p.186; © Konstantin Sutyagin – Fotolia.com, p.189; © Vladislav Gajic – Fotolia.com, p.195; © Rex Features, p.203; © PeteG – Fotolia.com, p.208; © Mike Booth / Alamy, p.209; © PA Archive/PA Photos, p.214; © Tjall – Fotolia.com, p.221; © Dan Sparham / Rex Features, p.222; Illustration by Dermot Flynnn / Dutch Uncle Agency / Photo by Andy Rudak @ Mark Gibson; courtesy of DDB London, p.230; @ Mark Henley/PANOS, p.239; @ Patrick Seeger / Photoshot, p.242; Zoe Ryan Starstock/Photoshot, p.245; PA Wire/PA Photos, p.248; Alex Segre / Rex Features, p.253; © World Pictures/ Photoshot, p.254; © James Steidl – Fotolia.com, p.261; Andrew Tobin/Scoopt/Getty Images, p.262; Daniel Berehulak/Getty Images, p.265; With kind permission by Eggxactly, p.266; With kind permission by Totseat, p.269; Jack Guez/AFP/Getty Images, p.271; Ian Gavan/ UPPA/Photoshot, p.276; With kind permission by Waterstones, p.280; Alexander Nemenov/ AFP/Getty Images, p.282; With kind permission by Plastic Logic GmbH, p.288; Talking Sport/Photoshot, p.289; © Dave Bartruff/Corbis, p.295; © endrille – Fotolia.com, p.303; PA

Archive/PA Photos, p.308; David Hartley / Rex Features, p.310; PA Archive/PA Photos, p.314; With kind permission by Metrow Foods, p.315; With kind permission by Tushingham Sails Ltd, p.316; © George Cairns / iStockphoto.com, p.322; © Jeffery Allan Salter/Corbis, p.325; With kind permission by Elle au Naturel, p.326; With kind permission by First Light Solutions, p.328; © Perrush – Fotolia.com, p.331; Photoshot, p.342; Richard Gardner / Rex Features, p.353; George Doyle / Stockbyte / Getty Images, p.354; © Roman Milert – Fotolia.com, p.363; Bob Hallinen/Anchorage Daily News/MCT/Photoshot, p.364; Graeme Robertson/Getty Images, p.366; Fairtrade Foundation, p.368; Facundo Arrizabalaga / Photoshot, p.371; Nicholas Bailey / Rex Features, p.375; With kind permission by www.labourbehindthelabel.org, p.378; With kind permission by War on Want, p.378, PA Archive/PA Photos, p.387

SPOTTING A BUSINESS OPPORTUNITY

An introduction to business enterprise

Business enterprise is about starting something of your own. It would most probably be a business, but it might be a charity, a pressure group or a sports club. The key is that *you* want to do it, and that it proves to be a success.

> '*Every teenager who wants to be an entrepreneur is a rescue from wanting to be on The X Factor or Big Brother.*'
> **Duncan Bannatyne, Dragon, *Dragons' Den***

After several years of talking about it, three young university graduates started up Innocent Drinks in 1999. They wanted their own business, to be able to do things their own way. Now it is Britain's market leader in fruit smoothies, with annual sales of over £35 million. Londoners are used to seeing its vans painted like cows, with a horn that moos. Innocent staff get a £2000 bonus for having a baby and can apply for a £1000 bonus to do something they have always dreamed of, such as travelling to Peru. Pepsi would pay a fortune to buy the business (easily £100 million), but the three founders like things just the way they are.

There are three main questions to ask about start-up:

1 Why?

2 Who?

3 How?

Why?

- The main motive for starting up something new is desire. People want satisfaction from a sense of achievement. If they could get it from their normal workplace, they might not bother. Terry

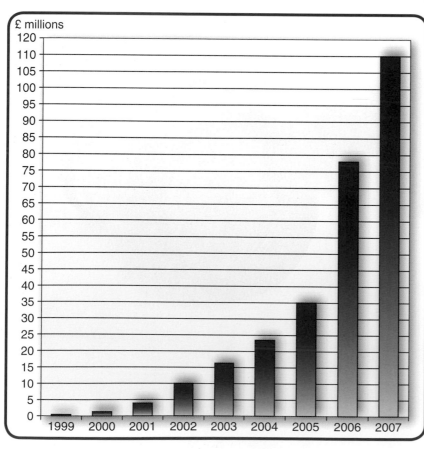

Annual sales 1999–2009, Innocent Drinks Ltd

Leahy, chief executive of Tesco, has become wealthy, famous and powerful from a life-time spent climbing the career ladder at one company. Many others find frustrations at work and want to break out, to give themselves a challenge.

- The next most important motivator is the wish to be your own boss. Independent decision making allows the individual to do things the way they think is best. Most jobs involve a degree of compromise. When you are running something for yourself you may not be able to afford the best, but at least you know that you will get the best you can afford. So the chef who hates working in a cramped kitchen with second-rate ingredients may long to be in a position to make all the decisions.

> 'We can spend our whole lives underachieving.'
> **Philip Crosby, quality guru**

- Then, of course, there is money. A person may start a burger bar because of the conviction that it will make a fortune. Such a person may dream of retiring early, with a beachfront house and a huge fridge packed with beer. The typical business to go for would be a franchise, in which the individual buys the rights to open a local branch of a business that already exists (and makes good profits). The Subway sandwich chain works in this way.

Who?

Successful start-up requires a huge list of qualities and skills, especially if starting up on your own. Among these are:

- personal qualities: determination; resilience (can bounce back from setbacks); enthusiasm; hard-working; decisive; willing to take risks.

- skills: can listen as well as speak; can plan and organise; can persuade; can manage others.

- resources: can find help when needed (finance or advice); may have exceptional knowledge of a special topic (e.g. building a website).

Of course, few entrepreneurs (business risk-takers) have *all* these qualities. But without quite a number of them, it will be hard to succeed.

> 'If you start off with a view to just making money, you'll probably make some, but you won't make a lot – you have to have a passion to succeed.'
> **Howard Hodgson, businessman**

How?

The most common way to start a new enterprise is to trial a business idea while still working, often from your own home. It is tried out in a limited way before committing too much money.

Duncan Goose, however, started One water as a social enterprise by giving up his regular job. It took him six months, without pay, to get the enterprise going. (The water is bottled

The profits from One water go to a water charity based in Africa

> 'A man is a success if he gets up in the morning and gets to bed at night, and in between he does what he wants to do.'
> **Bob Dylan, musician**

in Wales, sold throughout Britain and the profits go to a water charity based in Africa.)

When people need to raise capital to help them start a business, they write a business plan. This sets out the aims, the plan, the financial forecasts and financial requirements. If carried out professionally, a good business plan greatly increases the chances of getting funding. Crucial to a good business plan is a sensible sales forecast, based on independent market research.

Exercises

(A and B: 25 marks; 30 minutes)

A. Read the unit, then ask yourself:

1   Use the three points made under the heading 'Why?' to outline the motives of the graduates who started Innocent Drinks in 1999. (4)

2   Look at the bar chart on page 2. If Innocent Drinks' profit in 2007 was 20 per cent of its annual sales figure, how much profit did the business make? Show your workings. (3)

3   Explain why a younger person might prefer to start up a franchise rather than a wholly independent business. (4)

4   Without looking back at the text, briefly write down what you understand by the Why?, Who? and How? of starting a business. (4)

B.   Although 50 per cent of the working population are women, only 3.5 per cent of big business directors are women. And whereas 8 per cent of the UK population is non-white, only 1.5 per cent of big business directors are non-white. This may explain a huge amount of interest in business start-up among women and non-whites. Unfortunately, even then discrimination may apply. A recent survey showed that banks charge businesswomen a 1 per cent higher interest rate than businessmen.

1   Why might the figures 'explain a huge amount of interest in business start-up among women and non-whites'? (3)

2   How effective would you expect women to be at the business skills listed under the heading 'Who?' within the text? (3)

3   Outline two reasons why a bank might decide to charge businesswomen a higher rate of interest than men. (4)

Practice Questions

Bigger feet

A social enterprise

Duncan Goose was chatting in a pub with friends about how to make the world a better place. The idea emerged of a not-for-profit bottled water, in which all the surplus from trading would go to charity. Later, Duncan stumbled across the South African charity PlayPumps International. In summer 2004 he gave up his job to work, unpaid, on One water.

In parts of Africa, women walk several miles to a well, hand-pumping the water into flasks or plastic bottles, and then carry it home. PlayPumps International is a charity that provides villages with (free) water pumps, powered by children's roundabouts! The kids' energy in pushing the roundabout pumps water into a water tower. Then people can simply draw the water from a tap, instead of having to pump it themselves.

The bottling plant started operating in spring 2005, and One water started to be made available to shops in July. Since then, Duncan has achieved distribution in Morrisons, Waitrose, the Co-op and Total Garages. More importantly, over £1 million has been raised, which has financed more than 125 water round-abouts. For the first two years Duncan was unable to draw a salary. Now he can pay himself a small income and employ full-time staff. In 2008, sales of One water started to go global.

A play pump

Questions

(15 marks; 20 minutes)

1 Outline three qualities and/or skills shown by Duncan in founding One. (6)

2 Explain Duncan's motives in founding One. (4)

3 Discuss how Duncan could try to persuade teenagers to buy One water instead of the more familiar brands, such as Evian and Highland Spring. (5)

Understanding customer needs

There are really only three ways to start up a successful business:

1 Do something really new (and that people want).

2 Do something that already exists, but do it better.

3 Do something that already exists, but at lower cost.

All three rely on learning what people want and what they need, then combining this with a full understanding of what existing businesses are supplying. Any gap between what people want and what they currently get gives rise to an opportunity. Unfortunately, many gaps that look significant prove very hard to fill. One example is banking. A recent survey showed that 10 million people were dissatisfied with their current high street bank, yet few make a switch. Research might make a new bank account sound a winner, but customers might be too lazy to make the change.

> 'There's a gap in the market, but not a market in the gap.'
> **Peter Jones, Dragon, *Dragons' Den***

For a microbusiness

If the business is small, the owner does everything. S/he deals directly with customers and can therefore come to understand them fully. When prices rise, do customers notice, even grumble, or do they not really seem to care? The builder learns that customers get angrier about not sweeping up than serious building mistakes.

Good customer service is the key to success.

Yet plenty of small firms give poor service. There are bars where the staff are grumpy and shops that are dirty and messy. The bosses have forgotten that success comes from serving customers. At such places, the owner thinks that the world owes him or her a living; in fact, no business deserves to make a penny unless its staff are making an effort.

For a big business

Tesco plc has annual sales of £50 billion, with over 2000 stores, staffed by nearly 250,000 people. What chance is there that Tesco boss Terry Leahy will know all the customers' needs? In fact, he will know a great deal, because market research questionnaires will be recording what customers think and do. Beyond that, he will trust that local store managers understand their own area well enough to make good decisions. Part of Tesco's success has been that the company provides a wide range of products. The bargain-hungry shopper is satisfied, and so is the one looking for 'Tesco's Finest'. So Terry Leahy does not need to guess customer needs; he provides choice.

> 'An industry begins with customer needs, not with a patent, a raw material or a selling skill.'
> **Theodore Levitt, business thinker**

Market research

Collecting data

Many people starting their first business have a clear idea of the opportunity. They may be sure that 'everyone loves takeaway pizza'. This makes it important to check the facts. The starting point is **secondary research**. This means finding out data that already exists, i.e. second-hand information. Some of this is available free, by careful Googling or by visiting a public reference library.

In December 2008 Google could provide this secondary information about pizza takeaway:

● information from Key Note about the size of the pizza fast-food and delivery market in 2004 (£890million); this was available free, but 2008 figures were available only at a price of £1,500 (!) from Mintel

● newspaper reports explained that Dominos Pizza had enjoyed sales increases of 8.5% in its established stores in the 13 weeks to September 28th 2008. This showed that demand for pizza takeaways was holding up well during the 'Credit Crunch'.

In addition to research reports from Mintel and Key Note, government statistics are a useful (and free) source of secondary data. For instance, if you're thinking of opening a

kindergarten business, it's a great help to find out that the number of babies born in Britain rose by 14% between 2002 and 2007.

Having learned about the market background, it is time to consider **primary research**. This is first-hand research in which you find out the precise things you want to know from the people you need to talk to. When starting a business, the people you might want to talk to include:

● existing customers (currently buying from companies that will soon be your competitors)

● potential customers (those you might be able to persuade to buy for the first time)

● potential retailers (the shops that you hope will stock and sell your product)

The value of primary research is that it can tell you exactly what you need to know about your business. The problem, though, is that it is time-consuming and expensive to collect the data. For example, to find out whether your pizza should be priced at £9.99 or £12.99 might require interviewing more than 100 people. That takes time.

Qualitative and quantitative research

Primary research can be collected in two forms: qualitative and quantitative. **Qualitative research** is in-depth among relatively few people, but can provide insights that help a business make decisions. For example, a group of 8 people might be asked to discuss their pizza takeaway likes and dislikes. It might become clear that the most common complaint is about not knowing exactly when it will arrive – in which case this can become a major part of a new firm's advertising message: 'We'll deliver on time, every time'.

Quantitative research means collecting lots of answers to specific questions. Usually these questions are 'closed', meaning that the answers are limited to ticking a box such as 'Yes

– No' or 'Will definitely buy, will probably buy' etc. This type of research provides information such as that 20% of people like pineapple on pizza, but 80% do not. Quantitative research is usually gathered by interviewers using questionnaires, either in person or over the phone. Questionnaires can also be completed without an interviewer, e.g. on-line or by post.

Interpreting market research data

Research takes time and money to collect. The key to success, though, is to interpret its findings. With quantitative (Yes/No) research, it should be easy. There may be problems, though, in being sure that the figures mean what they say. For instance, one hundred people may say they prefer a thin base to their pizza, but can you be sure that the same is true of all pizza lovers?

Only if you are confident that the people who responded are typical of everyone can you be sure in the finding. If a young Bolton businesswoman asked 100 friends to fill in a questionnaire, the results only have meaning for young people in Bolton, not the whole market.

Qualitative research is even harder to interpret. If three or four people in a group discussion feel strongly about something, so what? For example, a few people may say they hate herbs on pizza. Should that be taken seriously?

Therefore market research findings are important and interesting, but need not always be taken seriously. A confident businessperson may be right to ignore some research findings, perhaps choosing to build a business that's a bit different and may not appeal to everyone's tastes.

Revision Essentials

Primary research – when a firm carries out first-hand research by field work, e.g. a questionnaire about customer perceptions of its products.

Qualitative research – in-depth research using depth interviews, used to find out customers' behaviour and attitudes.

Quantitative research – research involving large quantities of data, which allows statistical analysis of the results.

Secondary research – desk research; research that has been previously carried out or published for another body or purpose.

Exercises

(A and B: 25 marks; 30 minutes)

A. Read the unit, then ask yourself:

1 Explain why the boss of a small firm should find it easier to understand customer needs than the boss of a big firm. (3)

2 Outline two advantages to a firm of coming up with something really new, such as Maltesers (back in 1936). (4)

3 What problem might be caused for a firm that tries to improve profits by cutting prices? (2)

4 Outline the customer need that was met by: (4)

(a) McDonald's, started in America in 1954. (2)

(b) The teabag, first manufactured by Lipton in 1952. (2)

(c) Phones4U, started in 1996. (2)

B. On 29 June 2005 Sony announced the closure of one of its South Wales factories, with the loss of 650 jobs. The company explained that demand had slumped for 'fat telly' production, with flat screens accounting for 70 per cent of sales in Europe in 2005. These are produced by Sony in Spain. Sony was slow to see the customer demand for flat-screen TVs. Samsung dominates this relatively new sector.

1 Outline two ways in which Sony's managers should have known about customers' preference for flat-screen TVs. (3)

2 Do you think it is inevitable that factory workers suffer for the mistakes made by managers? (3)

3 Samsung outfought Sony by going for 'something really new' – the flat-screen TV. How might Sony respond in future? (3)

Practice Questions

EasyJet – soaring sales in hard times

August 2008 was a dreadful month for most businesses. With house prices down, but food and petrol prices up, consumers were cutting back. British Airways reported a fall in passenger numbers and Ryanair was struggling to make its low price message stick.

The summer winner proved to be easyJet. It flew 24 per cent more passengers in August 2008 than the 3.7 million it flew in the same month of 2007. Of course, in difficult financial times you can expect a low-cost airline to do well. But Ryanair (the cheapest airline of all) enjoyed only an 18 per cent sales boost in August 2008. So easyJet was the UK winner.

Nor is the explanation that easyJet opened up more routes. In August 2008 they sold 91.3 per cent of all available seats compared with 87.4 per cent in 2007.

So why easyJet rather than Ryanair? The answer lies in easyJet's better understanding of its customers. Ryanair thinks that all that people want is a cheap (and safe) flight. EasyJet is more aware of the other things passengers want, such as friendly service.

When flying, a great website to use is Skytrax. Passengers give ratings and comments about all the different airlines. Skytrax passengers give easyJet a 3-star rating (out of 5) and Ryanair 2 stars. Here are some of the comments made about the two airlines:

EasyJet customer comments, July 2008	Ryanair customer comments, July 2008
• 'New Airbus A319 very clean and relatively comfortable for the 1hr 10min flight. Departed to the minute. Cabin crew friendly and relaxed … couldn't ask more from a low-cost carrier' • 'Apart from the lousy boarding system the flights were perfect. Clean planes, on time'	• 'It is a low cost airline and provides low cost service … OK for short 45-minute flight, no good for any longer' • Carcassone – having checked in and been left standing at the departure gate for an hour, the 16.25 flight to Stansted was cancelled. Did Ryanair care? Not a bit … never again with an airline driven so much more by profit than customer care

Questions

(15 marks; 20 minutes)

1 Outline two ways in which easyJet seems to understand customer needs rather better than Ryanair. (4)

2 (a) How many passengers did easyJet fly in August 2008? (3)

 (b) If, on average, each passenger spent £80 with easyJet, what was the total revenue generated in August 2008? (2)

3 Which category do you think easyJet comes into: 'Do something really new'; 'Do something that already exists but do it better'; 'Do something that already exists but at a lower cost'? Explain your answer. (6)

Customer demand

Demand is the quantity of a product that customers want to buy. Of course, we may all *want* a brand new BMW, but not be able to afford one. For demand to be meaningful, it has to be backed up by the ability to pay. This is known as **effective demand**.

> 'You can hype a questionable product for a little while, but you'll never build an enduring business.'
> **Victor Kiam, chief executive, Remington**

Demand for bottles of Danone's brand Actimel depends on a number of factors:

1. The price of Actimel.

2. The price of rival brands, such as Yakult.

3. Fashion and taste. (Are consumers trying to spend money on their health?)

4. How easy is it to find and buy? (Distribution and display)

5. How well promoted is it? (The level and quality of advertising spending)

In the vast majority of cases, higher prices push demand down. A price increase for Pepsi would cut demand, especially if it made it more expensive than Coke. Price increases encourage customers to look for cheaper substitutes; and also may push products out of people's price range. As the graph shows, not all Chelsea supporters have a high enough income to spend £800+ on a season ticket. So the **demand curve** slopes downwards: the higher the price, the lower the demand.

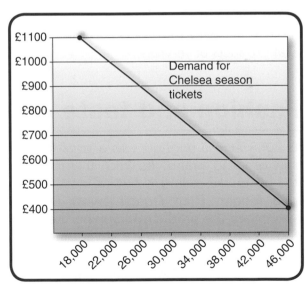

Demand for Chelsea season tickets

The price

The price of a product or service is a key influence on the level of demand. Occasionally a company may charge too low a price; customers may lose confidence and go elsewhere. A wedding dress for £99.99 might not win hearts and minds.

The price of rival brands

Although a Chelsea supporter would not switch to Crystal Palace just because of cheaper tickets, sales of *The Times* newspaper

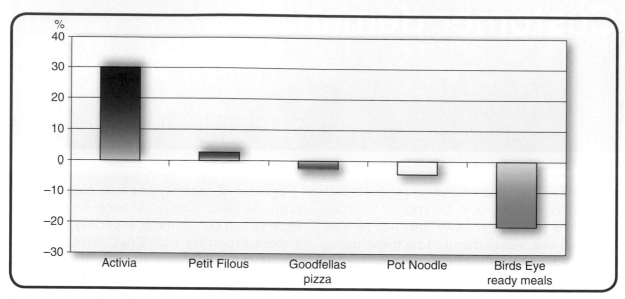

Percentage sales change 2007 compared with 2006 (Source: Nielsen figures quoted in *The Grocer*, 15 December 2007)

doubled between 1995 and 2005. During that whole period the price of *The Times* was cut far below that of its main rivals. So even if you leave your own price the same, sales could suffer because of a cut in the price of rival products or services.

Fashion and taste

In 2005 Activia yoghurt was a small-selling, slow-growing brand. Its 'bio' theme made it a bit quirky, ruling it out of most house-hold fridges. Then French owner Danone relaunched the product, scrapping the word 'bio'. It began an expensive advertising cam-paign based around 30-something women talking about 'that bloated feeling'.

The Activia advertising fitted into a time when people were thinking more and more about eating healthily. Sales shot ahead, from £28 million in 2004 to £117 million in 2007. While products such as Wall's Magnum and Coca-Cola were struggling, Activia was at the height of food fashion.

How easy is it to find and buy?

Small new brands from small producers can find it very hard to gain shelf space. Supermarkets stock thousands of profitable products, and are unlikely to take a profit-maker off the shelf to test out a newcomer. Major producers such as Danone (Actimel) or Müller (Vitality) have no such problem. Retailers such as Tesco are willing to test out new things, especially if there is the promise that the new product will be backed by extensive advertising.

How well promoted is it?

Three forms of promotion prove the most important:

1. Packaging gives the opportunity to create an image and help repeat-pur-chasers to find the product next time.

2 Advertising is the other image creator. Actimel has been styled as a product for young, active adults who want to boost their health and their enjoyment of life.

3 Sales promotion can boost short-term sales (e.g. offering trial packs at special prices).

In addition to the quality of promotion comes the quantity. In 2001 Danone spent £8 million advertising Actimel, at a time when sales were £24 million. So one-third of the sales revenue was spent on advertising, which was a remarkably heavy investment in the brand.

For individual products, other important influences on demand include:

- seasonality (e.g. toys in December and sunscreens in July and August).

- the weather: umbrellas, ice creams, roofing and fencing (sales of the latter jump after high winds).

> *'Brand loyalty is very much like an onion. It has layers and a core. The core is the user who will stick by your brand until the very end.'*
> **Chief executive, Procter & Gamble**

Product trial and repeat purchase

Demand is a function of getting people to try, then getting them to stay. In other words, product trial and **repeat purchase**. In most cases, advertising is the method to obtain trial, with the qualities of the product being relied on to achieve a high level of repeat purchase. The weakness of this approach is that advertising is an expensive way to get customers to try; and there is a risk of losing them if the image is not right for repeat purchase.

Successful products need to stand out.

Many new products flop when people drift away once the advertising stops. Producers have to make their brands strong enough to keep selling, even when advertising drops back. This has proved true for the Mars product Celebrations (sales are stable at about £75 million a year), though many other chocolate products struggle to keep selling beyond the trial stage.

Achieving repeat purchase requires not only a good quality product, but also distinctiveness. In other words, the product needs to stand out. Tango is a good quality sparkling orange drink, but unless it is advertised heavily, customers drift back to Fanta. Producers of toilet tissue suffer the same problem when up against Andrex, the dominant brand.

> *'Profit in business comes from repeat customers, customers that boast about your product and service, and that bring friends with them.'*
> **W. Edwards Deming, business guru**

Products such as cars and wedding dresses are bought infrequently – so repeat purchase is less important. For lower-priced, frequent purchases, such as chocolate bars or toilet rolls, long-term success relies hugely on brand loyalty and therefore repeat business.

Revision Essentials

Demand curve – the downward sloping line drawn to show how falling prices lead to rising sales (the 'curve' may be a straight line).

Effective demand – demand backed by the ability to pay.

Repeat purchase – customer loyalty reflected in regular purchasing.

Exercises

(A and B: 30 marks; 35 minutes)

A. Read the unit, then ask yourself:

1 Explain why demand might not be effective. (3)

2 (a) Draw a demand curve using this data for airline tickets from Manchester to Barcelona. (5)

Price	Demand (passengers per flight)
£140	55
£120	80
£100	105
£80	130
£60	155
£40	180

(b) Calculate how much money would be generated by charging £140 per ticket. (2)

(c) Calculate the selling price that generates the most money per flight. (4)

3 Identify two ways to improve the rate of repeat purchase for:

(a) L'Oréal hair colour products. (2)

(b) Sony PlayStation software. (2)

B. Each year Mars sells more than £125 million worth of Maltesers in Britain. The brand is 70 years old, but sales are still rising! The product is quite successful in other countries, but the British are the biggest Maltesers-eaters by far. Sales of Maltesers are more than twice those of Cadbury Flake.

1   Which two factors do you think are the main reasons for the high demand for Maltesers in Britain? Explain your reasons for each factor. (6)

2   Explain how Cadbury might try to boost sales of Flake:

(a) Over the next month. (3)

(b) Over the next two to three years. (3)

Practice Questions

Between 1997 and 2005, Sony dominated computer games. The Playstation (PS) 2 outsold Microsoft's X-Box by 5 to 1. In the lead-up to Christmas 2005, Sony's great concern was that the new X-Box 360 would gain an unstoppable market lead before Sony could launch its PS3.

In fact Sony was looking in the wrong direction. Instead of looking at American Microsoft, it should have been looking down the road, at Japanese Nintendo. The PS3 has struggled to make a real impact because Nintendo's Wii has been an unstoppable success. Its combination of being more fun to use and offering a wider variety of games has made it very hard to catch. Unusually, these benefits have been combined with a much lower price tag than the PS3.

Fortunately for Sony, the big money in consoles is in the games. In 2008, Sony's PS2 sold 140 million games – worth more than £3000 million. But this income will eventually dry up if the Wii continues to be the clear world number one.

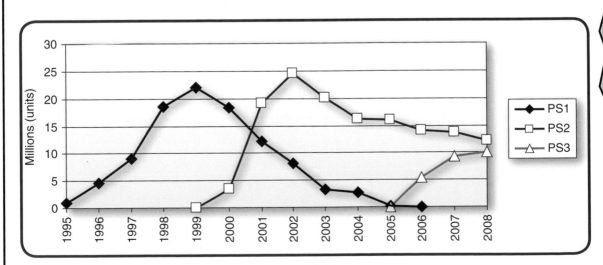

Annual worldwide sales of Sony PS1, PS2 and PS3

Questions

(25 marks; 25 minutes)

1 Explain the likely impact of seasonality upon sales of games consoles such as PS3. (3)

2 'Every boy in America wants a PlayStation this Christmas', said a Sony website in the 1990s. What might stop that demand turning into sales? (3)

3 (a) Look carefully at the graph. In the best sales year for each of the PS1 and PS2, how many extra PS2s were sold compared with PS1s? Show your workings. (3)

  (b) In 2004/5 Sony launched the portable PSP. Outline the evidence from the text and graph that Sony should really have been launching the PS3 at that time. (6)

4 Discuss what Sony needs to do to make its PS3 more successful than the Nintendo Wii. (10)

Market mapping

Years ago, the secret to business success was price competition. Spot a successful business, copy its idea and offer the same thing, but cheaper. Pepsi did this with Coke; Wrangler did it with Levi's; and supermarkets do it all the time with own-label versions of new products.

To a certain extent it still happens, but within a careful attempt at mapping the market. This means setting out the key features of the market on a diagram, then plotting where each brand fits in. For example, in the chocolate market, key features include:

- luxury versus everyday eating (e.g. Flake versus Dairy Milk);

- filling versus light (e.g. Snickers versus Maltesers).

A **market map** based on this idea would look like the diagram which follows.

A business such as Cadbury would spend a substantial sum each year (perhaps £100,000) gaining the **market research** evidence to get this market map right. In other words, it would usually be based on the opinions of thousands of customers. Armed with this information, a decision could be taken, such as to work on a new product that has a luxury feel *and* is filling. In the recent past, Cadbury has tried a praline chocolate bar to fill this gap in the market; but no one has launched a brand successfully.

The idea of market mapping is to identify gaps, to show where a sector is overcrowded, and to stop a producer becoming over-reliant on one sector. Mars is very strong in the filling, everyday sector (Twix, Mars and Snickers), but this is a declining sector, as people worry about their weight. So the 1990s launch by Mars of Celebrations was a very clever move.

For most businesses, the difficulty is in identifying the key factors to use in the mapping exercise. These might include:

- high-priced/low-priced;

- for the young/for the old;

- modern/traditional;

- for men/for women.

Companies decide on the 'right' factors after careful market research. Talking to customers may show that young and old have

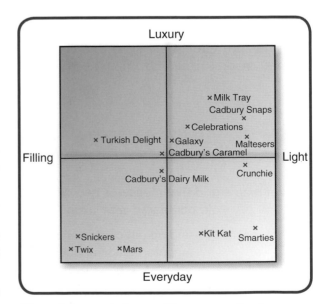

Chocolate market map (Source: author's estimates)

The everyday sector of the chocolate market is declining as people worry about their weight.

Talking Point

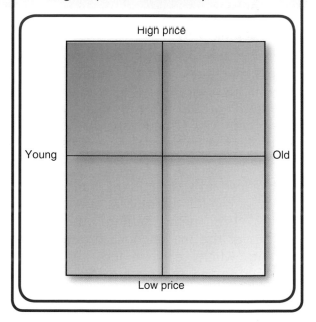

Where do these fit on the market map?
- Nintendo Wii (in the games console market)
- Jaguar (in the car market).

similar views about chocolate, whereas men and women think differently.

Market mapping is also very useful for a new small business, for example in building services. A good look through the Thomson Local directory may show lots of emergency plumbers, but few offering to fit luxury bathroom suites.

Of course, there remains a potential problem. Perhaps there is a gap because there is no effective demand locally. So further market research may need to be carried out. The fact that market mapping is not a magic solution should not stop it being used. All business decisions require thought; no single method provides guaranteed success.

Revision Essentials

Market map – grid that measures two different aspects of the brands within a market (e.g. young/old compared with luxury/economy).

Market research – finding out customer opinions and actions, usually by interviews and by gathering information about sales.

Exercises

(A and B: 20 marks; 25 minutes)

A. Read the unit, then ask yourself:

1   Suggest two reasons why it may no longer be enough to produce cheaper copies of product ideas. (2)

2   Explain why it suggests in the text that 'the 1990s launch by Mars of Celebrations was a very clever move'. (4)

3   (a) Look carefully at the chocolate market map. Identify two possible market opportunities for a new company entering the market. (2)

   (b) For one of those market opportunities, outline a product that you think might appeal to consumers. Suggest a price that you think would be appropriate. (5)

B.   For her recent GCSE project, Aliesha drew up a market map of her local area (Brixton, South London). She identified that there were many takeaways and cafes offering Caribbean food, but nowhere offering a smarter restaurant for special occasions. Her market research showed that 32 per cent of adults locally thought they would go to a smart Caribbean restaurant at least once a year. Aliesha was able to show that this business could be very profitable.

Brixton, South London

1   Outline one way in which Aliesha might have carried out her market research. (3)

2   Construct a market map for takeaways and fast-food outlets in your local area. Use as the scales: 1. expensive–cheap; 2. for young people–for older people. (5)

Practice Questions

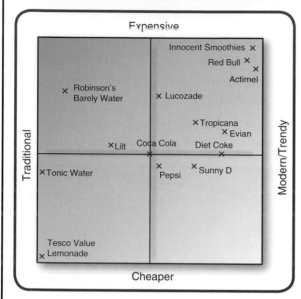

Soft drinks market map

Between 2004 and 2008 the market for soft drinks has been transformed. In the past, soft drinks were targeted mainly at children. Fizzy drinks dominated, especially colas and lemonades. Huge social transformations have changed that. The big sales successes of recent years have been:

- Probiotic drinks, such as Yakult and Actimel.

- Red Bull and other energy drinks.

- Fruit smoothies, selling at £1.50 to £2 for a small bottle.

- Bottled water, especially brands such as Evian.

The market for colas remains huge – especially for diet varieties – but the rising stars are more adult-orientated. The soft drinks market map shows that although there are thousands of brands, there still seem to be large gaps.

Questions

(20 marks; 25 minutes)

1 (a) Explain two benefits a soft drinks firm might gain from studying a market map. (4)

  (b) In this case, outline two conclusions Coca-Cola might reach from the soft drinks market map. (4)

2 Suggest two reasons why adults may be more interested in soft drinks nowadays. (4)

3 Discuss how a company might deal with a brand for which sales are falling, such as Lucozade. (8)

Competition – role and limitations

In 1981, when you moved into a new house you did not phone everyone to tell them. You did not have a phone. You applied to British Telecom (BT) to get a line for a phone. It took between one and three months. Within five years the position was transformed. For the first time, the government allowed competitors to enter the market for phones. BT quickly responded by speeding up their services and increasing choice. The arrival of competition improved things for the customer.

> 'Competition generates energy, rewards winners and punishes losers. It is therefore the fuel for the economy.'
> **Charles Handy, business guru**

Competition is often the biggest headache for a new, small business. The business may identify a profitable market gap, but what if another firm arrives at the same time as you? Instead of being the only Thai restaurant in the village, there may be two – both half empty. Even if you get there first, your success may simply attract copycats.

This is why starting a business requires self-confidence and a willingness to take risks. Competitors may arrive early, making it very difficult, but they may not. It took British Airways four years to respond to easyJet's introduction of online booking for aircraft seats. In the meantime easyJet built up its profitability so that price-cutting by British Airways was no longer a serious threat.

EasyJet built up its business by offering online booking

Benefits of competition to consumers

Benefits include:

- firms are forced to offer good products and a good service.

- firms are forced to keep prices down.

- in order to break away from fierce price competition, firms will try to bring in new, **innovative** products or services.

These consumer benefits place firms under constant pressure. A bright new idea will soon be copied by rivals. A profitable service may be undermined by price-cutting. This is clearly the case in businesses such as pizza delivery, where one firm's 'buy one get one free' is quickly matched by rival offers.

Drawbacks to competition

Competition can force businesses to do things they would prefer to avoid. With high rents, city-centre bars have to get good trade on Fridays and Saturdays. If your rivals have special deals or 'drink as much as you like for £10' offers, you join in or close down. Similarly, if other banks have relocated their customer call centres to India, you may feel that you have to cut your own bank's costs by following them.

Fierce competition may force firms to:

- cut costs by cutting staff – bad for the staff and perhaps bad for customers.
- take short-term action, such as price-cutting, that may damage the long-term health of the business.
- adopt **unethical** practices, such as dumping waste materials or injecting water into meat (bacon often has 15 per cent extra water pumped into it, to make it easier to charge a price that customers think is good value for money).

One pizza delivery firm's 'buy one get one free' is quickly matched by rival offers

The pressure itself is a good thing. It stops anyone getting complacent. If a football team is so wealthy and dominant that it wins matches and trophies without playing well, the outcome is bad for everyone.

> 'Competition brings out the best in products and the worst in people.'
> **David Sarnoff, former president, RCA**

Revision Essentials

Innovative – a new, perhaps original, product or process.

Unethical – an action or decision that is wrong from a moral standpoint.

Exercises

(15 marks; 15 minutes)

A. Read the unit, then ask yourself:

1 Identify two methods a new business might use to break into a competitive market. (2)

2 (a) Explain why shoppers might benefit if a new supermarket chain arrived to challenge Tesco's number one position in the UK. (3)

   (b) Outline two possible drawbacks to Tesco's shop-floor staff if a fierce competitor arrived. (4)

3 (a) Why might it be unethical for a bar to run an offer such as 'drink as much as you like for £10'? (3)

   (b) Why might competition force a bar to run such an offer anyway? (3)

Practice Questions

In May 2004 Wizz Air flew its first flight from Poland to London. Based upon the ideas of Ryanair and easyJet, it was Central and Eastern Europe's first low-cost airline. Cleverly financed, it operates new Airbus planes, but to secondary airports such as Luton and Liverpool rather than Heathrow or Manchester.

Within 11 months Wizz had flown 1 million passengers and by September 2007 the figure was up to 4.5 million. Wizz operates very full aircraft and is already profitable. By March 2008, Wizz had 19 Airbus planes, with 80 more on order. If you want a trip to (beautiful) Budapest, it will cost about £3.20 one way, as long as you book a few months ahead. When booking only a day or two ahead, the price is more like £75.

Wizz has had an immediate impact upon airlines such as British Airways and the Polish airline LOT. Before Wizz, a late-booked return trip from London to Warsaw cost over £500. Today BA charges £170 – but it would be £110 on Wizz.

(Source: www.wizzair.com)

Questions

(20 marks; 25 minutes)

1 Outline three ways travellers to Poland could benefit from the arrival of Wizz Air. (6)

2 In the short term Wizz is succeeding because it is the only substantial low-cost airline in Central and Eastern Europe. Outline two problems it may face when new airlines open up. (4)

3 (a) It took 11 months for Wizz to fly its first million passengers and by 2007 it was flying 4.5 million a year. Identify three things that may have led to this rise in sales. (3)

   (b) Discuss whether it would be unethical for Wizz to deliberately undercut the prices of LOT, with the intention of driving LOT out of business. (7)

Analysing competitor strengths and weaknesses

To start a business successfully you need to know where and how to fit into the market. In 2008 any business trying to launch an MP3 player had to acknowledge that iPod held the centre of the market. Its mixture of 'cool' and 'must-have' gave it a 70 per cent **market share**. For a new company, the strength of the iPod meant either giving up or finding small weaknesses that could provide small opportunities. For a new, small business, as for Sony or Samsung, the starting point was to look carefully at the iPod.

Analysing something means breaking it down into its component parts. Yes, iPod users love their iPods; but do they like everything about them? And what if the same person has an iPod and a Nokia and a Sony PSP? They might love them all, but find it irritating to carry them all round at the same time. So it is vital to study the strengths and weaknesses of competitors.

How to carry out the analysis

There are three ways to analyse the competition:

1 Customer research.

2 Retailer research.

3 Breaking the product/service down.

Customer research

Customer research is one way to analyse the competition

Get groups of consumers talking about how, when and why they use the rival product or service; what exactly their experience has been, before and after buying; and whether they would buy the same thing again – and if not, why not? Before Sammi Garnett started up an Italian restaurant in Northampton, she and her boyfriend simply asked around at pubs in the town for views of the existing places to eat. She learnt that nowhere offered a good deal for office parties of eight or more people, and chose to make that a feature of her restaurant. It proved very successful, providing 25 per cent of all her business.

Retailer research

Your competitors may be loved by the public, but hated by the trade (i.e. the wholesalers and retailers who distribute the product). The supplier of Indian ready meals to Morrisons may sometimes deliver late or send the wrong quantities. This could be a golden opportunity to break into a market. So a food producer may decide to change its plan for a new range of Italian meals, and focus on Indian instead.

Talking Point

You're thinking of opening a fashion shoe shop next to a big Asda store. What analysis should you carry out on your huge competitor?

Breaking the product/service down

When a new iPod is launched, the first buyer is likely to be the big rival, Sony. Its engineers take the iPod apart to identify exactly what is inside and to analyse how the product has been made. They want to know if a corner has been cut, creating some possibility that Sony could offer better sound or faster downloading. James Dyson started his huge business by taking apart a Hoover vacuum cleaner and seeing that he could come up with a better way to sweep carpets.

What conclusions can be drawn?

To start up successfully, you need to know as much as possible about the market, the customers and the competitors. Having done that, you can make some decisions. Ferrero is a huge chocolate producer in Italy (and has worldwide brand successes such as Tic Tacs,

Ferrero Rocher chose to avoid head-on competition with Cadbury

Ferrero Rocher and Nutella chocolate spread). Its company motto is 'Be unique. Never copy'. When it came to Britain it assessed the strength of Cadbury and decided not to fight it. Instead it launched brands such as the Kinder Egg, Kinder Bueno and, of course, Ferrero Rocher. They are all successful, but none of them offers straightforward chocolate – because that is Cadbury's strength.

So Ferrero decided to avoid head-on competition. It found ways to appeal to **market segments**, such as children. In other cases, the decision may lead to a much more direct approach. Anyone analysing the UK market for women's clothing between 1998 and 2008 has spotted weaknesses at Marks and Spencer. Some, such as Matalan and Primark, decided prices were far too high. Others, such as Zara and Topshop, decided the clothes were too old-fashioned, and that M&S reacted far too slowly to fashion changes. So both developed an approach based upon speed: quickly turning new catwalk styles into ready-to-buy clothes.

For a new business starting up locally, careful analysis of the local competition is a must. If all the rivals are really strong, you may decide not to start up at all. Unless you know how you can be better, you should not risk your money. Usually, though, businesses are far from perfect. The small grocer may be cramped and unfriendly. The cinema may have one screen and be uncomfort- able. If you can build your strength on your competitor's weakness, the result should be successful.

Revision Essentials

Market segments – sections of a market focused upon specific types of customer, such as children.

Market share – one brand's sales as a percentage of all the sales in the market.

Exercises

(20 marks; 25 minutes)

Read the unit, then ask yourself:

1   Outline two business benefits from holding a 70 per cent share of a market. (4)

2   If you were about to start up a business selling packets of home-made fudge, what might you learn from retailer research? Outline two ideas. (4)

3   Discuss the value of Ferrero's motto ('Be unique. Never copy') when competing with other firms. (6)

4   Explain why a large firm such as Ferrero might decide to avoid head-on competition with another large firm such as Cadbury. (6)

Practice Questions

In August 2005 Sam Harrison opened Sam's Brasserie and Bar in Chiswick, west London. He had been working on plans to start his own business for several years, since returning to England from two years working in different restaurants in Australia.

Sam's idea for a restaurant came from looking at the competition. He looked at what was available in the area and then set about trying to offer something differ- ent in terms of style and personality. The brasserie & bar is open all day and the

style is relaxed, so people come and go when they want to.

This idea proved a great success. Within a month of opening, customer numbers were 1000 a week, with an average spend of £35 per person. This revenue was much higher than expected, which meant that the business moved into profit quickly. In 2006 Sam's Brasserie won the *Time Out* Best Local Restaurant, and in 2008 the *Evening Standard*'s award for London's Best Value Restaurant. At the end of 2007, Sam opened another brasserie in Balham, south-west London.

Sam's Brasserie (http//www.samsbrasserie.co.uk/contact.aspx)

Questions

(20 marks; 25 minutes)

1 (a) Explain the weakness that Sam identified among his competitors. (3)

   (b) How did his plans turn this weakness into a strength for his own business? (3)

2 Sam says, 'We need to continue to build this business and work hard to keep the customers coming'. Outline three factors that are likely to be important for Sam's Brasserie to keep getting repeat business. (6)

3 (a) If sales continued at the rate mentioned in the text, what was the annual revenue from Sam's first year in business? (3)

   (b) Outline the costs that Sam will have to allow for before he can calculate the profit generated by the business. (5)

Understanding the need to add value

Many shops sell Walkers crisps at 35p per pack. The pack weighs 30 g, which is about 1p of potatoes. In the pack is oil, salt and flavouring, but even adding in the cost of the packaging, the total cost per unit could not be more than 3p. So turning potatoes into crisps adds value. It 'creates' value by making the customer willing to pay extra. In the case of crisps, turning 3p into 35p adds 1100 per cent to the value of the potato (33/3 x 100). That's good business.

> 'The real issue is value, not price.'
> **Robert Lindgren,** *Harvard Business Review*

Is **adding value** a rip-off? Not necessarily. A sandwich sold for £1.50 may contain ingredients costing 40p. So the baker is receiving £1.10 for two slices of bread. Assuming 20 slices in a loaf, that's selling a loaf of bread for £11 instead of £1. Yet when people are going out, they do not want to have to take butter, cheese, tomato and a knife with them. They would rather buy a sandwich. They are happy to pay for speed and convenience.

How to add value

Added value is the difference between the cost of materials and the selling price. Value can be added either by pushing the price up or by cutting the costs. Usually it is by adding in a feature that makes the item more valuable to the customer. That enables the price to be increased.

A sandwich is more than its ingredients – it has added value

Different ways to make the item more valuable to the customer are:

● **convenience and speed:** in Britain, most people will pay extra to save their own time, as shown in the table below.

Adding value by adding convenience

Chicken curry and rice	Price per person (£)
Cook your own	1.00
Add Sharwood's bottle sauce to chicken	1.25
Buy supermarket ready meal	2.50
Buy takeaway	3.50
Go to restaurant	4.75

- **good design:** a beautifully designed dress might sell for £200, while one using exactly the same quantity of material might sell for just £20.

- **high quality manufacture or service:** a Lexus sells at £50,000 because it is regarded as one of the best-made cars in the world; it never breaks down and is like sitting in a huge leather armchair.

- **the brand name:** a Nike swoosh adds tens of pounds to the 'value' of a pair of trainers; a Mercedes badge on the front of a car adds thousands of pounds to the value of a new car; cleverly, the 1999 start-up of Innocent Drinks quickly established this brand name as an indication of quality, freshness and originality.

- **a unique feature:** a USP, or **unique selling point**, is something that makes the product worth paying extra for (e.g. a family car with flat-screen TVs and headphones in the back of the front passenger seat).

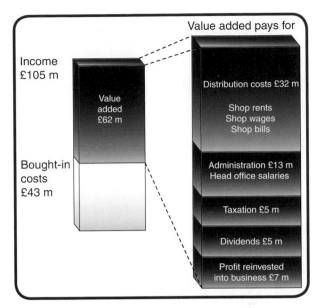

What the value added pays for: Ted Baker

Talking Point

How could you add value to a white t-shirt?

The importance of value added

People starting businesses often forget about the everyday costs. There are obvious ones such as electricity and phones, but also others such as the cost of 'wastage' (theft plus damaged goods), or the cost of recruiting and training new staff. All these costs have to be paid for out of the value added. So there needs to be a big enough difference between price and bought-in costs to allow internal costs to be paid for. The fashion clothing company Ted Baker adds £62 million of value to its £43 million of bought-in costs (such as clothes made by outside suppliers). The diagram above shows that the shareholders receive £5 million of the value added; the rest is spent within the business or paid in tax to the government.

As the diagram shows, value added is a necessity in business, not a luxury. Value added pays the wages, pays the bills and generates the profit needed to finance future growth. When starting up, every firm needs to think hard about whether the business idea adds enough value to be profitable. These are some business ideas that may have a market, yet do not have enough value added to be worthwhile:

- hand-washing cars;

- a dog-walking service;

- home-tutoring students on a one-to-one basis.

Good businesspeople recognise that high value added comes from clever ideas, presented well and delivered efficiently. That, in turn, makes it possible to run a sustainable, profitable business.

> *'What we obtain too cheap we esteem too little; it is dearness only that gives everything its value.'*
> **Thomas Paine, eighteenth-century political thinker**

> *'Consumers buy products, but they choose brands.'*
> **Procter & Gamble saying, from 'P&G 99'**

Revision Essentials

Adding value – creating something of a higher value to a customer than its bought-in costs.

Unique selling point – a feature of a product or service that is not shared by any competitor.

Exercises

(A and B: 25 marks; 30 minutes)

A. Read the unit, then ask yourself:

1   Why do staff rely on the business's skill at adding value? (2)

2   Briefly explain the sources of the added value in these cases:

   (a) A £4 box of Celebrations chocolates. (3)

   (b) A £48 ticket to see Chelsea play Newcastle. (3)

   (c) A £2 cup of coffee at Starbucks. (3)

3   Identify the USP that each of these firms is keen to establish:

   (a) Ryanair (1)

   (b) L'Oréal (1)

4   What might be the consequences of Ted Baker deciding to increase value added by cutting its £43 million spending on the clothes it buys in from suppliers? (4)

B. The Oban Chocolate Company began in November 2003, backed by £9500 of funding from a local Scottish Islands enterprise agency. At their shop, cafe and factory premises in Oban, Helen Miller and Stewart MacKechnie make hand-made chocolates in the basement for sale upstairs. Good quality chocolate is not cheap, but by making fancy, unusual products, such as 'hot chilli truffles', value is added. Visitors also get a whole experience, including a visit downstairs to see the chocs being made. The problem,

Hand-made chocolates

potentially, is that depending on tourists may mean very little trade in six to eight months of the year.

1 High value added is great for a business, but only if sales volumes are also high.

 (a) Why may the Oban Chocolate Company have a problem? (4)

 (b) What might they try to do to increase their sales volumes? (4)

Practice Questions

Callum and Jamie were bored with work. Both 21 years old, they had trained as plumbers, but it was getting dull working for British Gas. Jamie heard at a pub that there was a Snack Wagon for sale – fully equipped with gas, electricity and a fridge. Within three days they had found £3000 each to buy the van. Their plan was to place the van permanently on a busy road between Wimbledon and Croydon, then employ someone to do the cooking. Callum and Jamie's role would be to keep the van supplied and to make key decisions such as pricing.

The pricing decisions were largely drawn from their experience of local snack bars: teas and Cokes at around 60p, big burgers at about £1.50 and just the occasional item rising above £2. They were able to set down a few details, as shown in the table above.

In addition to these costs, there would be overhead costs such as rent, energy and labour costs. They allowed £350 per week for these. They served their first burgers in April and by October were making a modest profit. That same month they sold the business for £10,000. They had decided it was time to move out to Spain, to make a living from plumbing, and later to start up another business.

Item	Components	Bought-in costs per unit	Selling price
Cup of tea	Bag, milk, sugar, plastic cup, spoon	8p	60p
Burger	Frozen hamburger, onions, bun, ketchup, paper napkins	25p	£1.50
Chips	Frozen chips, oil, paper cone, salt	15p	£1.00

Questions

(20 marks; 25 minutes)

1 How can a good location add value to a business such as Callum and Jamie's? (4)

2 (a) How much value is added by making a cup of tea on this Snack Wagon? (2)

 (b) Why would it be wrong to call this value added figure 'profit'? (4)

3 Outline two ways in which Callum and Jamie might have added more value to their snack bar, enabling the business to be more profitable. (4)

4 Discuss the limits to ever-greater added value, in a business such as this Snack Wagon. (6)

Assessing a franchise opportunity

When you have set up a business successfully in one location, the race is on to do the same elsewhere. If you do not 'copy' your idea, others will. Yet how can a small business quickly clone its own idea, many times over? It is hard to start up one business outlet, let alone lots of them.

One answer to this problem is franchising. This means selling the rights to use your business idea and methods at a specific location or area. The person or business buying the rights therefore has to do all the work to make it a success. You, as the franchise owner, must ensure you select someone who will do a good job – and therefore not damage the image of your business.

Currently, there is no better example of this than the Subway chain of sandwich shops. It was started in 1965 by a 17-year-old (Fred de Luca) in America. He borrowed $1000 and set up a single outlet. Its success led him to open others, but he saw much bigger prospects, so started selling franchises in 1974. By 2008 there were 30,000 Subway outlets worldwide, boasting sales of more than £7000 million a year. The first Subway came to Britain in 1996 and by 2008 it was Britain's biggest seller of sandwiches, pushing Tesco in the number two spot. By 2010 the company hopes for 2000 franchise outlets in Britain – the same number as McDonald's. Subway's success has forced McDonald's and Burger King to start selling their own versions of 'deli' sandwiches.

What's in it for the franchise owner?

Expanding a business is expensive and difficult. Opening stores requires a huge amount of capital. For example, a Burger King typically costs £500,000. Selling franchises brings money in, instead of paying it out; and it

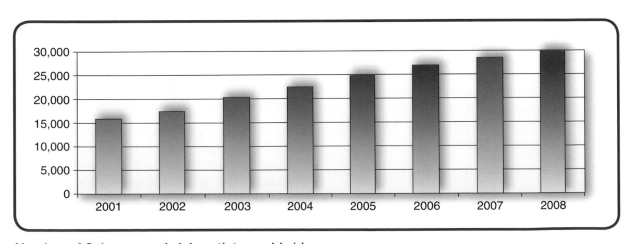

Number of Subway sandwich outlets worldwide

saves having to employ huge numbers of managers to check up on every aspect of the store openings. Key benefits of expanding by selling franchises include:

- Enables a firm to expand its sales quickly; this helps fill gaps that other firms will fill if you do not get there first.

- Franchise owners not only sell a franchise, but also receive a share of all future sales. Burger King (the franchise owner) receives 5 per cent of the sales revenue of every one of the 11,000 outlets worldwide; in addition, every outlet has to buy their supplies from Burger King, so the central company makes profits there too.

- You, the franchise owner, can concentrate on developing new products and services, and on good marketing and advertising; this was the basis of McDonald's huge success for many years.

Being part of a franchise may enable you to benefit from major marketing campaigns

Talking Point

Should Tesco sell franchises in their Tesco Express outlets?

Why buy a franchise rather than start up independently?

Starting a business from scratch requires a remarkable range of skills. Anyone can have a bright idea; and lots of people are good at one thing – cooking, perhaps. Yet there is a huge gap between being a good cook and running a successful restaurant. More than anything else you need to:

- identify a menu and an image that customers want;

- work out how to run the operation efficiently;

- find the right suppliers;

- market your business effectively.

It is not surprising that half of all new restaurants close within three years.

Key benefits of buying a franchise include:

- When you buy a franchise you not only buy your part of an image (e.g. McDonald's or BSM – the British School of Motoring), but also a method for doing things (e.g. the equipment for making a milkshake, plus the instructions on how to make it, clean the equipment, and so on).

- An individual outlet could never afford image-building TV advertising; being part of Subway or McDonald's enables you to benefit from major marketing campaigns.

- As the products and methods of working have been pre-tested, the chance of mistakes is lower; therefore the failure rate is lower with franchise start-ups; this, in turn, means that banks are much more willing to lend to a franchise start-up than a brand new, independent operation.

A franchise start-up takes on the brand, products and methods used by the other outlets

How to identify a suitable start-up location

When you've decided which franchise you want to buy into, the next question is where to put it. There are four steps to go through:

1 Which city/town?

2 Which part of the city/town?

3 Which immediate features, i.e. what do you want to be close to?

4 Which is the right match between these and other factors such as shop size and cost?

1 There is room for a Subway or a McDonalds in every city or medium-large town in Britain. The same is not necessarily true of other franchise businesses. An adventure travel business franchise would thrive in a university town, but struggle where there are fewer young adults. Franchises such as 'Just Wills' and 'Newcross Nursing' will do better in towns with many older people, such as Bournemouth or Eastbourne.

2 Having decided on the town, the single most important question will then be whether to aim for the centre or the outskirts. Clearly the centre will have more people walking by, but parking may be a problem and the rents will be much higher. The table below shows the extraordinary differences in annual rents in different parts of London.

3 The immediate features may be all-important. London's Bond Street has huge rents because businesses such as Bulgari and Versace are determined that their main London store should be at

London shop locations	Size of the shop	Annual rent (as at Jan 2009)	Cost per sq ft	Notes
Hoxton Market	670 sq ft	£10,200	£15.20	In trendy area near Hoxton Square
Clapham Park Road	625 sq ft	£25,000	£40.00	Recently fitted out as a bar
Barnes	1,050 sq ft	£65,000	£61.90	Corner shop site in wealthy area
Covent Garden	6,800 sq ft	£730,000	£107.35	15 year lease on shop opening in Spring 2009
Bond Street	1,080 sq ft	£351,000	£325.00	Posh Bond Street has Britain's highest shop rental costs

London's poshest shopping address. For a Subway, the key immediate feature may be to be close to a station, where there are always lots of people walking by. For a business such as Subway, the more pedestrians, the higher the sales.

Other key immediate features in choosing a location may include:

- Easily accessed, preferably free, parking
- Bus stop outside or nearby
- Open space at the back, if a garden would boost summer trade
- Open space at the front, if tables are allowed there
- Where other, comparable businesses are located, e.g. a DIY shop close to a carpet shop

4 The final decision requires an entrepreneur to balance three things:

- the habits and needs of customers
- practical requirements such as 'shop floor space of at least 1,000 sq ft'
- the cost of the lease and the cost of fitting/decorating the premises

This is a really difficult balance to strike. The table on the preceding page shows how the cost per square foot (sq ft) can vary massively. So you might start your Subway franchise in a terrific location that is always busy, yet find that the annual rent makes your fixed costs too high to allow a satisfactory profit. Alternatively, you might play it too safe, getting a cheap location but never generating enough revenue to pay all the other costs, such as wages, heating and advertising.

It is a business cliché that: 'the three most important things in retail are location, location, location'. That emphasises the importance and difficulty of the final decision. It also implies that the decision should be tilted towards a good and therefore a more expensive location. It may seem wrong to be paying five times the rent to be at one end of the street rather than the other. Yet if the expensive end has the station and other busy shops, the high rent is probably money well spent.

Take the example below of two shops in the centre of Manchester, both of 950 sq ft. One is in the busy Arndale Centre, the other in Oldham Street. The rent in the Arndale Centre is about three times higher, but it should bring in double the revenue of the Oldham Street site. In this case, despite the rent being three times higher, the profit is much greater from the busier location. This will not always be the case. What is essential is that every entrepreneur should make careful estimates of revenues and costs before finally deciding on location.

	Arndale Centre, Manchester		Oldham Street, Manchester	
	£s	Total £s	£s	Total £s
Annual sales revenue	£600,000	£600,000	£300,000	£300,000
Annual rent on 950 sq ft shop	£102,000		£36,000	
Other fixed costs	£56,000		£44,000	
Variable costs	£360,000		£180,000	
Total costs	£518,000	£518,000	£260,000	£260,000
Profit		£82,000		£40,000

Why might an entrepreneur not want to buy a franchise?

Franchising is a halfway house towards running your own independent business. When buying into a franchise you are bound by the rules of the franchise owner. This might be very frustrating for an experienced businessperson who wants to be their own boss. The rules may force them to offer products that might sell well nationally, but not locally. Among the other possible drawbacks are:

- Royalty payments of as much as 8 per cent of revenue are common. A typical franchise outlet might have an annual sales figure of about £300,000, so an annual payment of £24,000 is being made. That is no problem when things are going well, but between 2002 and 2005 sales at UK McDonald's outlets fell by 25 per cent. It would be very annoying to pay large **royalties** when sales and profits are falling.

- Not all franchises are good ones. The Pierre Victoire chain of restaurants had over 100 franchise outlets when it collapsed; franchisees were left with no back-up and a terrible image from a failed business.

Talking Point

If you decided to start a business, would you prefer to be independent or buy into a franchise?

Conclusion

As with any other business opportunity, buying a franchise carries major risks. The buyer needs to check the financial records of the franchise owner and talk to existing franchisees to find out whether they are happy with the service they are getting for their royalty payments. Without doubt, though, buying a good franchise is one of the best ways to start your own business. Having had success with a franchise, an **entrepreneur** could try to start up something completely new later on.

> *'There are a lot of cowboys around.'*
> **Sir Bernard Ingham, president of the British Franchise Association**

Revision Essentials

Entrepreneur – someone who takes on the risk of starting up a new enterprise.

Royalties – paying a percentage of the sales revenue generated by a business or product.

Exercises

(A and B: 25 marks; 30 minutes)

A. Read the unit, then ask yourself:

1 Give two reasons why it is hard to develop a business rapidly. (2)

2 Identify two qualities Fred de Luca must have had to start his own business at the age of 17. (2)

3 Outline two problems that might arise if the franchise owner sold franchises to businesspeople who cut corners to make high profits without high standards. (4)

4 Why would a bank be more willing to lend money to someone opening a franchise outlet than someone opening a fully independent business? (5)

B. Ian Janes had spent ten frustrating years as a journalist, working on a shipping magazine. He had been saving for several years to start his own business. He had £45,000 in the bank and a burning desire to prove to his wife and parents that he could be a financial success. Ian loved eating out, and wanted to start a bar/restaurant. Now he had to decide whether or not to buy into a franchise operation such as Pizza Hut, or start something completely independently. He knew that, if necessary, he could borrow up to £100,000 on the value of the house he owned jointly with his wife.

1 Outline two reasons for and two reasons against Ian deciding to buy a franchise. (4)

2 Recommend whether he should buy a franchise or go independent. Explain your answer. (8)

Practice Questions

With Burger King, McDonald's and Pizza Hut all struggling in recent years, the most attractive-looking franchise opportunity is probably Subway. To do so, you have to pay a £6000 fee, and then gain approval from the company. They will check your financial position, your business experience and your hunger for success. If accepted, you will need to pay about £100,000 to get a store decorated and equipped by Subway's suppliers.

Once opened, you pay Subway 8 per cent of sales revenue as a fee, plus 3.5 per cent into the national fund for advertising. You will have the franchise for 20 years, with an option on another 20 years. With the average Subway outlet having sales of £250,000 a year, it is quite hard to see it as a hugely profitable business. Yet 70 per cent of franchisees go on to buy a second franchise, so they must be doing very well.

An impressive feature of the Subway model is its flexibility. Although most customers buy huge, foot-long, calorie-filled sandwiches, Subway has introduced a '7 under 6' promotion of 7 sandwiches that have fewer than 6 g of fat. This is part of a deliberate marketing strategy to avoid McDonald's problem of being associated with obesity.

Subway

Questions

(20 marks; 25 minutes)

1. Explain why someone wanting to start a business might wish to become a Subway franchisee. (3)

2. Outline three benefits the Subway company receives from selling additional franchises. (6)

3. (a) How much is a franchisee with the average level of sales having to pay Subway each year? (3)

   (b) Identify two benefits the franchisee is receiving for the money they are paying each year. (2)

4. Unlike Subway, some franchise owners take the franchisee's money and give very little in return. Explain two ways in which a businessperson should check out a franchise owner before handing over their money. (6)

Exam-style Questions

DON'T RUSH; check answers carefully

1. Karen is planning to open a new shoe shop aimed at expensive tastes. Identify two good reasons why she should carry out market research before getting started.   (2)

a) To see if there are enough locals who want to buy the type of shoes she plans to sell.

b) To find out the cost of renting shop premises.

c) To work out the precise profit for the first two years of running the shop.

d) To help decide on the right location for the shop.

e) To find out the best place to recruit shopfloor staff.

2. Which is the best definition of qualitative research?   (1)

a) Uses questionnaires to find out the opinions of customers.

b) Finds out in-depth answers from a small group of customers.

c) Asks questions among a large sample of potential customers.

d) It's a way of finding out what percentage of customers like your products.

e) Uses 'blind product testing' to find out what people really think.

3. Identify two important elements in creating a successful manufacturing business.   (2)

a) Using market mapping to find out your customers' likes and dislikes.

b) Adding value by keeping your prices as low as possible.

c) Protecting a technical invention by taking out a patent.

d) Using franchising as a way of stopping others copying your ideas.

e) Analysing the key features of what your competitors offer.

f) Using secondary research to find out what customers think of your new idea.

g) Make sure you keep your added value low enough to make a good profit.

4. Which two of the following competitor actions would make life tougher for Cadburys? (2)

a) A decision by Mars to cut back on its product range.

b) A decision by Nestlé to increase the price of Kit-Kat.

c) A Mars initiative to offer sweetshops a shorter credit period.

d) A 30 per cent increase by Mars in the advertising budget for its Galaxy chocolate.

e) A 30 per cent cutback in the amount spent by Nestlé on sales staff.

f) A decision by Terry's to drop its Terry's Orange Easter Egg.

g) A decision by Mars to reduce the price of Mars and Marathon bars.

5. Which is the best explanation of why Marks & Spencer does not franchise its Simply Food stores? (1)

a) The company does not want to have to manage too many stores on a day-to-day basis.

b) The company wants full control over the day-to-day management of these stores.

c) M&S knows that the government would not allow it to franchise these stores.

d) M&S does not want the expense of franchising; it would rather open its own stores.

e) It may be worried that franchised stores would be run better than its own managed stores.

6. You've always wanted to open a café and you're sure you've identified a gap in the market. A terrific site has become available near the station, and you can (just) afford the £15,000 cost of the lease. Which two of the following are good reasons to hold back? (2)

a) You're not 100 per cent sure that the business will be a success.

b) You have asked why this gap hasn't been filled already, but cannot find an answer.

c) You haven't got the capital to cover the cash outflows beyond the cost of the lease.

d) You've checked on the costs and found that a £2 cup of coffee has a variable cost of 15p.

e) You cannot see how the personal and financial rewards can ever be that great in this case.

f) You've read that house prices might fall by as much as 8 per cent in the coming year.

g) You're not sure you have all the skills needed to run a business perfectly.

7. Last week Aliyyah opened her Males' Nails business. The opening party was fantastic, and led to full bookings in Week 1. Now business has slowed right down and Aliyyah is wondering what to do. She has just £10,000 of capital left of the £80,000 she started with. Which two of the following actions do you advise her to take?   (2)

a) Hold another party, at a cost of £6000, leaving her £4000 for running the business.

b) Phone last week's customers to check their satisfaction and whether they'll return in future.

c) Use the £10,000 to run an advertising campaign in the local papers.

d) Go to the bank to arrange to borrow a further £20,000.

e) Think of ways to encourage customers to tell their friends about Males' Nails.

f) Put her prices up, to help cover her costs.

g) Close the business before she loses everything.

SHOWING ENTERPRISE

Introduction to enterprise skills

In August 2004 Duncan Goose gave up his day job to start a type of business. He wanted to sell bottled water at a profit, but use all the profits for charity. The charity was to be Roundabout, which helps tackle one of the biggest problems for African villagers – water. Villagers may have to walk a mile to a well, then pump the water by hand, then walk home with a full container. Roundabout puts a kids' roundabout on the well-head, so that when the children play, water is pumped up into a water tank above ground. Now villagers can get their water by turning a tap. Duncan's water is called One. Do look out for it.

To make One work required a huge range of enterprise skills. Duncan had to:

- **ask why?** Why did consumers put up with overpriced bottled water – often priced higher than milk, orange juice or Coke?

- **ask why not?** Why not have a not-for-profit water that could make people feel happy to pay the price?

- **think creatively** – about what to do with the profits; choosing a water charity makes the One story complete.

- **do it!** Many people talk about great ideas, but Duncan actually got up and did it. He spent months finding a suitable supplier of water, reading the laws that govern the sale of water and setting up the One website (www.we-are-one.org.uk).

- **show initiative.** When Bob Geldof announced the Live8 concerts in May 2005, Duncan found a way to make contact. One was approved as the only water available backstage at Live8 – gaining millions of pounds' worth of publicity.

> *'Anyone who has never made a mistake has never tried anything new.'*
> **Albert Einstein**

Just do it

In 1988 Nike launched the advertising tag line 'Just do it'. It helped the business grow to the multibillion dollar empire it is today. The phrase sums up the key enterprise skill, which is to make things happen.

Most adults watch too much and do too little. They watch football instead of play it. They watch soaps instead of talking to each other. They watch programmes about

A family may be rescued from a mountainside, having gone climbing without proper equipment or training. In this case, 'let's just do it' is reckless

people building their own houses, but stay in their armchairs.

Being enterprising means spotting an opportunity, then having a go. Of course, this could be disastrous. A family may be rescued from a mountainside, having gone climbing without proper equipment or training. In this case, 'let's just do it' is reckless. Similarly, businesses are set up by people who have no expertise, no skills and not enough capital. Yet a few examples of stupidity should not put people off. Bold ideas lead to exciting lives and potentially huge rewards – emotionally and financially.

Taking calculated risks

Risk is about chance. What is the chance that a particular outcome will occur? Large firms know that, over the years, only one in five new products is a success. So the chance of failure is four out of five. Does that mean firms should never launch new products? No, or eventually they will go out of business. They must either:

- make enough profit from existing products to fund five new product launches for every one success; or
- make sure that the one success is big enough to make up for the failures.

> *Great successes never come without risks.'*
> **Flavius Josephus (around AD 65)**

Recently the giant company Reckitt Benckiser analysed the £550 million UK market for household cleaning products. It appeared saturated with brands such as Cif, Mr Muscle, Dettol and Harpic. But Reckitt believed there was room for a product that would be seen as 'the *most* powerful cleaner'. It launched Cillit Bang with a brilliant, eye-catching TV commercial. The risk was great, but it has been a huge success. Sales have risen sharply within the Reckitt division that produces Cillit Bang.

What was the risk of failure? The development and launch costs of a product such as this are about £15 million. What was the benefit from success? A sales potential of between £50 and £100 million a year,

Who?	What?	How?
Richard Branson, Virgin	At 16, Branson left school to start a student magazine. His Virgin Group is now worth many billions of pounds. Key qualities: initiative; risk taking; a talent for publicity.	Branson has shown an unusual ability to spot opportunities, build a positive image for a business, then sell it on at a profit. He has had many flops (Virgin Cola, Virgin Bride, etc.), but the successes far outweigh the flops.
Bill Gates, Microsoft	Bill Gates founded Microsoft, aged 19, and today is the wealthiest man in the world. Key qualities: technical brilliance; determined; ruthless.	Together with Paul Allen, Gates wrote some brilliant software that was adopted by IBM in the earliest personal computers. Gates was quick to spot the business potential of software and the need to dominate a market.

Who?	What?	How?
Sergey Brin and Larry Page, Google	In their mid-20s, they borrowed money to start Google in 1998; by 2008 it was valued at over $140 billion. Key qualities: brilliant; creative.	Sergey and Larry not only had the genius to invent the Google search engine, but also persuaded a Californian investor to write out a cheque for $100,000 to 'Google, Inc.' before they had even opened a bank account.
Perween Warsi, S&A Foods Perween Warsi	Warsi began cooking Indian food in her kitchen, for sale locally, and built ready-meal specialist S&A Foods to a turnover of nearly £100 million. Key qualities: passionate; determined; a risk taker.	Warsi started by employing five women to work in her family kitchen; she pestered Asda for six months before they tried her products, then rented a factory when Asda gave her a contract. S&A Foods now produces Thai, Indian and Italian meals for Tesco and Asda. Warsi is one of Britain's richest women.

generating profits of perhaps £20 to £50 million a year. That was a risk worth taking.

> 'Educated risks are the key to success.'
> **William Olsen, chief executive**

Goods and services

The skills required in starting a business can be different when providing goods or services. Goods are products, which can be manufactured or assembled far from the customer. A delivery driver may provide the only regular contact with the customer. Services, however, imply regular customer contact, e.g. serving customers at a sweetshop or waiting tables at a restaurant.

Whether a business is based on producing goods or supplying a service, risk-taking and initiative are important. But other skills will differ. For example the ability to enjoy dealing with people will be crucial in a service business, but less so when producing goods.

The key differences between providing goods and services are listed in the table below:

Goods	Services
Can be produced anywhere and then transported to the customers	Must be located where the customers want to buy (which may mean high rents, e.g. in London's Oxford Street)
Quality has to be built in, e.g. good design and high reliability	Quality is affected by personal service and therefore whether staff are well motivated
Factories can be very expensive to get started, due to the high machinery costs	Service businesses can often be started small (and cheaply), then built up later

Exercises

(A and B: 25 marks; 30 minutes)

A. Read the unit, then ask yourself:

   1   Why could 'just having a go' be disastrous? (3)

   2   Does being enterprising have to be about making money? (3)

   3   What is the evidence that launching Cillit Bang was a risk worth taking? (4)

   4   Outline one example of enterprise you have seen recently. It could be in your local high street or in a non-business setting. (5)

B. On the first day of the 2005/6 Premiership season, Fulham introduced a new idea. By the manager's dugout were two exercise bikes for substitutes to warm up. Manager Chris Coleman said the idea was to bring the heart rate of the subs up to the level of the players on the pitch. This could help reduce warm-up injuries.

   1   What 'Why?' question had the Fulham staff been asking themselves? (2)

   2   Was the Fulham management being enterprising? Explain your answer. (5)

   3   How might the players feel about this new idea? (3)

Practice Questions

An Enterprising Olympics

At the 2008 Olympic Games, the big international battle was between America and China (with Britain making a shock appearance among the golds). At the same time a huge business battle was taking place. The mighty Nike versus Germany's finest – Adidas. And the winner was? – Puma!

For Nike and Adidas, the big idea for 2008 was to win big in the vast Chinese market. Adidas spent £100 million as the official sponsors of the tournament and of the Chinese Olympic committee. Every Chinese gold medal winner appeared on the podium dressed in the official track-suit and trainers – with the three-stripe Adidas logo everywhere. Yet Nike spent nearly as much money sponsoring 22 of the 28 Chinese teams at the games. So the runners ran in Nike shoes (then, if they won, changed into Adidas for the medal presentation!). Both Nike and Adidas claim to have been the winners in the battle for Chinese customers during and after the games.

Although the big news in the UK was about British golds, for the rest of the world the big story was the 'Lightning Bolt'. The Jamaican sprinter Usain Bolt came to dominate the games. And his lightning feet were in neither Nike nor Adidas.

Usain Bolt

Tiny Puma had been clever enough to sign up Usain Bolt when he was a relatively unknown 17-year-old. Yes, he had already won the 200 metres at the World Youth Championships, but he was as well known for partying as for his running. At the time, he had never competed in a 100-metre race!

When competing with companies as huge as Nike and Adidas, smaller firms have to be especially enterprising. Puma's approach has always been to be quicker on its feet than its giant rivals. Sponsoring the world's fastest man may prove to have been one of its best ever pieces of business.

Questions

(15 marks; 20 minutes)

1   Apart from identifying Usain Bolt as the right person to sponsor, outline two other ways in which a small business could be 'enterprising' when competing with giants such as Nike or Adidas. (4)

2   Sponsoring a 17-year-old sprinter is a perfect example of a calculated risk. Explain what the upsides and downsides might be. (4)

3   Why may it be easier for a small firm to 'Just Do It' than a large business such as Nike? (7)

Thinking creatively

Why?

Creative thinking stems from asking questions. Three-year-olds can drive their parents crazy by constantly asking why. 'Why are those sweets in the toilet?' (A condom machine) 'Why are raspberries red?' and so on. In fact, just such a question about raspberries made the producer of Slush Puppy decide to make the raspberry flavour a blue colour. Then the red and blue would make a more eye-catching display.

When kids start going to school, they soon learn that asking why is not welcome. Teachers want to get on with things, not get

'Disneyland will never be completed, as long as there is imagination left in the world.'
Walt Disney (1901–66)

bogged down in lots of questions. More is the pity. The ability to ask why is at the root of creativity and innovation.

Some significant 'Why?' questions of recent times are set out in the preceding table.

Why not?

It is also vital to ask 'Why not?' The three-year-old is trying to find out the way the world is. Creative thinkers also ask why the world cannot be different. In 1933 Percy Shaw became the inventor of one of the world's most widely used ideas. Driving home in

Significant 'Why?' questions of recent times

The 'Why?' question	The answer	The business response
Why are oil supplies running down?	Rising car ownership worldwide.	Hybrid cars, part-petrol and part-battery, such as the fuel-efficient Toyota Prius.
Why are people getting fatter?	Too much fatty fast food.	McDonald's menu changes towards salads, vegetables and fruit.
Why do older women look older?	Wrinkles and loose skin.	Anti-ageing, anti-wrinkle and firming creams.

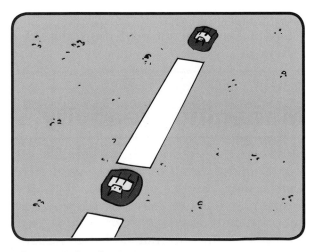

'Catseyes' reflector

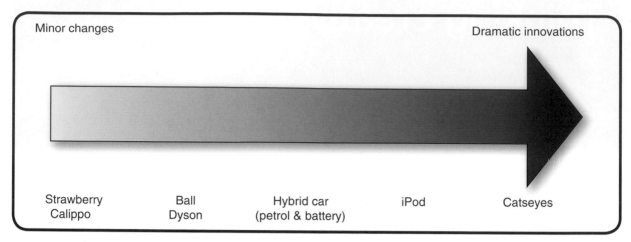

Minor changes — Dramatic innovations

| Strawberry Calippo | Ball Dyson | Hybrid car (petrol & battery) | iPod | Catseyes |

Creativity scale

dense fog he nearly drove off the road and crashed, but was saved by the flashing eye of a cat sitting on a fence. Two years later he patented 'Catseyes', the invention that made him a fortune. Brilliantly, he made a reflector with a rubberised top that would give when cars ran over it. And the action of pushing down the rubber top wipes the reflector clean – just like a cat's eye blinking.

Many 'Why not?' questions are much less significant than Percy Shaw's; for example, Why not have a strawberry-flavour Calippo ice lolly? Such an obvious idea might be hugely significant if it proves a huge commercial success.

> *'An essential aspect of creativity is not being afraid to fail.'*
> **Edwin Land, inventor of the Polaroid camera**

Managing creativity

Most of us have lots of creative thoughts. We look in an ice cream cabinet and wish there were a mint choc ice or a mango lolly. The problem is that we may not tell anybody about these thoughts, or – worse – we may try to tell someone, but find that nobody listens. It follows that creativity may only

have meaning if it is backed up by effective communication. Percy Shaw had his idea and developed it himself. Most of us have neither the money nor the ability to achieve this.

Well-run businesses encourage the sharing of creative thoughts. Great ideas may come from the shop floor as much as from management. Good managers encourage this. The ghastly superbug MRSA arises from poor hygiene in hospitals. Good, well-motivated

Sharing creative thoughts with colleagues is good for business

staff should quickly come up with ideas on how to stop it. Unfortunately, many NHS managers think they know best, so the problem remains acute.

For some businesses, creativity is the basis of the operation. A good example is Codemasters Ltd, a UK private company that produces games software. It has grown from a bedroom in 1986 to employing 450 people on a 90-acre site in Warwickshire. It is Europe's largest privately owned software business. Among its key games are Brian Lara Cricket, Colin McRae Rally and LMA Football Manager. A quick visit to its website (www. codemasters.co.uk) shows the importance of creativity. It also shows the potential rewards, as 50 jobs were being advertised in August 2008, including software development jobs at up to £70,000 plus bonuses.

> *'The man who has no imagination has no wings.'*
> **Muhammad Ali, greatest ever boxer**

Creativity and competitive advantage

In January 2009 Wrigley launched a new product, 'Extra Ice Mints'. Priced at 97p in pocket-sized tins, the plan was to appeal to young adults. This would open up a new sector, as brands such as Polo and Extra Strong have been bought mainly by older people. Wrigley had found a creative way out of its difficulties in 2008. Cadbury's launch of Trident Gum had dented sales of the Wrigley chewing gum brands. Wrigley wanted a way to achieve growth that side-stepped the Cadbury problem.

Wrigley believed that it had two sources of competitive advantage in the broader confectionery market:

1. Customers trusted Wrigley to provide good, long-lasting mint flavour

2. Younger customers saw Wrigley as a brand for them (compared with older brands such as Trebor or Werther's).

Competitive advantage is a term given to any factors that help a business succeed when fighting direct rivals. In its core market of chewing gum, Wrigley's key competitive advantage in Britain is that it has a 90% market share. That ensures that its products are displayed in every sweetshop in the country. There are two main ways to achieve competitive advantage: keeping your costs lower than any other producer, so that you can always win battles based on low prices; and, making your products stand out more than any others, perhaps because they have a trendier or classier image.

Good examples of the importance of creativity in achieving competitive advantage include:

- Ryanair using every creative opportunity to bang home its message that its flights are the cheapest

- Lucozade repositioning what was once an energy drink in a glass bottle, bought by older people when they felt weak! In 2008 Lucozade Energy and Lucozade Sport had combined UK sales of £340 million – more than Pepsi-Cola

- Cadbury's launch of its Crème Egg Twisted bar in May 2008; it helped boost sales of the Crème Egg brand by 16.3% in 2008, reversing a 4% fall in 2007.

Exercises

(25 marks; 25 minutes)

A. Read the unit, then ask yourself:

1 Outline two benefits from asking the question 'Why?' (4)

2 What might be the answer and the business response to the following questions?

   (a) Why are organic foods so expensive? (4)

   (b) Why has Sainsbury's lost out so badly to Tesco? (4)

3 Suggest two ways in which managers can encourage staff to be creative. (2)

4 Why is creativity particularly important for staff in a business such as Codemasters? (6)

5 How can creativity help achieve competitive advantage for a car manufacturer? (5)

Classroom exercise

(This should take about 20 minutes; if longer, ask each group leader to give some feedback; someone could summarise each group's answers on a whiteboard or flipchart.) Get into groups of about four people and appoint a leader. The leader's job is to appoint a secretary/note-taker, and to make sure everyone answers the following questions:

1 Which are your top three favourite chocolate 'countlines' (bars, bags or tubes of sweets you pick off the shop counter)?

2 Describe how you eat your favourite chocolate countline (probe: 'in detail, please').

3 Are there any bars you dislike? Why?

4 How many countlines have you eaten in the past seven days?

5 What is your opinion of these three ideas for new countlines?

   (a) CrunchieFlake: a chocolate flake studded with pieces of Crunchie honeycomb.

   (b) FizzyFruits: chocolate-coated balls containing fizzy fruit candy in different flavours.

   (c) Crisp 'n' Cool: a Cadbury milk chocolate bar wrapped in special foil that keeps it from melting.

   Probe – for each idea, find out:

   ● Whether the group would buy it to try it.

   ● What price they think it would be.

   ● Whether they think they would buy it regularly.

   ● Which of the three they think would be the biggest seller and why?

6 Ask everyone to stop for a moment to consider whether they can think of a great new countline. Get them to be as detailed as possible; get the comments of others.

Deliberate creativity

Most people think that great ideas come from flashes of inspiration. There is the famous story of Isaac Newton in his garden, seeing an apple fall to the ground and thinking 'gravity'. In fact, most creative ideas can be put down to patterns of thought. They have specific causes that lead logically to answers.

> *'The secret to creativity is knowing how to hide your sources.'*
> **Albert Einstein, genius**

Take the Apple iPod, which fused the idea of portable music (from the Sony Walkman), MP3 downloading, portable hard-drive storage (from laptops) and smart design (from Apple computers). Nothing revolutionary, but the parts were combined together to generate a brilliant multibillion pound innovation.

Professor Dennis Sherwood has been studying creativity for many years. He believes people can be taught to come up with bright new ideas. He calls this method **deliberate creativity**.

The essence of deliberate creativity is to get groups of people focused on what they know; to describe, perhaps, the TV show *Who Wants to be a Millionaire?* If six people each write down ten things about *Millionaire*, some will be duplicated, but many points will be different. Perhaps 30–40 different points will emerge. These might range from 'a £1 million top prize' to 'one player sits in the centre, facing the questioner, in the middle of the audience'.

Having described the topic in detail, the trick is to focus on one element and ask how it might be different. What if the player didn't 'sit in the centre, facing the questioner, in the middle of the audience'? How else might things be done?

Perhaps a quiz show might be less relaxed and more edgy if the player and the questioner were standing up? And what if there were no audience? And perhaps more than one player? This way of thinking enabled the BBC to devise *The Weakest Link* soon after *Millionaire* became a TV sensation.

The professor's key point is that ordinary people can come up with good new ideas if

Newton in his garden, saw an apple fall to the ground and 'discovered' gravity

they are helped to think through a deliberate process. In his book *Innovation and Creativity*, Professor Sherwood recalls a workshop he held with managers at Nestlé, the maker of KitKat and Yorkie. When someone wrote down about chocolate that 'you eat it', he asked the questions: How might this be different? What else might we do with chocolate? Among the answers came.

- Use it as a fragrance, for perfumed soaps, shampoos, air fresheners, and so on.
- As a fire alarm(!) – using its melting point as a way of identifying that a room was getting dangerously hot.

> *'By far the greatest flow of newness is not innovation at all. It is imitation.'*
> **Theodore Levitt, management guru**

Talking Point

Was the invention of the Big Mac a result of creative genius or deliberate creativity?

These unusual ideas came from people who would never think of themselves as 'creative'.

Evaluating ideas

Coming up with great ideas is not enough, however. There remain two key stages:

1 Evaluating whether a 'great idea' is also a good, sensible, workable idea.

2 Bringing the idea to reality.

To judge a new idea, Professor Sherwood recommends the clever idea of another professor – Edward de Bono (mainly famous for mind maps). De Bono warns that people in groups influence each other. A good new idea might be rejected because one individual is in a bad mood. He therefore suggests that those involved in evaluating ideas should have specific, different roles (one cheerleader, one cautious, etc.). Professor Sherwood uses this approach to suggest that there are seven key roles, often represented

Benefits
Identifying the number and likely scale of the benefits.

Constituencies and feelings
Which groups of people will be affected by the idea, what is their likely reaction and how can these factors be managed?

Solutions
What solutions can we identify to the problems identified by the black, red and white hats? How can they be overcome?

Process
Who will be responsible for what, if we carry the project forward?

Issues to be managed
Identifying the risks and how they are to be managed.

Data
What data do we have and do we still need to take an informed decision? How reliable are the sources? And how do we handle uncertainty in the data?

Actions
What actions should we take? Have we enough information to take a decision now? Or should we carry on with the analysis phase?

Professor Dennis Sherwood's seven key roles

as different coloured hats (i.e. whoever wears the hat has to fulfil that role). These seven key roles (or hats) are described in the figure on the preceding page.

The point is simple. Staff will only generate ideas if they feel they are given a fair hearing. If bright ideas are encouraged, but then quietly killed off in the evaluation phase, no one will waste time coming up with more. The coloured hats approach ensures that every idea is given a chance.

Of course, good ideas can still fail if they are poorly carried out. The cost overruns on the Channel Tunnel have condemned the project to being permanently unprofitable. It simply cost too much to build. And many newly launched soft drinks or chocolate bars sound great, but simply do not taste quite right. Those practical problems can be put down to poor management.

> 'The creativity that emerges from the company comes from the many ideas of the people who are here.'
> **John Rollwagen, chief executive**

Exercises

(A and B: 25 marks; 30 minutes)

A. Read the unit, then ask yourself:

1   What evidence is given that the iPod may have been a result of deliberate creativity rather than inspiration? (3)

2   Use the chapter to identify four steps to achieving successful deliberate creativity. (4)

3   Why might it be useful to give the yellow hat to the person who has come up with the idea being discussed? (3)

4   How might a firm such as Tesco encourage staff to come up with new ideas for improving the business? (5)

B. Encouraging and using ideas 'from the floor' can have dramatic results, as at BMW's Mini factory at Cowley, Oxford. The BMW Group has announced that suggestions from staff at Cowley have saved the company £10.5 million in two years. Of the 14,333 suggestions staff put forward, three-quarters were put into action. They ranged from cutting unnecessary use of paper to more complex engineering solutions.

1   Give two possible reasons for turning down a number of the suggestions. (2)

BMW Group Plant Oxford

2 What is the most likely explanation for the high number of suggestions from the Cowley staff? Explain your reasoning. (3)

3 Discuss whether the staff should get a financial reward for the suggestions that are put into action. (5)

Practice Questions

Ideas are the new currency

Businesses and organisations want creativity from their employees and see it as a key competitive advantage in a modern economy.

'There are two main uses for creativity,' insists Dr Edward de Bono. 'The first use is to do what you are doing in a better way. This may mean doing it faster, at less cost, with less waste, with higher quality or in a simpler way.'

Then there is a second use of creativity, which is to do better things, he says. 'This means new products and services, or adding new values to existing products and services.'

But can we all be creative? And if it is not a scarce resource, why is it prized so highly? After all, we all know what someone is talking about when they refer to another person as a 'creative type'.

In fact, creativity can be useful in all areas of business, and everyone has got the ability to be creative, the thinkers believe. 'As with any skill (cooking or skiing for instance) some people will become more skilful than others. But everyone can learn to be creative. It is not a mystical gift,' insists Dr de Bono.

(Source: www.bbc.co.uk, 28 June 2004)

Questions

(20 marks; 25 minutes)

1 (a) Outline two ways companies could benefit from a more creative workforce. (4)

   (b) Explain how a company's sales revenues might be affected by doing things 'in a better way'. (5)

2 Dr de Bono says 'anyone can learn to be creative'. Explain how this view compares with the ideas of Professor Dennis Sherwood. (5)

3 Do you think that we can all be creative? Explain your thoughts on this topic. (6)

Invention and innovation

Invention means having a totally original idea, and showing how it can work in theory. **Innovation** means putting a new idea into practice. This could be either by bringing a new product to the market or by getting an organisation to try a new way of working.

> 'Necessity, who is the mother of invention.'
> **Plato, *The Republic*, 427–347** BC

Invention

In business, the ideal invention is one that can be patented. A **patent** makes it unlawful for anyone to copy your idea for 20 years after the patent has been taken out. This system provides the incentive for inventors. After all, if a bright new idea could be copied straight away, why spend time and effort in the first place? Many years without competition guarantees a high level of profit for the inventor.

The Patent Office will only grant a patent if the invention has never been shown publicly, if it is a significant step forward in thinking and if it has a practical application. A patent can be taken out on a new way of making something (e.g. the Dyson method for carpet sweeping, using 'cyclones' instead of vacuums).

Inventions have made huge differences to people's lives. They include the internal combustion engine (invented in the nineteenth century, and still the way petrol-driven cars work); the television; and many life-saving drugs such as penicillin (kills bacteria) or warfarin (stops blood clots). Not all inventions are so significant, yet small-scale changes can be important for businesses. The Walls ice cream Solero was launched in the early 1990s, backed by a patented method for creating a smooth-textured fruit ice. Before then, ice lollies always had a glass-like, hard texture. The effect was huge, with the Solero brand achieving sales in excess of £1000 million in Europe alone.

For a new, small business, patenting an invention can be a difficult, expensive start. The problem is partly that the fees charged by the Patent Office may be quite high, possibly amounting to thousands of pounds. More serious still is that breaking a patent is not a criminal offence. So there are no

Invention means having a totally original idea

James Dyson

Great inventions that were not patented

Invention	Invented by	Exploited by
The World Wide Web	Tim Berners-Lee, Britain	Yahoo, Google and many others
Light bulbs	Thomas Edison, America	Philips
Internal combustion engine	Nikolaus Otto, Germany	Daimler, then everyone else

> 'An amazing invention – but who would ever want to use one?'
> **Rutherford Hayes, having made a call on Alexander Graham Bell's telephone in 1876 (Source: www.thinkexist.com)**

police raids on those who unlawfully copy a patented idea. The patent holder has to take the copier to court – and that is expensive. Despite this, the huge success of James Dyson's patented 'dual cyclone' cleaners has shown the value of spending a bit of time and money on obtaining patents. The table on the right shows some examples of great inventions that were not patented, meaning the inventor received little or nothing.

A different type of invention is the creation of a new piece of writing, drawing or music. The creator is automatically protected from this being copied thanks to **copyright** law. This means that anyone playing an Amy Winehouse record in public owes Amy a song-writing fee. Similarly it is, in effect, theft to photocopy this book without asking the author's permission.

Innovation

The company that makes the best use of a new idea may not be its inventor. The innovator is the person or company that finds a way to make a new idea work. There are two types of innovation:

1. **Product innovation:** new product ideas brought to the marketplace, such as probiotic yogurt drinks (Actimel, Yakult, etc.).

2. **Process innovation:** new ways of working (e.g. McDonald's use of factory-style production in its restaurants; before McDonald's, food was made to order, which was slower and more expensive).

Tim Berners-Lee, the inventor of the World Wide Web

Some companies make innovation their key competitive advantage, such as L'Oréal in hair care or Danone in foods. Ten years ago, the best example would have been Sony in electronics, but the company has lost out in many sectors, such as televisions. As Sony's innovativeness declined, so did its sales and profits. By contrast, L'Oréal has become the world's biggest cosmetics business, largely through continuous innovation. Anyone wanting a hair colour product would trust that any L'Oréal product would be at the cutting edge.

In effect, gaining an image as an innovative company is a way of adding value. It makes your brands worth more to the consumer. Are you worth it? Of course you are.

> '*Innovation distinguishes between a leader and a follower.*'
> **Steve Jobs, founder of Apple and the man behind the iPod (Source: www.Woopidoo.com)**

Revision Essentials

Copyright – protection for a creator against his/her work being copied.

Innovation – putting a new idea into practice.

Invention – showing how an original idea can work in theory.

Patent – registering a new way of producing something, to establish sole rights to its use.

Exercises

(20 marks; 25 minutes)

1   Give two reasons why a successful patent is likely to lead to high profits for the inventor. (2)

2   Reread the section about patents under the heading 'Invention' (page 57) and then explain why a brand name cannot be patented. (4)

3   Are the following examples of product innovation or process innovation?

   (a) A new car fuelled by solar power (launched in Spain, not Britain). (1)

   (b) A cinema chain changing from a national call centre to providing the telephone number of the local cinema. (1)

   (c) A new service offering door-to-door collection and delivery of dry cleaning. (1)

4   Innovation can be expensive, for example L'Oréal's stream of new product launches. Why is it vital, therefore, that innovative products should have high added value? (4)

5   Reread Steve Jobs' quote about innovation (above).

   (a) Explain what it means. (3)

   (b) Explain why it matters in business to be a leader rather than a follower. (4)

Practice Questions

Innovation in car sales

August 2005 was a poor month for car sales in America. Sales fell, especially for bigger trucks and 4x4 vehicles. A rare bright spot was the 115 per cent increase in the sales of the Toyota Prius. This innovative car offers a combined petrol and electric engine. In town it runs in electric silence, with no exhaust emissions and with terrific fuel economy. If the driver wants to put his/her foot down, the on-board computer kicks in the petrol engine, so that the car can overtake or reach a 70 mph motorway cruising speed.

First launched in 1997, the Prius was seen as an oddity by the motor industry. With, in effect, two engines, it cost about £3000 more to make a Prius. Yet Toyota only charged an extra £2000 for it. Sales were poor and profits much poorer. Then in 2003 Hollywood stars took up the car, to show their environmental consciences. Even more importantly, the leap in petrol prices between 2004 and 2008 made it seem a sensible choice for ordinary drivers. Demand blossomed, leading to a three-month waiting list for the cars. In 2008, Toyota announced that it would increase its 2009 output of Prius cars by 70 per cent! Toyota's innovation is paying off.

The Toyota Prius was taken up by Hollywood stars to show off their environmental conscience

Questions

(20 marks; 25 minutes)

1 (a) Over 8000 Prius cars were sold in America in August 2004, how many were sold in 2005? (3)

(b) Explain what could cause a three-month waiting list for those wishing to buy the Prius? (4)

2 During 2005 many American and European car producers announced that they were starting work on their own hybrid cars.

   (a) Outline two reasons why they waited so long after Toyota's 1997 launch of the Prius. (4)

   (b) Discuss whether the other American and European companies may have left it too late to succeed by copying Toyota's approach. (6)

3 How might the image of all Toyota's car models be affected by its success with the Prius? (3)

Business risks and rewards

Two years ago Trevor Peake put all his savings – £22,000 – into opening a clothes shop. He had always loved black, gothic clothes, and thought that a specialist shop could succeed in south London. Short of capital from the start, Trevor never had the range of stock he wanted. He also had neither the money for advertising nor the time to wait until word spread that this was the place for goths to come. Four months after it opened, his shop closed down. After he sold off his stock (very cheaply) and paid his debts, Trevor was left with just over £400.

> 'You miss 100 percent of the shots you never take.'
> **Wayne Gretsky, US ice hockey star**

Business is risky – at every stage and at all times. Even giants such as McDonald's, Coca-Cola and Marks and Spencer have suffered just when most people thought they were too big to suffer. The riskiest stage of all, though, is at the beginning. Of new businesses 36 per cent fold within three years, and only 10 per cent make significant profits.

Risks can yield rewards

In 1984 two teenagers, Richard and David Darling, moved on from playing computer games to writing them. They produced the games for fun, but then tried advertising them in popular computer weekly. A £70 advertisement brought in £7000 worth of orders. In 1986 they formed a company, Codemasters Ltd. It went on to produce some of the longest-lasting games software brands, such as Colin McRae Rally and LMA Football Manager. In summer 2005 it held the number one spot in the games chart with Brian Lara Cricket. Today the business has over £100 million of sales per year, employs over 400 people and is worth around £250 million. Risking £70 on an advertisement has resulted in fabulous wealth and an amazing achievement.

> 'I've been rich and I've been poor. Rich is better.'
> **Frank Sinatra, singer and actor**

Codemaster product Brian Lara Cricket

What are the main risks?

Businesses start when one or two people have an idea and push it through. It may be a market stall; it may be a shop; or it may be a scientific or design breakthrough. Putting it into practice will be difficult, because there are so many things to think about and so many things to get right. At the start, the main pitfalls are:

1 **Making sure you really know what the customer wants.** If a new business is to succeed, it must have something new and different. It cannot just be one more pizza takeaway. Whatever is unique about the new business is a risk. Customers must be attracted to the unique feature, and stay attracted. In the 1990s Cadbury launched a series of new chocolate products (Strollers, Wispa, Wispa Gold). All sold well for a while, as people bought one or two. But over time they drifted back to their regular favourites, and these brands were dropped.

2 **Making sure you can deliver on your promises.** Many new firms generate hype, but let the customers down (e.g. the 'great new club' that proves a bit dull, or the clothes shop that never seems to stock your size or the colour you want).

3 **Getting the financing right.** The single most common reason for start-up failure is lack of working capital. Entrepreneurs work out how much will be needed for the builders, the equipment, the computers and the vehicles. Yet they underestimate the need for capital to keep the business going day by day – to pay the wages, the

What are the main risks?

At the start	In the early days	When growth is rapid
Identifying a market gap big enough to be profitable.	Making sure your initial customers come back for more.	'Overtrading' – sales growing faster than you can cope with financially.
Raising (more than) enough capital.	Running out of cash during the off-season.	Struggling to manage rapid rises in staff, especially middle management.
Getting the right people working in the right way.	Running out of energy and self-belief when times are tough.	The entrepreneur owner may struggle to be a good manager.
Building a base of initial customers.	Coping with competition when it arrives.	The boss and staff may become complacent, so the rise leads to the fall.

suppliers, the gas bills, and so on. This daily (working) capital will eventually be funded by the revenue coming in from customers, but many firms start slowly. A shop in Leeds that sells sports trophies took three years before the revenues were sufficient to support the business. (Now it is thriving, but the owner is thankful that he was able to borrow £16,000 from his mother to tide him over in this difficult period.)

> '*The man who makes no mistake does not usually make anything.*'
> **William Magee, philosopher, 1889**

What are the main rewards?

Becoming wealthy

Starting a small business can generate huge returns. Most working people struggle to save much from their salary. They may be comfortable, but can never become rich. Starting a business creates the possibility of selling it once it is established. It could be sold completely, or part of it could be sold to outside shareholders, by 'floating' the business on the stock market. In 1990 Tim Slade and Jules Leaver raised £12,000 to open their first Fat Face sportswear shop. In May 2005 they sold the business for £100 million. They had planned to float Fat Face on the stock market, but a private buyer offered a better deal.

In 1972 a 23-year-old started a market stall in London, selling clothes imported from Thailand. A year later he used the profits from the stall to open his first shop, calling it Monsoon. The business kept growing, largely from reinvested profits, and Peter Simon (the founder) kept adding new stores. In 1984 he spotted the opportunity for a new type of shop, Accessorize. Today there are over 250 Monsoon and Accessorize shops and the business makes annual profits of around £50 million. The Simon family still owns 75 per cent of the business, making them one of the richest families in Britain.

The excitement

Excitement comes from taking risks (i.e. the risks generate the rewards). It is the difference between riding a bike on the flat and riding it down a steep hill; or watching

Excitement comes from taking risks.

Brazil play football compared with watching Germany. At every stage in starting and building a business, risks have to be taken and new skills have to be learnt. This provides the buzz that makes it exciting to be an entrepreneur.

The control

Many people dislike being told what to do, especially if they do not respect their boss. For such people, starting up on their own may be ideal. They can then make their own decisions and, if necessary, their own compromises. People with this motivation may struggle, though, if they start to employ others who have different ideas or standards from their own.

'Rewards should be proportionate to risk.'
Harvard Business Review, 1986

Exercises

(A: 15 marks; 20 minutes)

A. Read the unit, then ask yourself:

1   What did Trevor Peake do wrong? (3)

2   If you are opening your own shop, how can you make sure that you really know what the customer wants? (3)

3   How does the experience of Peter Simon compare with the three points made under the heading 'What are the main rewards?'? (4)

4   Of new businesses 36 per cent close within three years. Should that put people off starting up on their own? (5)

B.

Zoom: Business start-up failure

On Tuesday 26 August 2008, 74-year-old Robert Hainey booked two £350 return tickets to Ottawa, Canada. He and his wife were flying on Zoom Airlines to visit family to celebrate their golden wedding anniversary. The £700 was paid by debit card and was withdrawn from his bank account on Thursday 28 August. On that same day Zoom collapsed. Mr Hainey says he will inevitably lose his £700.

Zoom airline

Zoom started in 2003 when Scottish brothers John and Hugh Boyle saw an opportunity for a low-cost airline based in Canada. Having started with routes from Canada to Glasgow, the business expanded rapidly. It operated point-to-point routes avoided by the bigger airlines, such as Glasgow to Ottawa. To keep its investment costs down, Zoom leased older second-hand planes such as the Boeing 767 and 757. EasyJet and Ryanair, by contrast, only have brand new planes – expensive to buy, but more fuel-efficient and therefore cheaper to run.

Comparison of Zoom's and Ryanair's business plans

Zoom Business Plan	Ryanair Business Plan
● Low prices, undercutting standard airlines	● Lowest prices, undercutting all other airlines
● Quickly developing routes from a variety of different locations, e.g. five airports in Britain alone	● In first five years, focused just on Dublin then London Stansted, to keep fixed costs as low as possible
● Free in-flight meals and entertainment; full service at low price	● No-frills service; charge for all extras; keep costs to the minimum
● Second-hand aircraft; cheap to acquire; expensive to operate	● Brand new planes; big investment but low fuel costs and maintenance
● Long-haul routes: no scope for working the planes harder than standard airlines	● Short routes and quick turnaround, allowing more flights per plane per day

Business start-ups don't come harder than launching a new airline, but it should have been relatively easy for the Boyles. John knew the travel industry extremely well; and made £56 million when selling his 'Direct Holidays' business to Airtours in 1998. He also knew enough to start the business as a private limited company. Yet, from the start, there were reasons to doubt the logic behind Zoom. As shown in the table above, Zoom was set up as a relatively high-cost operation, yet planned to attract customers by cutting prices.

Between 2003 and 2006 Zoom expanded rapidly at a time when fuel prices were low and the economy was strong on both sides of the Atlantic. Late in 2006 the Boyles struck a £5.7 million deal with the Bank of Scotland to help finance a major expansion. From 2007 Zoom would open route from Gatwick to JFK New York – directly taking on Virgin, British Airways and many others. In June 2007 this service began, with flight prices starting at £129 one way.

Even after the dramatic rise in fuel prices in the early months of 2008 (which added £27 million to its total fuel bill), Zoom's growth seemed unstoppable. On 21 April 2008, Zoom advertised for more staff: 60 at Gatwick and another 62 cabin crew. In June 2008 the

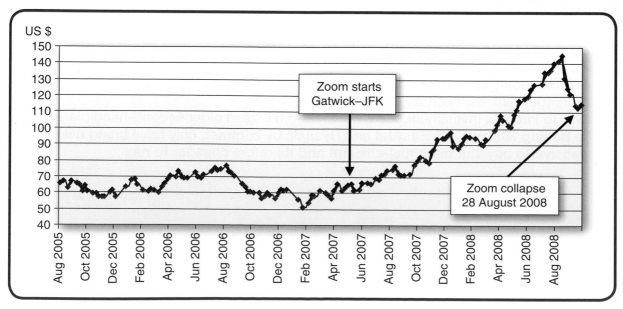

World oil price August 2005–August 2008

International Air Transport Association (IATA) changed its world airline profit forecast for 2008 from +$4.5 billion to −$2.3 billion. It stated, 'Oil is changing everything'. Yet in July 2008 Zoom announced further growth, opening up a new route from Gatwick to San Diego, California.

The first public sign of trouble came on 27 August, when the airline leasing company impounded a Zoom aircraft at Calgary airport for non-payment of the monthly rent. It was like someone having their car seized because of a failure to keep up with the payments. It proved to be that the leasing firm had been owed £2 million for some months. When word spread, things quickly fell apart. Imperial Oil, owed £750,000 by Zoom, refused to let Zoom fill up its planes at Gatwick unless there were cash payments. With no cash around, the business imploded. More than 700 staff lost their jobs instantly, more than 2500 passengers were left stranded and Zoom has left debts of £60 million.

The Boyles announced that the majority of the 40,000 customers who had paid for flights over coming months would get their money back. This was announced as if the brothers would be helping out from their personal wealth. In fact all it meant was that people who had paid with a credit card would be able to claim their money back (because of the credit card industry's insurance scheme). Those paying by cheque or debit card would lose everything. Thousands of people will lose many hundreds of pounds. When firms collapse, there is rarely anything left to share out among the suppliers, customers or staff.

Questions

(30 marks; 35 minutes)

1 Examine two key mistakes made by the Boyles in the development of Zoom. (6)

2 (a) What was the importance to the Boyles of starting the business as a private limited company? (4)

(b) Is it right that the Boyles should be protected from any further personal losses following the collapse of Zoom? (8)

3 The text identifies oil price as one reason for the collapse of Zoom but also queries whether the business plan ever made sense. Discuss which of these is the more important explanation for the failure of the business. (12)

Practice Questions

Red Bull risks and (huge) rewards

In 1982 a jet-lagged 25-year-old Austrian (Dietrich Mateschitz) tried a cheap local energy drink while working in Thailand: 'It cured my jet lag in seconds.' The drink was called Krating Daeng, which translates as Red Bull. There had never been a product like it before in the West, either in taste or effect. It was packed with sugar, caffeine and taurine. Mateschitz spent years talking to the cautious Thai producer and in 1985 founded Red Bull GmbH

Red Bull was launched in Britain in 1993

in Austria. The Thai company received 51 per cent of the shares; Mateschitz had the other 49 per cent and was to be the chief executive (and still is).

Early taste tests were discouraging. 'Most people said it was disgusting and created a sticky mouth,' one former employee recalls. Bars initially refused to stock it, seeing it as an overpriced medicinal or health-related product, rather than a mixer. Mateschitz remained certain that it would be a hit. To create a youth-oriented 'underground' feel for Red Bull, he deliberately restricted supply and refused to advertise. He paid students and DJs to host parties where the drink was served. Young Austrians caught the bug and by the early 1990s Red Bull spread to Germany.

Red Bull was launched in Britain in 1993 and now sells over £100 million of high-priced cans in shops alone. Worldwide, Red Bull reached sales of $1 billion in 2001, and $2 billion by 2004. Also in 2004 Mateschitz decided to buy the Jaguar Formula 1 motor racing team for £60 million. This built on several years of sponsoring extreme sports – to back the Red Bull image as an edgy, though non-alcoholic, drink.

Mateschitz took huge risks, but has reaped huge rewards. The Red Bull business is believed to be worth well over £1000 million. It rivals Pepsi-Cola for profitability and worldwide impact. Quite an achievement for a cheap energy drink from Thailand.

Questions

(20 marks; 25 minutes)

1 (a) Outline two risks Mateschitz faced when launching Red Bull in Europe. (4)

   (b) Explain how he overcame these risks. (4)

2 Surprisingly, Red Bull has never faced competition from a major soft drinks firm. How well do you think a 'Coca-Cola Energy' drink might do today against Red Bull? (6)

3 Discuss what Mateschitz has gained from starting up Red Bull, using the three factors identified under the heading, 'What are the main rewards?'. (6)

Calculated risks

Risks in business (and in life) are unavoidable. Well-run firms think about the risks that may turn against them, then estimate the possible impact. For example, the cost of dropping out of the Premiership is said to be about £20 million. Apart from the top five sides, each of the other clubs will think about the chance of relegation and the cost. If there are 3 relegation places for 15 teams, there is a 20 per cent chance of relegation *every year*. So a wise club chairman would have a plan for how the team would cope. Sadly, the past experience of teams such as Nottingham Forest and Southampton suggests that not every club does this.

> '*Take calculated risks. That is quite different from being rash.*'
> **General Patton, famous soldier**

Sweetshops that run out of ice cream on hot days may make the customer go somewhere else next time

Upside risk

Of course, luck does not have to be bad. New products can prove to be unexpected successes. New clubs can get great launch publicity and never look back. No one expected the first Harry Potter to be a worldwide smash – even the publisher, Bloomsbury Publishing. In 1995 Bloomsbury made a loss of £391,000. It offered an advance of £2500 for a 'quirky little book' called *Harry Potter and the Philosopher's Stone*. Today, author J. K. Rowling is one of the richest women in Britain and Bloomsbury Publishing makes annual profits of up to £20 million.

Ideally, firms should plan for the unexpected ups as well as downs. The most

Harry Potter author JK Rowling

obvious reason is to help cope with the success. High sales may be an embarrassment if you cannot keep up with them. Sweetshops that run out of ice cream on hot days not only lose an opportunity to sell, but may also make the customer go somewhere else next time.

Calculating risks

There are two elements to risk:

1 What is the chance of it happening?

2 What is the cost of it happening?

Big firms, such as Nestlé or Johnson & Johnson, know that only one in five new products is successful. So four out of every five (80 per cent) are flops. Yet companies such as Johnson & Johnson are constantly launching new products, backed by expensive TV advertising. Why?

They do it because, on average, it takes them five new product launches for every success. They know that a flop will cost them around £10 million. A success, however, can easily bring in £50–100 million. So four flops costing £40 million are outweighed by one star product. That's intelligent, calculated risk. Here, the rewards outweigh the risks, so the risk:reward ratio is favourable.

New firms will not know the chances of success or failure in their particular business; and will not know the costs involved. So new, small firms find it much harder to calculate risk and reward.

Drawing the right conclusions

For a small firm there is more to consider than just risk and reward. There are also the consequences. When Bloomsbury risked a £2500 advance to J. K. Rowling, it was not going to break the bank, even if Harry Potter proved a flop. But if a small firm takes a big step, failure may drag the business down.

Clearly it is vital to think not only about the chance of something going wrong, but also the consequences. Microsoft can risk £100 million on a technology that may or may not work. £100 million is only 2 per cent of the money it keeps in its bank account. For a small firm, risking £10,000 may be risking the whole future of the business.

Clever businesspeople therefore try to weigh up:

● The chances of success or failure.

● The costs or benefits of success or failure.

● The implications for the business as a whole.

Learning from your mistakes

A key part of taking risks is to accept that some will prove a mistake. Well-run businesses see learning from mistakes as key to success. The 2008 banking crisis came about partly because earlier mistakes had not proved costly. When house prices were rising, lending to people who struggled to pay hardly mattered to the banks. The property could be sold at a profit and everyone won. But when times got tougher, mistakes proved much costlier. Few bankers will forget the lessons they learnt in 2008/2009.

> 'If you do it right 51 per cent of the time you will end up a hero.'
> **Alfred Sloan, president, General Motors**

> 'The policy of being too cautious is the greatest risk of all.'
> **J. Nehru, India's first prime minister**

Exercises

(A and B: 20 marks; 25 minutes)

A. Read the unit, then ask yourself:

1 Outline two significant risks that might be faced over the coming year by a small sports shop in your local high street. (4)

2 Explain why a firm should benefit from calculating the risks involved in its operations. (4)

3 Only 1 in 20 newly published books becomes a sales success. How does the experience of Bloomsbury Publishing explain why new books keep getting published? (5)

B. Skye and Ted Barton took over the family fish and chip shop when Skye's parents retired. The business kept them going financially, but seemed to be going nowhere. Skye looked into buying the shop next door, to create the space for a sit-down restaurant section. She was sure that would attract office workers at lunchtime. Her calculations showed that it would cost £18,000 and could generate an extra £9000 profit a year. But Ted rejected the idea, saying, 'You can't be certain. There's a real risk that your figures are wrong.'

1 Describe Ted's attitude to risk. (3)

2 Explain why it is necessary for all businesspeople to be willing to take risks. (4)

Practice Questions

Allan Leighton, former boss of Asda, on risk

My definition of 'business risk' is some activity you're prepared to take to push the business forward with a pretty good chance of success.

My style is probably high risk. But under my criteria I have always approached it as a calculated gamble. The most important thing is that businesses won't grow without taking risks. But you can reduce that risk. That's in the quality of the planning and how well it's carried out.

What kills business is complacent staff. Complacency is always the greatest risk. That's why people get it wrong. What happens with complacency is, one, you get further away from the customer; the other is you get further away from your people.

You have to stay very close to the

customer and your people. The people who tell you it first are the customers … If you listen to the customer, you'll see if you are getting complacent or not. You've got to find ways of doing that.

(Source: adapted from questions posed by Pamela Shimell, author of *The Universe of Risk*, www.pearson.com)

Allan Leighton, former boss of ASDA

Questions

(20 marks; 25 minutes)

1 (a) Why may it be 'that businesses won't grow without taking risks'? (4)

(b) Why might 'complacency' be a risk? (3)

2 Explain how Allan Leighton's thoughts on risk compare with the quote in the text (see page 71) from Nehru, former prime minister of India. (5)

3 (a) Outline two benefits of staying 'very close to the customer'. (4)

(b) Allan Leighton is clear that risk is not just about decisions, but also how well they are carried out. How may it help if the boss stays close to staff ('your people') as well as to customers? (4)

Other important enterprise skills

To be enterprising requires more than creativity and a taste for risk. An enterprising individual is one who can:

1 Think ahead.

2 Make connections.

3 Show initiative.

4 Make decisions.

5 Show leadership.

> *'The only thing we know about the future is that it's going to be different.'*
> **Peter Drucker, management guru**

Think ahead

There are two main parts to thinking ahead. The first is to be able to see what people will want in the future. On 2 September 2005 HMV announced the launch of a music download service (charging 79p per digital song). Coming three years after the launch of Apple's massively successful iTunes service, the HMV boss admitted the company had moved too slowly. He said, 'We were unsure whether the digital delivery of music would become a viable and worthwhile market'. Not much evidence of enterprise there, then.

The second part of thinking ahead is to anticipate problems or opportunities. In July 2007 Bloomsbury Publishing launched the final Harry Potter book. The Harry Potter series had sold more than 400 million copies. Now what was Bloomsbury going to do? To the company's credit, it had thought ahead. By December 2007, it had built up a cash pile of £48 million, making it easy to buy out a primary school publishing business in early 2008.

Make connections

In business, one thing leads to another. To have an idea of how everything connects together is vital. For instance, having the Olympics in London in 2012 has huge implications for many firms, especially in the hotel trade. The enterprising hotel manager must think ahead. How will 2012 be? What will need to be done beforehand? What might life be like afterwards? After the 2008 Olympics, Beijing was left with too many new hotels in the wrong location for tourists and business travellers.

A useful approach is to draw up a mind map. This encourages you to think about the option, and about how things link together. The figure on the following page shows a mind map for a small London hotel chain, thinking ahead to the Olympics. It would be a way to think about the whole picture.

Show initiative

Initiative is crucial. It means not waiting for orders or until you see what everyone else

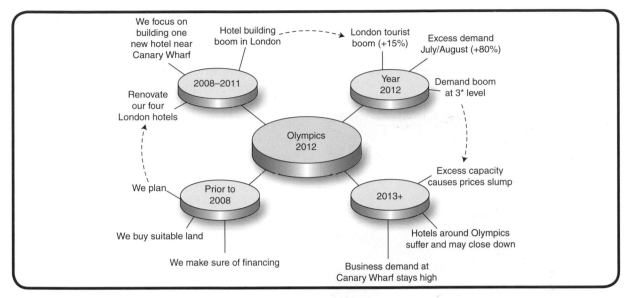

A small London hotel chain, thinking ahead to the Olympics 2012

is doing. It requires you to be bold, decisive and willing to accept that you might get it wrong. The initiative might not be as huge as Apple's move into the phone business with its iPhone. Here are other good examples of initiative:

- Cadbury's market research manager uses a large part of her budget to explore customer opinions of white chocolate-based face creams; if a successful new product emerges, she will be the hero; if not, the company may start to doubt her judgement.

- Jamie Oliver's initiative in approaching Greenwich Council to get permission to carry out his school dinners experiment.

Only through initiative can a business hope to be first into a market; and only by being first do you have a chance to make a real impact.

Talking Point

How could you use your skills to launch a profitable business for the 2012 Olympics?

Make decisions

Decision making is crucial. Not only when initiative could be taken, but also in response to difficulties. A hairdressers with three outlets may have one that is losing money. Decisions are required. Perhaps the outlet should close or perhaps it needs a revamp. When the bankrupt bookstore chain Dillons was taken over by Waterstones, over half the shops were found to have been losing money for years. But no one did anything about it!

To make decisions successfully, the key is to find out as much information as possible, from as many sources as possible. Most important are your staff and your customers. Ask for views and opinions, then decide, and carry the decision through without hesitation.

In early September 2008, Newcastle was in disarray. Popular manager Kevin Keegan was threatening to resign unless he was given

'Ever notice that "What the hell" is always the right decision?'
Marilyn Monroe, film star

control over player transfer dealings. Club owner Mike Ashley had to decide whether to back his manager or Dennis Wise, his executive director of football. Ashley chose Wise, but not necessarily wisely.

Newcastle United Football club

Show leadership

Leadership has a lot to do with qualities such as decisiveness, initiative and the ability to think ahead. One more element, though, is the personality and the character to make people believe in you. This might be helped by self-confidence, but in fact some excellent leaders are quite shy. Some are great at one-to-one chats, but less comfortable when speaking in public or when chatting in a group of people. Although Richard Branson comes over very well on TV, he is said to be very shy and often tongue-tied.

Good leadership needs to be based on good judgement about the right decision or initiative, plus the determination to see things through. It also requires an ability to make people want to share the leader's path (i.e. to help achieve his or her aims). This requires either charisma or the ability to make people respect and believe in him or her.

> 'A leader is a dealer in hope.'
> **Napoleon Bonaparte, soldier and French emperor**

Different leadership approaches

Leader	Approach to leadership	Outcome
Alex Ferguson	Tough, almost bullying; very decisive; brutally honest.	Gains huge respect from staff.
Richard Branson	Full of initiative; friendly and sociable.	Love and respect from staff; inspirational.
Tony Blair	Decisive; persuasive; claims to listen, but seems not to hear.	Gets what he wants, but results can be divisive.

Exercises

(A and B: 25 marks; 30 minutes)

A. Read the unit, then ask yourself:

1   Explain how a business can benefit from a leader who thinks ahead. (3)

2   If you were the boss of a company, outline two actions you could take that would encourage staff to show more initiative. (4)

3   Looking back to September 2008, did the Newcastle board make the right decision? Briefly explain your answer. (3)

4   Outline one strength and one weakness of your own, which would affect your ability to be a successful leader. (4)

B. Joy Marsh, boss of a small advertising agency, was worried about the effect of rising expense account spending. When she asked her staff, they were equally puzzled about the possible cause. At a board meeting a director mentioned production quality problems since the head TV producer had left the agency. Joy then spent two days with the TV production team, to try to understand the issues. This made her realise that staff were spending more on their expense accounts to give posh lunches to unhappy clients. She solved the problems within a week by hiring a top producer from New York.

1   (a) Outline the connections Joy made. (3)

   (b) Explain the benefit to the business of making those connections. (4)

2   Outline two leadership qualities shown by Joy. (4)

Practice Questions

Cool dinners

Jamie Oliver, celebrity chef, took the initiative to alter the diets of nearly 30,000 school kids in Greenwich. He soon found three massive problems: a budget of only 37p per meal, the fact that most 'dinner ladies' could not cook, and that many school 'kitchens' only had equipment for reheating food. Then came the biggest problem of all: that the pupils did not want freshly cooked, inventive food. They had grown up with fat-laden foods such as Turkey Twizzlers and chips, and did not want to change.

There were times when Oliver felt like giving up. 'I'd be getting hassles with the contractors, hassles with the school, hassle with the kids and hassle with the council,' he remembers. 'The responsibility felt enormous. It was like everything was down to me and I had to reassure everyone that it was going to be fine, when inside I felt like ✳✳✳✳.'

Jamie Oliver

But gradually everything fell into place. The menus worked out, and the processed food was consigned to history. A contract for proper meat was negotiated with Harvey Nichols, retailer to the rich and famous, which worked out cheaper than the previous one for processed chunks with a wholesaler and, biggest achievement of all, the kids started eating Jamie's food. 'It was a close-run thing,' he says. 'When we first abandoned the processed food, most of the kids abandoned us. It was only when we had a spell of really nasty weather and the kids couldn't be bothered to go elsewhere that they started coming back.'

(Source: *The Guardian*, Tuesday 15 February 2005)

Questions

(20 marks; 25 minutes)

1   (a) Outline three enterprise qualities shown by Jamie Oliver. (6)

   (b) **Which one of these qualities do you think was the most important in his success in this case? Explain why. (5)**

2   Jamie managed to keep going when times were tough. How important do you think determination might be in a successful leader? (4)

3   Outline the evidence in the text about the satisfaction Jamie gained from his school dinners initiative. (5)

Exam-style Questions

DON'T RUSH; check answers carefully

1. Which of the following is the best reason to use a mindmap when making a decision? (1)

a) It's a way of listing out all the advantages and all the disadvantages.

b) It encourages deeper thought about how one thing leads to another.

c) It's a way of identifying all the Strengths, Weaknesses, Opportunities and Threats.

d) It encourages you to think 100 per cent positively, and therefore avoids the risk of negativity.

e) It makes you balance rewards against risks.

2. This year looks a tough one to start a housebuilding firm, but that's exactly what Tamara and Callum plan to do. They have £40,000 in cash savings and can get a mortgage of £180,000 on their 3-bedroom house. They think they will need £210,000 to build their first house, which they have the skills to do themselves. They plan to sell it for £250,000. Which two of the following qualities will be the most important for them in the coming year? (2)

a) Showing leadership.

b) The ability to persuade.

c) Willingness to take risks and make decisions.

d) Using mindmaps.

e) Making effective use of deliberate creativity.

f) The ability to analyse competitor strengths and weaknesses.

g) Determination.

3. Which of the following is the best definition of deliberate creativity? (1)

a) Making sure that creativity is one of the factors for selecting every new member of staff.

b) Carefully selecting the most able staff to be the creative stars of the business.

c) Deliberately hiring staff with top results on degree courses such as 'creative arts'.

d) Selecting one aspect to a product or a problem, then asking 'How could it be different?'

e) Making sure to check every new idea out on the public, especially those in the target market.

The following two questions (4 and 5) are based on this passage of text:

Leyla and Karim are about to open a Turkish café, selling Turkish and English breakfasts, but only Turkish foods at lunch and in the evening. Leyla worked for a year at her father's Turkish café in a fruit and vegetable market, so she understands what busy customers want. They have chosen a location just 150 metres from their home in Southfields, South London. There are three cafés nearby, so they feel confident that it's a good location. The business is to get started as an unlimited liability business.

4. Which three of the following risks are of the greatest concern in their launch? (3)

a) That their choice of location might not be for businesslike reasons.

b) They may make too many mistakes due to lack of experience with customers.

c) They may lack the initiative to succeed.

d) They have not thought about the exchange rate of the £ with the $.

e) They have not yet checked on the prices charged by their local rivals.

f) They haven't asked why there is no Turkish café at that site at the moment.

5. Which of the following is the right term to describe Leyla and Karim? (1)

a) Business leaders.

b) Enterpreters.

c) Entrepreneurs.

d) Business managers.

e) Company directors.

6. Carly and Owen plan to spend £100,000 opening a night club. Research shows that a successful club can make a £500,000 profit over a five-year period. A flop would make nothing. They think there's a 50/50 chance of success or a flop. From the following, pick the one statement that gives Carly and Owen the best advice on what to do. (1)

a) Open the club. A chance of making £500,000 is too big to turn down.

b) Don't open the club. A 50 per cent chance of a flop is too high.

c) Don't open the club. £100,000 profit a year is no better than the sum invested.

d) Open the club, but only if you can afford to lose £100,000.

7. What's the best statement of the difference between invention and innovation?   (1)

a) Inventors think of new ideas, but only innovators show how they could work.

b) Innovators think up new ideas, but only inventors show how they could work.

c) Innovators find a new use for existing inventions.

d) Inventors think up new ideas; innovators bring a new idea to the market.

e) Innovators reject all existing inventions and come up with something original.

PUTTING A BUSINESS IDEA INTO PRACTICE

Introduction to getting it right

In spring 2004 Trevor and Ray started a company making and selling high quality garden furniture. Although young, they had more than ten years' experience between them in this business, and had spotted a gap in the £500 to £1000 price range. They would sell directly from a website, advertised in garden centres and gardening magazines. The business was based in their home town of Carlisle.

Before starting, they estimated the sales they would achieve and all the costs involved, month by month. They used these figures to get a bank loan to help provide the £48,000 it cost them to start up. As the bar chart below shows, the early months were a struggle, but after the 'terrific quality furniture' was mentioned in a BBC TV gardening programme, sales went crazy in July.

Trevor and Ray had to hire 12 extra carpenters to match production to the level of demand. They only hired three permanently, with the rest on weekly contracts. This was fortunate because in January 2005 Carlisle was put under four feet of water by flooding and the factory was ruined. It took three months to start up again. Several other local businesses closed and never reopened. Trevor and Ray had made sure the previous summer to treat their July/August boom as a lucky windfall. They banked the **profit** rather than spent it, and were able to use that money to rebuild the business after the floods.

From business idea to business success

Many new businesses fail. No one is sure of the right figures, but probably no more than half are successful. In many cases this

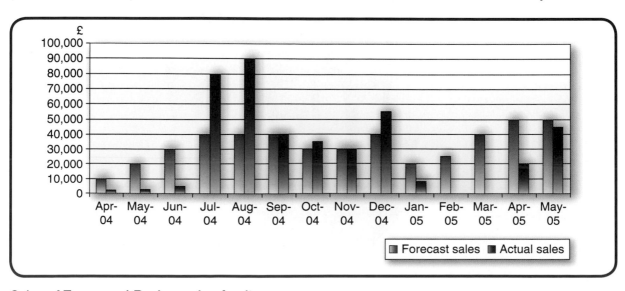

Sales of Trevor and Ray's garden furniture

Flooding in Carlisle in January 2005

is because too little thought has gone into it. People start up second-hand bookshops or little teashops because they want to. Husband and wife may agree, 'It would be lovely to run our own bookshop'. In fact, it may prove quite depressing to run a bookshop if hardly anyone comes in.

Talking Point

Would these business ideas succeed or fail?

- an online weekly magazine, *Celeb Fashion First!*, costing £20 a year
- a mobile pizza van to be positioned outside your school at lunchtime.

In other cases people may have a great business idea. They may have thought it through with care and intelligence. Yet the business may flop. Good ideas do not automatically become great successes. This is because many businesses are complicated to run effectively. For example, to start up and run a restaurant effectively, you have to:

1 Find a great location.

2 Negotiate an affordable rent.

3 Design a stylish restaurant and a workmanlike kitchen.

4 Get it built, equipped and decorated on time and not too expensively.

5 Appoint high quality, well-motivated staff.

6 Train them well and keep them motivated.

7 Agree the right menus to appeal to the customers you want.

9 Set prices at the right balance between customer 'value' and your own profit.

9 Keep ordering the right quantity and quality of supplies (meat, fish, etc.).

10 Keep the atmosphere in the restaurant as lively and enjoyable as possible.

11 Make sure that every customer receives fresh, hot food without long waits between courses.

Keep the atmosphere in the restaurant as lively and enjoyable as possible

And so on and so on, lunchtime and evening, every week for 52 weeks a year. One bad experience may mean a customer never returns; and if that customer is a restaurant reviewer, he or she may turn hundreds of people away from the restaurant. The following quotes from national newspaper restaurant reviews in 2005 and 2006 demonstrate the point (both about restaurants charging £90 to £100 for a meal for two): 'The potato was so grossly oversalted you'd be reported to social services if you fed it to a three year old.' 'Sliced bread turned up warm on the outside and frozen in the middle. The second lot was still stone cold in the middle and the end piece was hard and stale.'

Success requires a clear plan, enthusiastic leadership, effective organisation and a bit of luck. It starts with a realistic forecast of sales. How many customers are likely? And how much will they be prepared to pay? A clothes shop might attract 400 visitors on a Saturday, but only 50 may buy something, perhaps with an average value of £20. The Saturday takings may seem great at £20 x 50 = £1000, but what if the clothes cost £500 to buy, the wage bill is £250 and other bills amount to £150? With costs of £500+£250+£150=£900, there is only £100 profit on the Saturday. The theft of just one expensive dress might wipe that out.

So a sales forecast must be compared with the costs to make an estimate of the profit. If the profit seems too low, the entrepreneur should think how to boost it. Should prices be increased? Or should costs be reduced? Or should a different location be found to attract more customers? The thing to avoid is to start a business and only realise later that it never had much chance of success. For example, Stelios, the founder of easyJet, launched a chain of internet cafes called easyInternetcafé. He later closed many of them down because the amount charged per hour could not cover the costs of the business.

Financing the start-up

Having worked out a profitable business idea and set out a believable forecast of **revenues** and costs, it is time to raise the capital to start the business. The key to persuading others is for them to be sure that you are backing the idea with as much money as you can. No lender would provide more than half the launch capital. They want the entrepreneur to have risked at least half the start-up capital. And lenders are sure to want security for their money. In other words, they want their money backed by specific assets, such as property. If the business fails, the bank seizes the assets that are the security on its investment. The entrepreneur may lose her/his whole investment, but the bank will probably be okay.

Although financing the start-up can be difficult, the rewards may be huge. Bebo was started by British entrepreneur Michael Birch in 2005. It quickly became the world's third largest social networking site. In March 2008, Birch sold Bebo to AOL for £417 million. Not bad for three years' work.

As shown in the table below, although every company has share capital, not all have borrowings. Those that do tend to use the flexibility of a bank overdraft in preference to

The social networking site BeBo

the rigidity of a bank loan. Very few receive any form of government grant/allowance to help in the process of starting up.

Sources of finance for small companies in Britain

Share capital	100%
Overdraft	53%
Leasing	27%
Medium-term loans	24%
Grants	6%

Source: *Finance for SMEs*, University of Warwick, 2005)

Conclusion

To start a successful business requires a great idea and a great plan for making it happen. A good understanding of finance is important, because profit can only happen if costs are kept below the value of the sales. Investors demand the opportunity to make good profits. So business leaders have to know how to build a good level of sales, and how to keep costs down. In a business such as Ryanair, this is part of the everyday thinking of every manager. No wonder Ryanair has been such a success.

Revision Essentials

Billion – one thousand million (1,000,000,000).

Profit – revenue minus costs. This is the surplus that can be used to reward shareholders or to invest in the expansion of the business.

Revenue – the value of sales (i.e. the number of customers × the average amount they spend). This does not allow for costs.

Exercises

(25 marks; 30 minutes)

A. Read the unit, then ask yourself:

1   Look at the sales graph for Trevor and Ray's business. Then calculate:

   (a) The extra sales in August 2004, when comparing actual with the forecast figures. (2)

   (b) The sales shortfall in April 2005, when comparing actual with forecast sales. (2)

(c) The approximate total sales lost because of the flooding. Show your workings and explain your reasoning. (5)

2   (a) Reread the 11 steps identified for setting up a successful restaurant. Identify six steps to setting up a successful clothes shop. (6)

       (b) Explain which two you consider the most important and why. (4)

       (c) Outline two ways in which luck might affect whether or not a new clothes shop is successful. (4)

3   Outline one reason why a bank insists on its loans being backed by security. (2)

Practice Questions

Scoop ice cream – start-up success

When Matteo Pantani arrived from Italy to approach estate agents about a central London location for an ice cream parlour, most turned him down. They had all seen ice cream shops enjoy a super first summer, then collapse from negative cash flow during the winter. At the time he was looking – late 2006 – the economy was buoyant, so estate agents saw no reason to take a chance on such a high-risk business.

Yet, by Autumn 2008 Matteo's ice cream parlour 'Scoop' was a great success in London's Covent Garden. After a long time looking, Matteo found premises of the right size close to a busy area for tourists and Londoners. And he was starting to look for other locations for Scoop2 and Scoop3.

So why did Scoop succeed where others have failed? A good start is that Matteo thinks that selling high quality ice cream is 'like selling happiness ... £2 for ten minutes of happiness'. His thrill from running the business is his pride in his product, and in people's reactions to it. He is working 16-hour days, so he needs to enjoy it!

The key is that Scoop attracts regular customers. The fantastic quality of the

Scoop ice cream

Italian ice cream plus the range of flavours keeps people coming back for more. The ice cream is made from high quality ingredients and is made in fresh batches every day, on the premises. For Matteo the only downside is having to get up extra early to find the time to make all the ice cream.

But having a good product is not enough. Matteo is sure that, 'If I just made ice cream the business would be closed by now. I had to market it – through the website [www.scoopgelato.com], by coming up with special ice cream promotions and going round to restaurants offering samples – to get them to buy my product.'

The Scoop start-up shows that there is room for business based on passion, determination and commitment to the product and the customers. Matteo is sure that he will make good profits for his investors and himself, but that's only as a result of his success in 'selling happiness'.

Questions

(25 marks; 30 minutes)

1. Outline the main enterprise skills shown by Matteo in starting Scoop. (4)

2. Examine two factors that were important in turning Scoop from a business idea into a business success. (6)

3. On balance, do you think starting Scoop was high-risk or low-risk? Explain your answer. (8)

4. Which factors might prove important when Matteo expands Scoop by opening two more ice cream parlours? Explain which single factor is likely to be the most important. (7)

Estimating revenue

Ted Draycott's alarm goes off at 3.45 every morning. He drives from Watford to Covent Garden market to buy the best and freshest fruit and vegetables. If strawberries are 32p a punnet and the weather forecast is good, he might buy 4 dozen boxes (nearly 1000 punnets). He expects to sell them on for 45p, so that Watford's greengrocers can charge the public 95p or £1. If the buying price is 50p he might buy only a dozen boxes, especially if rain is forecast.

Ted's skill is an ability to make quick, accurate **sales forecasts**. If he gets things wrong he may run out of strawberries halfway round the town, leaving some of his greengrocer customers angry. Or he might buy too many and find himself pleading with people to take the fruit off his hands, perhaps at a cut-down price.

On a good day, Ted can make £800 profit between 3.45 and 10.45 a.m., leaving

Ted needs to make quick, accurate sales forecasts of what to supply to Watford's greengrocers

himself free all afternoon and evening. On a bad day he may take 12 hours to barely cover his costs. In fact, his profit averages £2000+ a week, so you can see that he's doing pretty well!

For a bigger business, such as Innocent Drinks, there needs to be a bit more certainty. If Ted has a bad week, he can cut down, to stop spending too much. Innocent employs over 50 people and has a wage bill of £40,000 a week. It simply cannot afford to have weeks where no money is made or where revenues are expected, but do not turn up. Nor will Tesco accept, 'Sorry, we haven't any strawberry smoothies this week; there's been a rush on them and we've run out.' Every business needs to find a way to estimate **sales revenue**.

Sales revenue comes from the number of things you sell multiplied by the price you charge. If Yeovil Town FC sells 7000 tickets at £20 each, its revenue is £140,000. Yeovil decides its own ticket price, so the uncertain factor is the level of demand. Will it sell 7000 tickets (£140,000) or 5500 tickets (£110,000)? Even for such a well-run club, the difference of £30,000 is very important.

Price

For some businesses the price cannot be estimated with full confidence. At the start of 2008, BP might have expected that its petrol pump price would average £1.00 per litre. In fact, it proved to be nearer to £1.15. In Africa, farmers producing coffee could have hoped for a price of 60p a pound in March 2008, but by May they were receiving only 50p. The near 20 per cent fall in their incomes condemned them to desperately low living standards.

Prices cannot be estimated with confidence when:

- The business operates in a market where prices change in the short term due to variations in supply and demand.

- Competition is direct and fierce (e.g. Ryanair competing with easyJet).

- You are launching a new product and cannot be sure of the consumer response (e.g. the original Xbox launched at $399, but the price was cut to $299 within a few weeks).

Talking Point

Richard Branson's Virgin Galactic plans to offer space tourism: five minutes of sub-orbital weightlessness in space. How might he decide on the right price per flight?

Quantity

Occasionally, the demand for a product or service can be judged with confidence. Robbie Williams concert tours have always sold out, so it seems safe to expect them to sell out next time round (but what about Michael Jackson?). Similarly, sales of Heinz baked beans are extremely predictable. They will have seasonal peaks and troughs (sell more in the autumn and winter), but Heinz managers know that, so they will be able to forecast with a high degree of accuracy. The precision of the revenue estimate will be helped by the strength of the brand. Not even Tesco could decide to stop stocking Heinz beans; nor could a huge advertising campaign for HP beans hurt Heinz. A revenue forecast made for six months' time by a

Sales of Heinz baked beans are extremely predictable

Heinz director would prove very accurate. Therefore the business can make sure it has the right quantity of machinery, staff and raw ingredients. Managing this type of business is easy.

It is quite different when trying to plan the revenues for a posh London restaurant. Customers will usually be a mixture of wealthy Londoners, businesspeople and visitors to London. The restaurant could be full this week, but in six months it might have been emptied by:

- a newspaper review that condemns it as dull and overpriced.

- an economic slowdown, leading to cutbacks in luxury spending.

- terrorism or other reasons for people to avoid London.

Conclusion

The point can be summed up in this way: revenue is the quantity of sales multiplied by the price. In some cases this is easy to predict; in many other cases it is virtually impossible. For every business the circumstances are different. This affects the ability of the firm to run smoothly and efficiently. Most managers would rather have a stable revenue of £1 million a month than a revenue that averages £1.2 million, but in an erratic way. This is because predictable revenues allow firms to keep costs low enough to make a good profit. Revenues that jump around make it much harder to trade profitably.

Revision Essentials

Sales forecasts – estimates of the future level of sales to be achieved by a new or existing product.

Sales revenue – the total value of sales made within a period of time, such as a month. To find the value, multiply the quantity sold by the price.

Exercises

(30 marks; 30 minutes)

A. Read the unit, then ask yourself:

1 (a) What is the formula for calculating a company's sales revenue? (2)

   (b) If a bus company sold 4000 tickets a day at £1.20 each, what would be its daily sales revenue? (2)

   (c) If you knew that selling 500 shirts produced a revenue of £7500, what would be the price per shirt? (3)

2 Explain briefly whether it would be easy or hard to predict next year's selling price for:

   (a) Cadbury Dairy Milk chocolate. (3)

   (b) The world price for oil. (3)

3 Why may direct and fierce competition make it difficult to estimate prices with confidence? (3)

4 Outline two ways in which a business could use accurate forecasts of future sales. (6)

5 Give two reasons why a revenue forecast made for six months' time by a Heinz director would prove very accurate. (2)

6 Explain briefly whether it would be easy or hard to predict next year's sales volumes for:

   (a) Topshop clothes. (3)

   (b) The Sun newspaper. (3)

Practice Questions

Japan has always been a tough market for US firms such as Microsoft. The Xbox games console has been a big flop there. Yet Apple seems to have cracked it. SoftBank Mobile, Apple's exclusive provider of the iPhone2 (3G) in Japan, grabbed 215,400 'activations' in July 2008, more than half the market. 'We believe our large net growth was an iPhone effect,' SoftBank representatives said.

Japan's cultural barriers

Many people predicted that Apple's phone would flop in Japan, a market where electronic hardware is usually more sophisticated than other countries. Apple's original iPhone could not be used in Japan because it was too low-tech. Other critics pointed out that the iPhone lacked a variety of elements unique to the Japanese mobile market. These include the ability to enter Japanese characters such as the pictographs shown that many people in the country consider essential in mobile messaging.

Differences in the Japanese market previously frustrated Apple's ability to increase Mac sales there, as many Japanese, particularly the youth demographic, now use smartphones in place of full-sized computers. Microsoft has faced similar problems in trying to sell its Xbox game consoles in the country, where tastes in gaming software simply differ.

From the makers of iPod

A factor that has helped launch the iPhone 3G in Japan is that Apple's iPod is already wildly popular there. In addition to brand recognition, the Japanese market also seems to be attracted to Apple's simple, easy to use interfaces, which are not a strong point in other existing devices being sold in the Japanese market.

Similarly, while Japanese phones are revered for their exceptional hardware styling and features, they also sport complex menus that are difficult to navigate and services that are often impractical to use, leaving many of their pioneering features ignored. As one reader noted, 'most phones in Japan felt like you're running Windows 98'.

Questions

(20 marks; 20 minutes)

1 Outline two possible reasons why the Microsoft Xbox console has been a flop in Japan. (4)

2 Examine the difficulties Apple may have faced if sales of the iPhone 3G proved much higher than expected. (6)

3 Discuss why a business moving into a market such as electronics in Japan would need to carry out careful research in order to forecast sales. (10)

Estimating costs

What do you think it would cost to start up a business making potato crisps? After all, the attractions are clear. A bag of Walkers selling for 35p weighs only 30 g. As potatoes can be bought for 33p a kilo, the potato inside the bag costs about 1p. There's oil, salt and flavourings as well, but not conceivably coming to more than 2p in total. If the packaging materials cost another 1p in total, our 35p bag cost 3p to make. No wonder Gary Lineker looks so pleased with himself.

Of course, it is not that simple. There are many other costs: the factory rent, the cost of machinery, the salaries of the research and development staff who think up the new flavours, and the marketing people who plan the advertising and promotions.

The costs of making potato crisps

For someone thinking of starting their own business, estimating costs is one of the hardest things to do. The starting point is to realise that there are two types of cost: **fixed costs** and **variable costs**.

Variable costs

These are costs that vary with the quantity sold and therefore the quantity made. They are costs that relate directly to making the sale and therefore making the product. If Walkers runs a brilliant new advertising campaign and crisp sales double, they will have to buy in twice as many potatoes, twice as much packaging, and so on. These are variable costs. They rise and fall in relation to sales and therefore output.

Examples of variable costs include:

- **raw materials** (e.g. potatoes for making crisps; cocoa beans for making chocolate).

- **bought-in components** (e.g. spark plugs for making cars; headphones when making iPods).

- **energy** used in the production process (e.g. gas for cooking in a restaurant).

- **piece-rate labour**, which means paying people per unit of work (e.g. £2 per pair of jeans made; commission paid to sales staff would also be a variable cost).

Fixed costs

These costs do not change as output changes. They are fixed in relation to output. Take the rent on a clothes shop, for example – it must be paid, whether sales are terrific or awful. Therefore it is fixed. Note, though, that the landlord can put up your rent, so the fact that it is a fixed cost does not mean it never changes.

Fixed costs are often related to a time period rather than sales or output. Rent, for instance, might be paid per month, as might staff salaries.

Examples of fixed costs include:

- **salaries** of permanent staff.

- **rent and (council) rates**.

- **marketing spending** (the budget for this will be set at the start of the year, and will not rise just because sales rise).

- **machinery and equipment**, which might include delivery vans.

Stop and think, what are the fixed costs and what are the variable costs of running:

- A Topshop branch?

- Manchester United FC?

- A kebab shop?

Then look at the answers in the table below.

Getting the numbers right

If you plan to open a kebab shop, it may be easy to decide which are the variable costs

A Topshop branch

Separating fixed and variable costs

Type of business	Fixed costs	Variable costs
A Topshop branch	Rent and rates Staff wages and salaries Security and insurance costs Lighting and heating Regular redecoration	Buying clothes from suppliers Carrier bags Damage/wastage/theft (which rise and fall depending on how busy the shop is)
Manchester United FC	Players' wages Staff salaries Ground maintenance	Programme and ticket printing Cost of pies/food bought in Cost of beer/drinks bought in
A kebab shop	Rent and rates Staff wages and salaries Lighting and heating Insurance costs Irregular redecoration	Buying in the meat, bread, salad, potatoes (or frozen chips) Energy (gas, etc.) for cooking Paper bags and other packaging

and which are the fixed costs, but what will the *exact* figures be? The only way to find out is to work at it. A trip to a local estate agent will tell you what rents are likely at different parts of the high street (they might vary from £600 to £4000 a month, depending on location). The estate agent will also know the level of council tax/rates on different properties. A look in the jobs advertisements in the local paper will show the hourly pay rates and salary levels locally. A few phone calls to insurance companies will give an idea of the insurance costs. A builder could give a quote on the cost of turning the shell of an empty shop into a kebab shop, with the electrics, gas and water in the right places. So most of the fixed costs can be established fairly easily.

It may be harder to estimate the variable costs. A Google search would get you the names of doner kebab meat suppliers. (I have just done this, and learned that a doner kebab grill/display machine costs between £650 and £1005. From a phone call I have been offered kebab meat to make 450 kebabs for £135 – that's 30p per kebab!) Of course, without experience you cannot be sure that you would really get 450 portions from the meat; so a sensible businessperson would be very cautious in estimating costs. To be on the safe side I would allow 60p in meat variable costs (plus the cost of pitta bread, salad, etc., so perhaps 80p in total).

Getting research done

Having completed my research, I can estimate the following totals:

- fixed costs of the kebab shop: £1200 per week.

- variable costs per kebab: £0.80.

I can now calculate the **total costs** at different levels of business. Most importantly, if I carry out research into potential sales levels, I can estimate the costs involved. For example, if research shows that 600 customers will come per week, my total weekly costs will be: 600 x £0.80 = £480 (variable costs) + £1200 (fixed costs) = £1680 (total costs). As long as the estimated revenues are higher than this figure, there is money to be made.

Revision Essentials

Fixed costs – costs that do not change when sales/output changes.

Total costs – all the costs of making a specific level of sales (i.e. fixed costs plus total variable costs).

Variable costs – costs that change in direct proportion to changes in sales/output.

Exercises

(20 marks; 25 minutes)

A. Read the unit, then ask yourself:

1 Explain the difference between fixed costs and variable costs. (4)

2 A greengrocer buys punnets of strawberries for 50p and sells them for £1. She must also pay £120 in weekly rent and £180 for other fixed costs.

   (a) What is the total cost of selling 500 punnets per week? (2)

   (b) What is the total cost of selling 1000 punnets per week? (2)

3 Identify two fixed costs and two variable costs of running:

   (a) A secondary school with 1200 pupils. (4)

   (b) A Tesco supermarket. (4)

4 Outline two reasons why people starting a new, small firm might make cost estimates that prove to be too low. (4)

Practice Questions

When the Choy Sum Chinese restaurant opened in Wimbledon, it was in a great position to estimate costs accurately. The owners already ran a Chinese five miles away in Fulham, so they knew how much to allow for the variable and fixed costs of their new outlet. Before opening, their plans showed:

Average price per dish	£4.40
Average variable cost per dish	£1.80
Fixed weekly overheads	£2000
Number of dishes sold p.w.	3000
Weekly revenue	£13,200

In fact, though, it proved harder than expected. The owners knew how much the ingredients *should* cost in a chicken and black bean sauce, but actual variable costs proved 25 per cent higher. The owners checked the figures carefully, trying to find whether staff were stealing food from the kitchens.

The explanation came in two parts. First, the restaurant manager at Wimbledon failed to attract and keep good chefs. So customers sent poor quality dishes back to the kitchen and the cooking had to be redone. The second problem stemmed from the first. Bookings were slow, with only 200 customers buying 1000 dishes per week, so fresh food went off and had to be thrown away.

Questions

(25 marks; 25 minutes)

1 If the forecast of 3000 dishes per week had been met, what would have been the total costs of operating Choy Sum, Wimbledon? (4)

2 Explain why sales proved lower than expected. (4)

3 Actual variable costs were 25 per cent higher than predicted; and the number of dishes sold was only 1000. What were the total costs of the business? How does that figure compare with the revenue generated from 1000 dishes sold? (6)

4 Identify two likely variable costs and three likely fixed costs of operating a Chinese restaurant. (5)

5 Choy Sum restaurant has now closed down in Wimbledon. To what extent can its failure be blamed on the owners' sloppy approach to estimating costs? (6)

Calculating and using profit

Profit is the difference between revenue and costs. It is calculated by the formula: **revenue minus total costs = profit**. If costs are greater than revenue, the result would be a negative number. That means making a loss.

Look at the position of British Airways. In 2002 it had a bad year and made a loss of £100 million. In 2008 its position was much better and it made a profit of £875 million.

For new, small firms, profit can be very difficult to achieve in the early days. Costs may be higher than necessary because staff have not yet learned to do things efficiently. Revenues may be low because word has not yet spread about the quality of the service you offer. W. H. Hales, a shop supplying and engraving sports trophies, took five years to become profitable. That was because it took that long for the word about the shop to spread among local football teams.

British Airways' operating costs and profit, 2002 and 2008

	2002	2008
Revenue	£8300m	£8775m
Operating costs	£8400m	£7900m
Operating profit	–£100m	£875m

Waiting for business

Forecasting profit

Unit 17 explained about estimating revenue, and Unit 18 showed how to estimate costs. Profit forecasts put these two estimates together. For a brand new firm it will be especially important that the forecast is done cautiously. In other words, cost estimates should allow for unexpectedly high figures; revenue estimates should allow for disappointing figures. If you start off with a gloomy forecast, the surprises should all be pleasing ones.

In this case, a new pizza takeaway business, Milano Pizza, had forecast a loss in its first year. It only expected to make a profit after 18 months of trading. In fact, it had a stroke of luck as the local Pizza Hut closed down! As a result, sales proved much higher than expected.

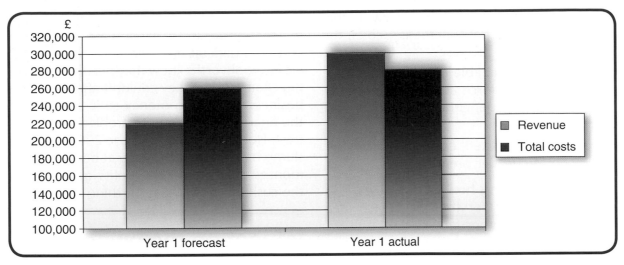

First year at Milano Pizza

What is the effect of over-optimistic forecasting?

The problem with optimism is that disappointment can cause serious problems. If managers forecast a £90,000 profit, they might plan to use the money to launch a new product. Money will be spent on researching the market, and perhaps testing a new product. This might be wasted if low profits make it impossible to finance the product launch. So forecasting should be done cautiously.

Using profit

The word 'profit' tends to suggest riches. In fact, reinvested profit generates 60 per cent of all the money invested to help firms grow. In other words, most of the capital firms use to finance growth comes from their own profit. Among the typical uses of profit may be:

- To invest in extra property or machinery, to help the business grow.

- To invest in more efficient systems or technology, to help cut costs.

- To help fund extra stocks of materials or finished goods.

- To pay out as dividends to shareholders, to give them an annual return on their investment.

The higher the profit, the easier it is to compete with the best firms around you. The best recruits want to go to the firms with the best prospects. High profits can help build a firm's reputation as a secure, attractive employer.

Talking Point

Identify the different ways profit might be used at:

a) Liverpool FC

b) the charity Oxfam

Dealing with losses

Business is not simple or predictable. A business that starts successfully may suffer a downturn in revenue if a new competitor opens up. Revenue may slip below costs, pushing the business into losses. This may not be too serious if it only lasts for a month or two, but lengthy periods of loss-making will force the closure of all but the richest businesses. To try to bring the business back into a profit-making position, the managers could:

- Try to boost revenues, especially if this can be done without increasing costs, for example a price increase.
- Act to reduce variable costs per unit (e.g. talk to the workforce about why and how to reduce wastage, either in a factory or a shop).
- Act to reduce fixed costs (e.g. consider moving to cheaper premises).

When considering how to cut losses, it is important to consider the effect each idea can have on the other factors. Cutting variable costs, for example, could damage sales if it is done by finding a cheaper, but lower quality, supplier.

Impact of profits and losses

Impact on the business

Profit is crucial if a business is to survive in the long term. It provides the rewards needed for the owners and the bankers, and gives scope for the business to expand or to change course in difficult times. In 2008 the managers at Woolworths knew they needed to make big changes, but they couldn't afford to. The business was losing money so it didn't have the finance to sort out its problems. By contrast, Honda responded to the 2008 car sales slump by paying staff to stay at home for two months. Years of good profits gave Honda the cushion to do the right thing.

Impact on the owners

Some owners get too excited when their new business becomes profitable. They spend freely on new cars, holidays and even houses. That would be fine if they had first put profits back into the business, i.e. made sure to build a cushion in the same way as Honda. The risk is that a bright start to a business might be followed by a tougher spell. Yesterday's BMW might become today's cash crisis. So it is important for owners to start up a business with some caution.

Exercises

(A and B: 30 marks; 30 minutes)

A. Read the unit, then ask yourself:

1 What is the difference between revenue and profit? (2)

2 Using the figures provided, briefly explain how British Airways turned a £100 million loss into a £875 million profit. (3)

3 Explain why, when making cost estimates, firms should allow for unexpectedly high figures. (3)

4 Look at the bar chart for Milano Pizza.

(a) Identify the forecast profit for year 1. (2)

(b) Identify the actual profit for year 1. (1)

(c) By how much did Milano Pizza's actual profit beat the forecast? (1)

5 After two difficult years since starting the business, Mark and Sima's coffee bar has made £8000 profit in the third year. Identify three possible ways this profit might be used by the business. (3)

B. Toni's ice cream van sells 150 ice creams a day at £1 each. The variable costs are 20p per ice cream and the fixed costs of running the van are £50 a day.

Tony's ice cream van sells 150 ice creams a day

1 What is Toni's profit per day? (4)

2 Toni's daughter wants him to put the price up to £1.20; she thinks sales will stay at 150 ice creams, but Toni is worried that sales will fall to 125.

(a) By how much will Toni's profit change if his daughter is right? (4)

(b) What will be the new profit if Toni is right about the price rise to £1.20? (4)

(c) Outline one reason why Toni might still want to keep the price at £1. (3)

The role and importance of cash

At the end of the year a business looks at its revenues and costs and works out the profit. Day by day, though, **cash** is more important than profit. Suppliers have to be paid, wages have to be paid, the rent and telephone bills have to be paid – with cash.

In business today the word 'cash' means more than the notes and coins in your pocket. Writing a cheque or paying by debit card is (just about) as quick as paying in banknotes, so it is regarded as the same thing. Whatever is in a firm's current account at the bank is just as useful as cash. Accountants use the term 'cash at bank' to summarise that it is the notes and coins you hold *plus* the money in your bank accounts. (From now on, when this book refers to cash, it always means 'cash at bank'.)

Why does cash matter?

Cash matters because, without it, bills go unpaid and a business can be taken to court

> 'In God we trust. All others pay cash.'
> **American saying**

and perhaps closed down. Staff expect to be paid every Friday, for example, and will not accept a boss saying, 'Sorry, I can't afford to pay you today. Hopefully we'll be okay on Monday.' Yet it is hard enough for individuals to *always* have cash available; if you are running a business with 15 staff and 150 customers, the problems are much greater.

On 10 September 2001 one British firm was celebrating winning a contract from a fourth major airline to supply it with steel cutlery. The following day's catastrophe at the Twin Towers in New York meant – worldwide – that all airlines were banned from using metal knives and forks. Overnight – and totally unpredictably – the firm's cash income dried up. It was spring 2005 before British airlines were allowed to begin using metal cutlery again. In the meantime the cutlery company had – somehow – to find the cash to keep going. A business that

Possible cash problems and consequences

A firm's possible cash problems	Consequences
Unable to pay the rent on time.	Landlord could evict you (e.g. you lose your prime-location shop premises).
Unable to pay staff reliably.	Your best staff find jobs elsewhere.
Unable to pay suppliers on time.	They may ignore you when they have some prime goods to sell (e.g. limited quantities of a hot new PS3 game).
Unable to seize a new business opportunity.	A close rival closes down and has stock available at knockdown prices, but you do not have the cash to buy it.

failed to find the cash to keep operating was Woolworths. It collapsed in November 2008 as a result of a cash flow crisis.

Problems managing cash

There are three factors that make it particularly hard to manage cash:

A toy shop may have problems managing cash because its sales are seasonal

1 Seasonal sales, such as a toy shop with 50 per cent of the year's total sales in December. For many months of the year trading is so poor that costs are not covered, so cash totals go down and down; it may be a struggle to survive until next Christmas.

2 When you have a few large customers, if one of them fails to pay on time, your cash position is squeezed badly. In November 2007, Alfred Wood and Sons, an 80-year-old family business, collapsed after its biggest customer stalled paying and then closed down.

3 When starting a business (e.g. if you are starting a restaurant there are huge start-up costs in the building and decoration, the kitchen equipment and the staff recruitment and training) cash can only start coming in when the doors

Talking Point

What problems managing cash might a business that manufactures fireworks have?

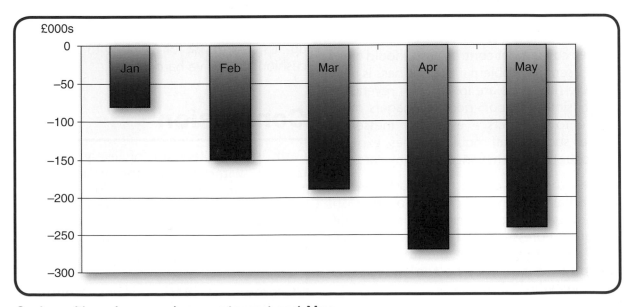

Cash position when opening a restaurant on 1 May

open for the first time, but business may start slowly until reputation spreads by word of mouth. This creates a cash position such as that shown in the figure below. If the business started up with £300,000 of finance, any cost overruns in the building work could have pushed the business under before it had even started!

How should cash be managed?

The key is to forecast the flows of cash into and out of the business. This topic (**cash flow**) is covered in the next unit. In addition to careful forecasting, a business must take care to:

● Negotiate a generous overdraft facility at the bank. A bank overdraft is a flexible way to borrow what you want, when you want and for how long you want. If you have no cash in your bank, but expect a fat cheque from a customer on Monday, you pay your £7000 salary bill today, Friday, using your overdraft. The cost of borrowing £7000 for three days would be less than £6 – well worth it to keep staff happy! Overdrafts (and other forms of borrowing) are explained fully in Unit 22: Raising finance.

● Keep costs under control; cash should never be a serious problem if the business is profitable (i.e. costs are lower than revenues). If business is poor, good managers make sure to cut costs – especially inessential ones such as staff mobile phones, expense accounts and renewing company cars.

● Keep the cash coming in. Most business in Britain is done on credit, not for cash. In other words, if Versace sells £400,000 worth of dresses to Harrods, the latter may be given two or three months to pay. A poorly run firm may be too soft on customers who fail to pay up on time. Firms allow customers an average of 70 days to pay up; but some firms allow over 120

days, which is four months! Waiting this long to be paid can strain a firm's cash resources and is no way to run a business.

Cash flow and business plans

When trying to raise finance from a bank or an investor, it is necessary to have a **business plan**. This sets out in detail the business opportunity and how the entrepreneur plans to succeed. Central to every business plan is a cash flow forecast. This will show how much cash is needed, month-by-month. It will therefore show investors how much cash the business needs to get started, and when the business will be able to pay the money back.

Writing a business plan forces the entrepreneur to think about every aspect of the start-up, including the risks of things going wrong. In this way, the plan should help to minimise the risk of something happening that is unexpected. Not even the best of business plans, though, would have helped someone realise in early 2008 that consumer spending would fall sharply in the autumn. So it's always wise to plan for an extra cash cushion, when starting a business. If your forecasts say you'll need £50,000 to start up, it's best to ask for £65,000 to give you a cushion to survive hard times.

Conclusion

Cash is the lifeblood of every business. Literally, without cash the business dies. Therefore it is vital to plan how much is needed and where to get it from. The best

> 'He that has lost his credit is dead to the world.'
> **George   Herbert,   17th   century Englishman**

possible source is from your own customers – making sure they pay up on time. It is also necessary to allow for the unexpected, which is why a large overdraft facility is a vital resource. Ideally you would use it rarely, to keep interest charges down. But when it is needed, its flexibility takes the pressure out of difficult financial situations.

Revision Essentials

Business plan – a formal document setting out a new business idea and how it is planned to make it succeed.

Cash – the money the firm holds in notes and coins and in its bank accounts.

Cash flow – the movement of money into and out of the firm's bank account.

Exercises

(A and B: 20 marks; 25 minutes)

A. Read the unit, then ask yourself:

1 Why do businesses think that money in bank accounts is part of their cash total? (2)

2 How might a house-building firm suffer if it lacks the cash to buy supplies of bricks in bulk? (4)

3 Outline two cash flow problems a British seaside hotel business might have. (4)

4 Before her first beauty salon opened, Moira Angell's builders took four months to complete the work – exactly double what they had promised. Outline two ways this would affect the cash position of the business. (4)

B. Look at the cash flow table (below) for a one-year-old women's clothes shop.

Cash flow for a women's clothes shop

All figures in £000s	January	February	March	April
Cash at start of month	90	94	85	83
Cash in	24	16	18	22
Cash out	20	25	20	22
Net monthly cash flow	4	–9	–2	0
Cash at end of month	94	85	83	83

Explain two ways in which the cash position of the business might be improved. (6)

Practice Questions

Cash crisis at Halifax Town

Halifax Town football club ('the Shaymen')

Cash is king in every business, but especially in professional sport. Before the start of every season supporters press their clubs to invest heavily to bring about success. Yet only a small number of clubs can succeed each year, so most will 'fail'.

In 2001 the failure of ITV Digital meant a drastic drop in TV income for all football clubs outside the Premiership. For Halifax Town FC ('the Shaymen') the financial problems were made worse by relegation. In 2002 Halifax dropped out of the football league – and quickly fell into administration.* By March 2003 the club was back in business and in 2005/06 reached the Conference play-offs. But by mid-2007 it again had a serious cash flow problem. Average crowds of 1600 people were rattling around a stadium built for 9500.

The underlying problem was simple: the business had operating losses of £30,000 every month. This meant that unless someone put £30,000 of their own cash into the club every month, it would go under. Towards the end of the 2007/08 season, the Shaymen were fighting on two fronts: to avoid relegation and to cope with debts that had, by now, reached £2.1 million. And, of course, the higher the debts, the higher the interest charges.

April 2008 saw the club survive the drop, and a pitch invasion by jubilant fans. A fortnight later the club's creditors (those owed money) rejected an offer of 2.5p in the £. This would mean that business–people looking to 'save' the club would have to find £800,000 just to pay its past debts (let alone finance its future ones). Worse was to come when the Conference expelled Halifax Town, forcing it to take a double relegation to the Unibond League North. The long-suffering fans have taken another beating.

With cash flow problems, prevention is much easier than cure.

*Administration occurs when the Directors realise they can no longer cope with the debts of a business, and call in a financial administrator.

Questions

(20 marks; 25 minutes)

1 What is meant by the term 'cash flow'? (2)

2 Identify and explain two reasons why Halifax Town's cash position became so serious. (4)

3 (a) What percentage of Halifax Town's ground capacity is being used by its average crowd? (3)

  (b) What cash problems might that lead to? (4)

4 Explain why, with cash flow problems, prevention is much easier than cure. (7)

Unit 21

Forecasting cash flow

Cash flow is the difference between the flows of cash into and out of a business over a period of time. For example, if a firm starts up by spending £20,000 of cash on premises and stock in its first month, but receives only £1000 from sales to customers, its month 1 cash flow is *minus £19,000*.

Cash flow forecasting means predicting the future flows of cash into and out of the

A brand new nightclub started with £250,000 of capital

firm's bank account. In effect, it means forecasting what the bank balance will look like at the end of each month. A cash flow forecast will usually be for a 12-month period. The table below, though, shows the forecast cash flow for the first six months of a brand new nightclub, started with £250,000 of capital.

The forecast is based on some key points:

- Building work is finished by the end of September, so that customers can start coming in in October.

- A launch party will bring the publicity and the customers needed for success.

- Costs will prove as expected, so the business never has to dip into the overdraft.

Successful cash flow forecasts require:

- accurate prediction of monthly sales revenues;

- accurate prediction of when customers will pay for the goods they have bought;

- careful allowance for operating costs and the timing of payments;

- careful allowance for other flows of cash, such as cash outflows when purchasing

Forecast cash flow for new nightclub

(Figures in £000s)	August	September	October	November	December	January
Cash at start	250	65	10	20	25	55
Cash in	0	0	85	65	115	55
Cash out	185	55	75	60	85	60
Net monthly cash	(185)	(55)	10	5	30	(5)
Cumulative cash	65	10	20	25	55	50

assets such as land, and inflows from raising additional capital, perhaps from selling shares.

This level of accuracy is very hard to achieve, especially for new, small firms. This is a key reason why the failure rate is so high among new firms. If cash flow proves much worse than the forecast, banks can be unforgiving. If a firm enters a period of **negative cash flow** without having discussed it with the bank, the consequences can be serious. If a bank loses confidence in a client, it can demand to have the overdraft withdrawn within 24 hours. This is likely to make it impossible for the business to continue trading.

The importance of cash flow forecasts

Forecasting cash inflows and outflows is always important, especially for three types of business:

- New firms.

- Fast-growing firms.

- Firms with erratic sales (e.g. a firework factory that only really brings in cash in

October and November – how will it pay its bills from January to August?).

Negative cash flow

When cash outflows are greater than inflows the result is negative cash flow. In other words, the firm is operating in the red. This is sustainable for a few weeks or months, as

A fireworks factory may only really bring in cash in October and November

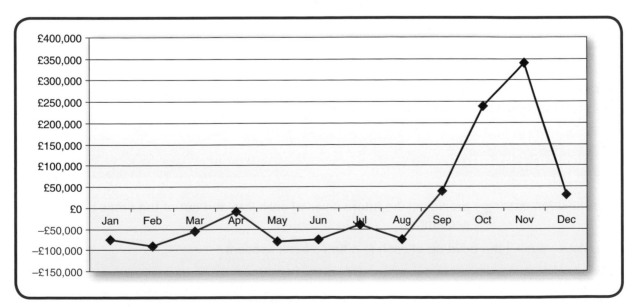

Monthly cash flow at a firework factory

long as the firm has an overdraft facility or other sources of capital. Ideally, though, the business should act to improve its cash flow.

There are many ways a firm can act to improve its cash position:

1 Cut stock levels (i.e. reduce the money the business has tied up in stocks of goods it means to use or to sell). If a firm cancels or reduces its orders to suppliers, stocks will steadily fall and so too will the amount of cash tied up. A £40,000 reduction in the levels of stock being held will place £40,000 in the firm's bank account.

2 Increase credit from suppliers (i.e. take a longer period before paying the companies that have supplied you with goods). This delays your cash outflows, which will improve the cash flow.

3 Reduce credit to customers. By giving less time to pay, you are getting your cash more quickly. This may cause some problems, if customers go to someone with longer credit terms. Overall, though, it may be better to deal with few, good payers than some who take ages to pay.

Cash flow problems and business failure

In autumn 2008 a fall in High Street spending hit many retailers. For Woolworths, prob-lems led to complete business failure. Having ordered its pre-Christmas stock months before, it had too much stock given the sharp fall in consumer spending. Worse, its suppliers started to worry about letting Woolworths have stocks on credit. Some demanded to be paid in cash; others asked to be paid more quickly.

Both these factors hit the company's cash flow. Customers were spending less cash, but suppliers wanted more cash – right away. When Woolworths went to its bankers to ask for a bigger overdraft, they refused. With the business unable to provide the cash to pay its bills, it fell into a position of **insolvency**. As no-one was willing to take over the company's debts, it ceased trading at the end of 2008.

Conclusion

Careful cash flow forecasting is the single most important way to keep a bank man-ager's confidence. That, in turn, makes it easier and cheaper to borrow some extra cash when the business needs it. The word 'careful' implies cautious. In other words, the bank manager will be impressed if a business keeps its forecasts of cash inflow quite low; while expecting the worst of cash outflows. If the cash position always turns out a little better than expected, who could object?

Revision Essentials

Cash flow forecasting – **predicting the future flows of cash into and out of the firm's bank account.**

Cumulative cash – **the build-up of cash in a firm's bank account.**

Insolvency – **the inability to repay debts as they become due.**

Negative cash flow – **when cash out is greater than cash in.**

Net monthly cash – **the month's cash inflow minus the month's cash outflow.**

Exercises

(25 marks; 25 minutes)

Read the unit, then ask yourself:

1   Give two benefits of cash flow forecasting for a new, small firm. (2)

2   Look at the table on page 110, showing the forecast cash flow for a new nightclub.

   (a) Explain briefly two reasons why the firm's cash has fallen from £250,000 at the start of August to £10,000 by the end of September. (4)

   (b) Explain briefly the likely effect on the firm's cash position if the builders worked too slowly, forcing the nightclub to open in November rather than October. (4)

3   Look at the graph on page 111, showing monthly cash flow at a firework factory.

   (a) Estimate each month's cash flow (read it off the graph), then add up the figures to estimate the firm's cash flow over the whole year. (5)

   (b) Why might the firework company have faced serious financial problems by August? (5)

4   Explain in your own words why it is sensible to forecast cash flows cautiously. (5)

Practice Questions

Thyme runs out

In April 2002 a famously mean restaurant critic wrote a glowing review of a new restaurant called Thyme, in Clapham, south London. He loved the cooking and the terrific value for money. By spring 2003 its two chefs were picking up an award for the Best New Restaurant in London. Thyme was packed every night and turning people away.

Frustrated by packing people into quite a small restaurant, the two chefs decided to look for bigger premises. In early 2004 they found a terrific space in Covent Garden, in central London. The rental payments on the lease were huge, so they decided to make the menu more expensive (one option was a 'tasting menu' at £100 per person!). For many months a huge sum was invested in creating a beautiful restaurant with the finest kitchen equipment and fittings, plus a huge wine cellar filled with expensive wines.

In November 2004 Thyme closed in Clapham and opened in Covent Garden. Initial restaurant reviews were positive about the quality of the food, but shocked at the prices. One reviewer noted that 'They have had the Thyme logo printed on the napkins and the knives. Clearly money has been no object'. He also noted that he and his wife were the only diners in the huge 86-seat restaurant. In July 2005 Thyme closed down. It had run out of cash.

Questions

(20 marks; 25 minutes)

1 Outline the likely cash flow position of the Clapham restaurant between mid-2002 and early 2004. (3)

2 Identify two causes of high cash outflows at the time of the move. (2)

3 Explain why a cash flow forecast would have been especially useful for Thyme during its expansion in 2004. (6)

4 Discuss the mistakes you believe Thyme's owners made that led to the July 2005 closure. (9)

Raising finance

In May 2007 Matteo Pantani opened an ice cream parlour in London's Covent Garden, called Scoop. It would be London's first real Italian 'gelateria', with ice cream (gelato) made freshly every day, on the premises.

It had taken about two years to get Scoop up and running – two years since Matteo received a text from a friend in London, asking him to come over from Italy and start a business. The start-up was financed by:

● Matteo and his friend's capital

● the same investment again, put in by two banker friends.

Within a year Scoop was doing so well that the four shareholders decided it was time to expand. The business was profitable, but it would be even more so if the ice cream could be made in bigger batches, then sent fresh every morning to more outlets. But to open more shops would need a lot more finance. Should the shareholders put more in? Should they look for other shareholders? Or should they go for a bank loan?

When raising finance there are three vital questions to ask:

1 **How secure is the source?** Capital raised by selling shares is kept within the business permanently, which means it is 100 per cent secure. Bank overdrafts, by contrast, can be cancelled at any time, allowing the bank to demand its money back within 24 hours.

2 **How expensive is the source?** When starting a business, capital can be expensive to obtain, because investors want high rewards to balance against the risk of possibly losing the money they invest.

3 **Is enough being raised?** Because capital is hard to raise and expensive to manage, many firms raise just enough to cover their expected needs. Unfortunately, it is hard to anticipate all possible problems in starting up and running a business, so it is wise to obtain at least 25 per cent more finance than seems necessary. This provides a safety net.

Short-, medium- and long-term finance

When raising finance, the first question to ask is about the timing of the cash requirement. Is the finance needed for a few weeks or for several years? If a business wants to buy a 10-year lease on a shop, there is clearly a need for 10 years of financing. Therefore it would be crazy to finance this via an overdraft, which is a useful, but expensive, way of borrowing money in the short term.

The rule is simple: short-term needs require short-term finance; long-term needs require long-term finance.

Long-term finance can be used to:

● provide start-up capital to finance the business for its whole life span.

Long-term finance can be used for the purchase of property

- finance the purchase of assets with a long life, such as property and buildings.

- provide capital for expansion, such as building a new, bigger factory or buying up another business.

  Medium-term finance can be used to:

- finance the purchase of assets with a two- to five-year life, such as cars, lorries and computer systems.

- finance a change of business strategy, such as switching marketing focus from Britain to the whole of Europe.

- replace an overdraft that is proving expensive.

  Short-term finance can be used to:

- get through periods when cash flow is poor for seasonal reasons (e.g. a seaside hotel during the winter).

- bridge gaps when large customers delay payment, leaving no cash coming in to pay the bills.

- provide the extra cash needed when a sudden, rush order requires a large sum to buy raw materials and pay overtime wages.

Types of long-term finance

Share capital

Ordinary shares give the buyer part-ownership of the business. If you buy 100 shares in a firm that has a total of 1000 shares, you own 10 per cent of the business. This gives you voting rights at the annual general meeting and entitles you to 10 per cent of any **dividends** paid from the firm's profits.

For the business, share capital has two key benefits:

1 The business has the capital permanently; if shareholders want to cash in their shares, they can only do so by finding someone else to buy them (usually through the stock market); they cannot get their money back from the company.

2 In a bad year no dividends need to be paid. Whereas interest payments to banks must be paid, no matter what, shareholders are not promised a dividend payment every year. So if the firm cannot afford to pay dividends, it need not do so; this makes share capital a safer source of finance than bank loans.

Drawbacks to businesses of share capital are:

- if lots of shares are issued, ownership gets spread thinly among many shareholders; this dilutes the power of the founders of the business. The key to retaining control is to keep hold of more than 50 per cent of the shares.

- if the business is listed on the stock exchange it becomes vulnerable to takeover bids. This might affect decision making within the firm, for example forcing the whole business to be greedier for profit than would otherwise be the case (because high profits mean a high share price, making the business expensive to take over).

Loan capital

Loan capital is any source of borrowing, probably from a bank. It might be in the form of a mortgage for as long as 20 years, or a bank loan for 5–8 years. The key features of loan capital are:

- interest payments must be paid on time or there is a risk of being taken to court and perhaps closed down.

- almost all loans are secured against the assets the firm owns; therefore failure to pay means losing an asset, such as buildings, shops or lorries.

- the interest charges may be fixed or variable; some firms like fixed rates (e.g. 7 per cent a year, fixed for the five-year life of the loan); others like variable rates.

Venture capital

Talking Point

In the Dragons' Den, entrepreneurs are trying to get venture capital investment. Why might an entrepreneur prefer venture capital to loan capital?

This is a combination of share and loan capital. Providers of **venture capital** will take risks, as long as they can share in the rewards. Therefore they want a share stake in the business, though often offering a bank loan in addition. For a young or growing firm, a venture capital company is more likely to provide finance than a large high street bank.

Profit

Over 60 per cent of all funds for business expansion come from the profits made by firms. This is the ideal source of capital, as it does not require the payment of interest charges or dividends. Well-run businesses fund as much of their capital needs as pos-

The dragons of Dragons' Den are venture capitalists

sible from the profits they make from their regular trading.

Types of medium-term finance

Loan capital

As for 'Types of long-term finance', above, but covering two- to five-year loans.

Leasing

This is a way of obtaining the use of important assets without ever buying them. Many company cars are leased. All this means is signing a contract committing the business to make regular payments on a car over a period that is usually two or three years.

Types of short-term finance

Bank overdraft

This is the most common form of finance. It must be understood in two parts. First, the bank grants the business (or individual) an overdraft facility, for example of £5000. This provides the right to keep spending until the bank account is £5000 in the red. The actual overdraft level is likely to vary day by day, and even hour by hour, as customers pay up or staff salaries are paid out.

Key features of a bank overdraft are:

- variable interest rate (i.e. the cost of borrowing money will rise if UK interest rates rise); this adds a degree of uncertainty to small business plans.

- flexibility: instead of having a £5000 bank loan, requiring payments each month based on the whole sum, a £5000 overdraft facility need only be dipped into occasionally. So if a firm only needs to borrow money for one day, it will pay 1/365th of the annual interest rate.

- the bank can demand full repayment of an overdraft within 24 hours. Many of the firms that go into **liquidation** have been finished off by banks that make this demand.

Trade credit

Small firms rely hugely upon good relationships with suppliers. Big companies can bully their way to get what they want from suppliers; small firms have to be nice or clever. If a supplier knows and trusts a customer, it may be willing to help when the customer is in need. For example, a small clothes shop may be able to persuade Stella McCartney

to keep supplying clothes even though the shop has not yet paid earlier bills. Getting a longer credit period is an effective way to raise short-term finance.

For small business start-ups, though, it is often impossible to obtain credit at the start. Suppliers demand to be paid cash in advance or on delivery. After all, they do not know whether you will be among the 30 per cent of firms that fail to survive their first year.

Conclusion

When deciding how to raise capital, the starting point is to identify how much you need and how long you need it for. Broadly, there are three options:

1 Loan capital.

2 Share capital.

3 Internal sources, such as reinvesting the profit the firm is making.

Most experts would then advise balancing out the capital; in other words, not relying too much on share capital and not too much on loans.

Revision Essentials

Dividends – payments to shareholders from the company's yearly profits. The directors of the company decide how large a dividend payment to make; in a bad year they can decide on zero.

Liquidation – selling off a firm's assets in order to raise cash to pay off the firm's debts.

Share capital – raising finance by selling part-ownership in the business. Shareholders have the right to question the directors and to receive part of the yearly profits.

Venture capital – a combination of share capital and loan capital, provided by a bank that is willing to take a chance on the success of a small to medium-sized business.

Exercises

(20 marks; 25 minutes)

Read the unit, then ask yourself:

1   Explain why the founder of a business is likely to care about keeping 51 per cent of the business's share capital. (4)

2   Identify whether the following situations require short-, medium- or long-term finance.

   (a) Buying extra stock for the Christmas period. (1)

   (b) Buying land nearby in case it is needed for expansion. (1)

   (c) Redecorating your restaurant. (1)

   (d) Buying a new company BMW for the managing director. (1)

3   Why is profit the ideal source of capital? (2)

4   Outline two possible advantages to an investor of buying shares in a business rather than lending it money. (4)

5   Explain why a fast-growing business might choose to obtain assets by leasing rather than buying them for cash. (3)

6   Explain the difference between an overdraft and an overdraft facility. (3)

Practice Questions

In 2006, a young mum, Donna Morgan (23), started up her own business called Baby Suds. She invested £15,000 of her savings. A family member put in a further £30,000, taking 50 per cent ownership. The business idea was a range of affordable, fun children's shampoos that are kind to the skin. They managed to find a manufacturer who could produce the right products. Their eventual product line-up was:

● Baby Suds Pineapple Shampoo and Detangler;

● Baby Suds Tangerine Hair and Body Wash;

● Baby Suds Banana Shampoo and Conditioner;

● Baby Suds 'Kind to Eyes' Baby Bath. [BL: end]

After an unsuccessful meeting with Asda, Waitrose proved much more enthusiastic and ordered 200,000 bottles. This required £40,000 of capital to pay the manufacturer, before the bottles could be delivered to the supermarket. The business could (just) afford this, but when sales took off, Waitrose required a further huge order that made extra finance necessary. Morgan tried to sell more shares for £125,000, but eventually borrowed the money needed.

With just 15p of profit per bottle, the business required at least 500,000 sales to cover its yearly fixed costs. In fact, by the end of its first year Baby Suds had made a profit of £61,000. With many other supermarkets queuing up to buy its children's shampoos, the business appeared to have succeeded.

Questions

(25 marks; 25 minutes)

1   Outline one possible reason why the founders only used share capital to finance the start-up of Baby Suds. (4)

2   The manufacturer who produced the shampoos required to be paid in advance. Explain why it may not have been willing to give Baby Suds any trade credit. (3)

3   (a) Given the information about the manufacturing costs of producing 200,000 bottles, what is the apparent production price per bottle? (3)

    (b) Given the 15p profit claimed per bottle, what appears to be Baby Suds' selling price to Waitrose? (2)

4   When further finance was needed, Morgan decided to borrow the extra money rather than sell more shares.

    (a) Outline two possible reasons why she may have decided against selling more shares in these circumstances. (4)

    (b) Discuss whether an overdraft or a bank loan was the more appropriate way for Baby Suds to borrow money. (9)

Objectives when starting up

People starting a new enterprise usually have one of three objectives:

1. A financial objective, such as to be rich.

2. A business **mission**, such as James Dyson in setting up his own bagless cleaner business; he was determined to prove that his idea would work.

3. A social mission, such as starting a charity aimed at improving water quality in African villages.

> 'To tend, unfailingly, unflinchingly, towards a goal is the secret of success.'
> **Anna Pavlova, Russian ballerina**

Financial objectives

When starting up, most entrepreneurs concentrate on survival. In other words, they want to bring in enough cash to pay the bills. They will only think about profit when the business is doing well enough to mean some cash is building up in the bank account. From then on, the owner can make decisions based on profit and therefore wealth. Innocent Drinks, founded in 1999, was estimated to be worth £100 million to Pepsi or Coca-Cola within eight years. It had always been profitable, but the key to its huge value was that both the American drinks giants could see huge potential from joining Innocent's quirky image to their own distribution muscle.

If a business is being set up with a view to making the owners rich, there are some key points to bear in mind:

- the product or service must have high value added (i.e. customers must be willing to pay a high price for something that does not cost much to make or provide); the Pizza Express chain is worth more than £400 million, and the value has come from the high prices that can be charged for tomato paste smeared on bread, which is what the average pizza really is.

- it must be possible for the product or service to be provided and sold to a large market, perhaps using mass production or a sales system such as franchising; this allows the good idea to be reproduced many times over.

- it must be possible to protect the idea from being copied by others. James Dyson took out **patents** to protect his new cleaner (and sued Hoover successfully).

Business mission

Many people start a business from a sense of purpose, even duty. They think they can do something better than anyone else. In 2005 the American Glazer family bought up Manchester United. Angry fans responded by setting up 'FC United' as their own team. The original Body Shop was started in Brighton because Anita Roddick could not find the type of cosmetics she wanted to use herself. Business ideas such as these may start up with no desire for profit other than to help finance survival and growth. Later, the owners may realise there is money to be made. Anita Roddick became very wealthy from Body Shop (over £30 million), even though it was not her original goal.

There are other sources of business mission. It may be that the individual is determined to start a business for personal reasons, such as to prove himself or herself. A surprising number of successful entrepreneurs are dyslexic (dyslexia is word-blindness, making it difficult to read and write), for example Richard Branson and Anita Roddick. Their feelings of failure at school are said to have motivated them to build dynamic business empires.

There are also many people who start a business because they want to be their own boss. They want to have more control over their working life than is possible when you work for someone else. John Cauldwell (billionaire boss of Phones4U) started work as a tyre fitter at a Michelin factory. His objective when he started his first business was to bring his life under his own control.

Social mission

The not-for-profit sector is becoming increasingly important. This refers to enterprises that are started with the objective of achieving a social goal, using business methods. A traditional example is a charity such as Oxfam, which is professionally run, but has the goal of helping to relieve suffering in developing countries. Today, firms such as One (not-for-profit bottled water) attempt to achieve the same objectives, but not necessarily as a charity (because charity status requires a great deal of paperwork).

Talking Point

Which staff are likely to be more motivated – those working for an organisation with a business mission or a social mission?

A leading social enterprise is Traidcraft, which began in 1979 and has built up its turnover to £15 million a year. All profits are ploughed back into the business. Traidcraft began the idea of 'trade not aid' by bringing coffee, tea and household items from developing countries and selling them in the UK. It helped to found the hugely successful Cafédirect and Fairtrade businesses. Both specialise in offering developing country producers guaranteed higher prices for their output, and then finding sales outlets in Britain. The founder of Traidcraft, Richard Adams, earns a salary from running the organisation, but his enterprising approach has never been in the pursuit of profit.

Other firms with social rather than profit motives include:

- the Coop Bank, which is owned by its members
- Waitrose and John Lewis, which are owned by their staff
- groups such as Greenpeace and Friends of the Earth
- social enterprises such as One Water.

Traidcraft product

Conclusion

It is a mistake to think that business is just about making profits. People run businesses because they can be challenging, rewarding and fun. They also provide the scope to achieve social as well as financial progress. Nevertheless, there will always be some firms that are interested only in profit. These may become the cowboy builders who charge high prices for shoddy jobs; or the financial institutions who encourage young people to build up debts they cannot afford. Just as every individual is different, so is every business.

Revision Essentials

Mission – something that a person passionately wants to achieve.

Patent – legal protection for the originator of a technical breakthrough.

Exercises

(15 marks; 15 minutes)

Read the unit, then ask yourself:

1 Why should someone starting a business for financial objectives make sure to identify a product or service with high value added? (2)

2 Give two reasons why an entrepreneur might be justified in trying to make as much profit as possible from his/her new business. (2)

3 Which of the following motives might influence you to start a business of your own?

(a) To be your own boss.

(b) To prove yourself.

(c) To get rich.

Pick one and explain why it matters most to you. (5)

4 Salvatore Falcone started his Italian bakery to have a business that could support his young family, then provide jobs for them when they grew up. Discuss whether his objectives could best be described as financial, business or social, or whether it is more of a mixture of the three. (6)

Practice Questions

Organic enterprise

The Soil Association was started up in 1946 by a group of farmers and nutritionists. Set up as a charity, its purpose was to campaign against the use of chemicals in farming. No one listened for many years, making it hard for the charity to keep going on the limited contributions given by members. Then, in the 1990s, people started to get interested in organic farming. Problems such as mad cow disease made shoppers more careful about the food they ate.

As interest rose in organic farming, the Soil Association's charity status ensured that people trusted it to certify which products are truly organic and which are not. By 2007, organic foods sales were said to have reached £2000 million a year and rising. The Association is at the heart of this, with 140 staff supervising the approval of most of the organic food sold in the UK. Having started as a small-scale social enterprise, the Association has become quite a powerful organisation. It remains a charity, however, run for and by its members.

The Soil Association's farmers campaign against the use of chemical in farming

Questions

(20 marks; 25 minutes)

1   (a) Explain the objectives of those who set up the Soil Association. (4)

       (b) At the start of the chapter, three types of business objective were identified. Into which of the three categories would you place this case? (1)

2   Explain why it might be important for a charity such as the Soil Association to control its costs as carefully as any business. (6)

3   Discuss why the Association's charity status ensured that people were more trusting of it than they might have been with an ordinary company. (9)

Exam-style Questions

DON'T RUSH; check answers carefully

1. Identify three important elements in making an accurate revenue forecast.   (3)

a) To have carefully worked out the fixed and variable costs for the coming period.

b) To have forecast all the cash that will flow into the business over coming months.

c) To have made a firm decision about the price to be charged for your product.

d) To know what the interest rate will be over the coming months.

e) To have worked out the seasonal pattern of sales in previous years.

f) To have a clear idea about the number of customers intending to buy.

g) To make sure of keeping the added value low enough to make a good profit.

h) To have a large enough advertising campaign to push sales up sharply.

Question 2 is based on this bar chart for XQ Ltd showing total cost of producing 1000 units.

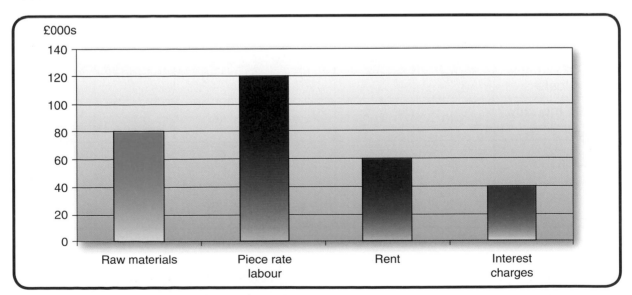

2. Calculate XQ Ltd's variable cost per unit

    £ _____   (1)

3. Identify the answer that only lists external sources of finance. (1)

a) Profit, venture capital and asset sales

b) Share capital, venture capital and overdrafts

4. Which two of the following would be businesslike objectives for starting a not-for-profit sports club? (2)

a) To gain a sense of achievement by creating something to be proud of.

b) To build a business strong enough to be sold for a lot of money.

c) To break even within the first two years.

d) To find a way to franchise the business.

e) To make the cumulative cash position of the club as high as possible.

f) To win trophies and therefore show how clever the management is.

g) To earn the income level needed to support the family.

Questions 5, 6 and 7 are based on this cash flow forecast for a swimwear producer.

All figs in £000s	April	May	June	July	August	September
Cash at start of month	150	250	360	490	520	520
Cash inflow	400	540	600	ii.	620	550
Purchases	120	170	200	290	270	230
Other running costs	180	260	270	360	350	340
Total monthly outflow	300	430	470	650	620	570
Net cash flow	i.	110	130	30	0	(20)
Accumulated cash flow	250	360	490	520	520	iii.

5. Which of the following gives the correct answer for all three missing numbers?

All in £000s (3)

a) i. 100 ii. 600 iii. 540

b) i. −100 ii. 620 iii. 520

c) i. 100 ii. 680 iii. 540

d) i. 100 ii. 680 iii. 500

e) i. −100 ii. 620 iii. 500

6. Which of the following is the best conclusion to be drawn from the cash flow table? (1)

a) The business looks sure to make a really good profit this year.

b) The cash outflows look far too high for comfort; they should cut them straight away.

c) With figures like these, the business could scrap its bank overdraft facility.

d) The figures look good, as long as the winter months do not eat too much cash.

e) The business should be able to make the monthly cash flows more stable next year.

7. Which two of the following might explain why cash outflow is forecast to be so high in August and September? (1)

a) Because of exceptionally high profit levels expected in those months.

b) The business may be expecting to buy a lot of stock in those months.

c) The company may intend to cut back on its advertising in those months.

d) The managers may intend to give customers longer credit terms from August.

e) The company may be intending to bring in big bank loans in those months.

8. Bejax and Co. makes kettles. Monthly sales are 5000 units. Each one has a variable cost of £8 and they are sold to shops for £12. The fixed costs per month of running Bejax are £8000. What is the monthly profit made by Bejax?

a) £12,000

b) £51,992

c) £60,000

d) £20,000

e) £52,000

f) £32,000

g) £108,000

Question 9 is based on this bar chart.

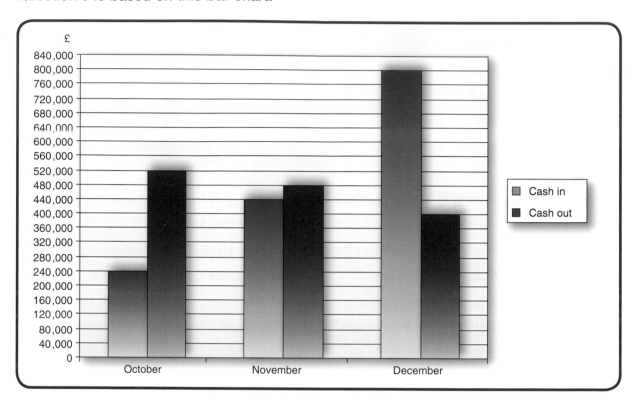

9. Calculate the net cash flow achieved by Hobart Ltd in the three months shown in the graph.

£ _____

(1)

MAKING THE START-UP EFFECTIVE

Introduction to effective start-up

In July 2000 Steve and Julie Pankhurst opened a website called Friends Reunited. It was to enable old school friends to get back in contact. It was completely free to register and use the site.

As they had no money for marketing the site, all their resources went into making the site as user-friendly as possible. By the end of 2000 they only had 3000 registered members, and just a tiny income from advertising. Early in 2001 the site was featured on a Radio 2 show, and tens of thousands tried to register. The computer system collapsed, but was put right overnight, and by February there were 19,000 members. With rising costs (they built up from a single computer server in January to 15 by the summer), they introduced a £5 charge for making contact with friends. This was well timed, as **word of mouth** enabled membership to shoot ahead to 1 million by August. By the end of 2001 it had risen to 4 million.

Friends Reunited continued to grow and develop until, in December 2005, ITV bought

Steve and Julie Pankhurst of Friends Reunited

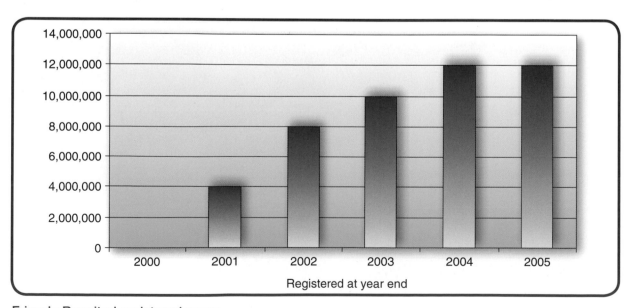

Registered at year end

Friends Reunited registered users

the site for £120 million, with a further £55 million to be paid in 2009, if profit targets are met. Steve and Julie are believed to get a quarter of this cash.

Making a start-up work

The keys to the success of Friends Reunited provide a model for every new business.

1. **Customer focus.** Julie and Steve believed in their **vision**: bringing people together. They encouraged people to write emails about how their reunions had gone, and tried to answer every one. They cherished stories like the first Friends Reunited engagement, then marriage, then – in August 2002 – baby. In response to customer feedback and ideas, they introduced Genes Reunited, to allow people to check their family tree, and bring together people who did not know they were related.

2. **Effective delivery.** The site has always done 'what it says on the tin'. Some businesses promise a great deal, but struggle to get the details right. This leaves the customer frustrated or even bitter. Friends Reunited does not charge for looking for an old friend. You only pay when you have found someone – and want to make contact.

3. **Intelligent business organisation and financing.** In its early stages, Friends Reunited became a **limited liability** business. This ensured that any serious financial problems for the business would not create personal liabilities for Julie and Steve. It also made it easier to bring in new investors to become shareholders in the business. This was essential, as the business was swallowing cash at an alarming rate in 2001. By the time of the 2005 sale, the Pankhursts owned just 25 per cent of the shares – but they were worth more than £30 million!

4. **Great management of people.** To cope with 2001's growth of over 1300 per cent (from 3000 to 4 million) was an astonishing achievement. It required rapid recruitment and training of new staff, all of whom worked from home until an office was opened in 2002. Julie Pankhurst, when interviewed in late 2001, said that she delegated a great deal to her 15 staff. In other words, she trusted staff to get on with things without checking up on them all the time. This is a great way to motivate employees, as long as they feel free to ask for help when needed.

Talking Point

Between 2006 and 2009 the online fashion business was growing very rapidly. What problems might that have caused?

Other factors in start-up success are:

- **Luck.** The best ideas can be undermined by bad luck, such as the launch of a holiday company focusing on the American South, two months before New Orleans was devastated by hurricane. In the case of Friends Reunited, the Radio 2 show came at the right time to push the business forward. Without it, Steve and Julie might have lost heart and given up.

- **Flexibility.** A business needs to be based on a clear idea, but the managers must be willing to change in line with experience. Friends Reunited was meant to be a totally free site, with income coming solely from advertising. The decision to start charging in early 2001 was crucial to provide the revenue to cover the costs of expansion.

- **Hard work.** The golfer Arnold Palmer once said, 'It's a funny thing, the more I practise the luckier I get.' In other words, hard work pays off. Julie and Steve had to work extremely hard during 2000 and 2003, both to keep everything working day by day, and to find the time to think ahead about new products and new ideas. The 2005 cheque for £30 million will have eased the pain!

Revision Essentials

Limited liability – where responsibility for paying the debts of the business is limited to the business, and cannot be passed on to the owners (the shareholders).

Vision – a clear view of what the business should be aiming for (e.g. bringing millions of people together).

Word of mouth – people speaking to each other about a topic or a business.

Exercises

(25 marks; 30 minutes)

Read the unit, then ask yourself:

1 Explain one reason why businesses should take word of mouth very seriously. (3)

2 Explain the importance of customer focus in running one of the following businesses:

   (a) Manchester United FC.

   (b) Primark.

   (c) McDonald's. (4)

3 How might effective delivery affect word of mouth? (4)

4 Outline two possible benefits to a business of having well-motivated staff. (4)

5 (a) Outline two occasions where luck played a factor in Steve and Julie's success. (4)

   (b) Discuss whether luck was the most important reason for Steve and Julie's success. (6)

Practice Questions

Having competed for three years at the White Air extreme sports festival on the Isle of Wight, Damon Breeze decided to start his own sports business. As one of the world's top kitesurfers, he was sure that his name would be a good basis for a website selling extreme sports clothing and equipment, from kitesurfing and mountaineering through to snowboarding and mountain-boarding.

Kitesurfer

He took advice from a business-minded aunt, then formed a limited company called Extreme Breeze Ltd. His aunt invested £18,000 and received 49 per cent of the shares. She urged him to keep focused on selling to the core market of young, male, extreme sports fans.

Damon had always been good with computers, but hired a specialist to build the site. It took three months and cost £14,000. It opened on 1 July 2005 and immediately made a sale. Because the business was so short of cash, it hadn't bought any stock, so relied on buying from suppliers and delivering to customers as quickly as possible. Several complaints came Damon's way, when deliveries were much slower than promised.

By October, enough cash had come in to start buying items for stock. This made it possible to deliver within the five days customers were promised. Even so, progress was quite slow. Damon was hoping to make sizeable profits within a few months of starting up the business. It was not going to be that easy.

Questions

(20 marks; 25 minutes)

1 Outline two weaknesses in Damon's business start-up. (4)

2 (a) What is meant by a 'limited company'? (3)

   (b) Explain why it was wise to set up a limited company in this case. (4)

3 Why is it usually very difficult to make sizeable profits within a few months of starting up a business? (4)

4 If you were invited to invest at this stage, what changes would you insist on beforehand? Explain your reasoning. (5)

Customer focus and the marketing mix

Every year Britain's business leaders are asked to vote for their 'Most Admired' business boss. For three years in a row they have voted for Terry Leahy, chief executive of Tesco. In a magazine interview, Leahy gave his 'Secrets for Success' as follows:

- Have a clear vision.
- Listen to your customers.
- Trust your staff to make decisions.
- Keep things simple.

This unit is about listening to your customers.

Customer focus

If you run a small, one-person business, **customer focus** comes from chatting to and learning from customers, face to face. This is much harder for Terry Leahy, as Tesco has tens of millions of customers. His solution is to leave his office every week and visit stores, staff and shoppers. This is time-consuming, but invaluable. He learns when shoppers are unhappy with the products or the service. Indeed he insists that every director and thousands of head office managers spend one week a year back in a store, stacking shelves and working at the tills. This keeps everyone focused on the key to the business – customer satisfaction.

Customer focus can enable a business to learn:

- about niggles/weaknesses

- how customers see you in relation to your competitors
- what else customers want (this might lead to new products or services)
- what customers do not want, or what they would quite like to have, but not enough to pay for it.

There are a number of different ways to achieve customer focus:

1 Train staff to be clear that customers are the purpose (and the paymaster) of the business. Ideally every employee should test everything they do by asking: how does this benefit the customer? The reason many people love the chefs Jamie

A mystery shopper can test the standard of customer service

Oliver and Gordon Ramsay is because this attitude shines through. Both show incredible determination to do their best, all the time.

2 Check regularly on customer views (e.g. by market research). This should investigate consumers' attitudes to different products and brands, their buying habits and their views on new product ideas.

3 Get senior managers to act as 'mystery shoppers' (i.e. acting as an ordinary customer to find out what happens when you shop at the Newcastle branch or phone with a query).

4 Ensure that targets set for staff are focused on customer satisfaction and not on short-term sales. On many occasions UK banks have been guilty of persuading customers to buy inappropriate financial products. Sales staff greedily pursued commission based on short-term sales – and sometimes cost customers thousands of pounds. Examples include endowment mortgages, personal pensions and 'precipice' bonds. Not only are such actions **unethical**, but they also damage the reputation of the business.

> 'Marketing is the whole business seen from the customer's point of view.'
> **Peter Drucker, management guru**

Marketing mix

It may not be enough to have a clear customer focus and to rely on word of mouth. If a market is already crowded with lots of brands, it may be impossible to get established without a heavy marketing campaign. Success will hinge on the marketing mix chosen by the company.

The marketing mix is the way in which a firm tries to ensure that the right product is being promoted in the right way and sold at the right price at the right place. The mix is often called the four Ps:

- Product
- Price
- Promotion
- Place.

Product

After careful market research, a firm should be able to design a product or service that will appeal to a specific **target audience**. This is the heart of the mix, and the other three factors should revolve around this. For example, Kellogg's Special K cereal has always been targeted at weightwatchers. Having the right product to appeal to the audience is then backed up by:

- the 'right' price – more expensive than other cereals, to help confirm that it is worth paying for
- the right place – distributed in supermarkets and grocers, but also sold at breakfast bars in health clubs
- the right promotion – focusing the TV advertising at women, with a voice-over emphasising health (the 'drop a jean size' campaign helped sales rise by 33 per cent).

Price

All consumers expect value for money; this means that price is always important. In many cases, having a low price may be crucial to achieving high sales, for instance when selling packets of sugar or butter. At other times, though, being 'cheap' may cause image problems. No one wants cheap baby food or cut-price perfume.

Most products are price-makers or price-takers. A price-maker has the market power to set prices that others have to follow. This can be true of new products (such as the Innocent Drinks smoothie, priced at an amazing £2 for a small bottle) or of established ones (such as Chanel No.5 perfume – £75 for a remarkably small bottle). Consumers see both these products as unique, and therefore are willing to pay a high price.

A price-taker is a product or service that has to be priced with reference to others in the marketplace. Perhaps it needs to be priced below the price leader (e.g. Tesco baked beans compared with Heinz); or perhaps the whole market is full of similar products (e.g. Esso petrol compared with BP or Shell).

Promotion

This is the way a firm can promote sales of its products. It lumps together methods of promoting the long-term image and sales of the business, using methods such as TV or cinema advertising, and short-term methods such as sales promotions (e.g. buy one get one free).

Most large firms are keen to use every £ spent on advertising to promote the long-term

> 'Build a better mousetrap and the world will beat a path to your door.'
> **R. W. Emerson, management thinker**

image of the product. Short-term boosts to sales can be at the expense of the brand image. Few firms would want to take such a risk.

Place

This is where (and how) the product is distributed, so that customers can get it when they want it. Mass market products usually seek as much distribution as possible. Coca-Cola uses the phrase 'an arm's length from desire'; in other words, they want such good

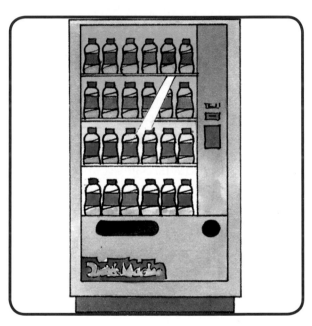

Vending machines are a way to achieve large-scale distribution

Examples of marketing mix in action

	Cadbury Dairy Milk	Starbucks
Product	Traditional-tasting chocolate aimed at a mass market (i.e. 'everyone loves . . . ').	Huge variety of coffees and other drinks; terrific space for sitting and relaxing.
Price	Priced competitively, to get high sales in the mass market.	Priced very high to fit in with the image of self-indulgence.
Promotion	Uses TV advertising and extensive promotional support (e.g. 25 per cent extra chocolate at the same price).	Very little advertising; relies on location and word of mouth.
Place	Widespread distribution through sweetshops, grocers and other outlets.	Locations are clustered, effectively swamping an area with Starbucks.

distribution that customers should only need to stretch out an arm to get a Coke. Coca-Cola wants this (which is why there are so many vending machines) because they know that the more people see Coke, the more they buy.

For other products, the same does not apply. Chanel hates cut-price retailers such as Superdrug selling its perfumes; its managers worry that cutting prices may damage the image of the brand.

Successful marketing mix

For success, a firm must make sure that its mix is coordinated and coherent. A classy product aimed at a classy market should have a high price, be promoted in classy magazines and stocked at the classiest shops. Similarly, a product aimed at the environmentally conscious buyer should have little advertising support, a moderate price premium and aim to be sold through a limited number of local outlets. The marketing mix puts the public face on a product or service. That face must make sense.

Revision Essentials

Customer focus – keeping your staff thinking about customers' needs and wants.

Target audience: – the part of the market your product is aimed at (e.g. women aged 15–24).

Unethical – doing something that is morally wrong (e.g. selling cigarettes to children you know are under 14 years).

Exercises

(20 marks; 25 minutes)

Read the unit, then ask yourself:

1 Why may customer focus be easier in a small business than in a big one? (3)

2 Outline two possible benefits to Tesco from getting all their directors to spend one week a year as shop-floor employees. (4)

3 Outline the marketing mix used by one of the following:

(a) Cadbury's Creme Eggs

(b) Tesco stores

(c) Ryanair. (5)

4 Why would 'buy one get one free' be a poor way to boost the long-term image and sales of a business? (4)

5 Explain one reason why Chanel may be right, and one reason why it might be wrong, in trying to stop Superdrug from stocking Chanel No. 5 perfume. (4)

Practice Questions

In early 2005 Twinings launched an 'Everyday Tea'. Before then, Twinings had only focused on special teas such as Earl Grey. Now it was going head-to-head with the big beasts, Tetley and PG Tips.

Twinings' marketing idea was to launch a tea with a comparable taste to Tetley and PG, but with a superior image, backed by the 300-year-old Twinings brand. TV commercials featured the actor Stephen Fry, known for his good taste and his Englishness. Twinings Everyday Tea would sell at a 20 per cent price premium to Tetley and PG. The new product would be promoted by £4.5 million spent on TV and radio advertising. The distribution would be through supermarkets and grocers, plus restaurants and hotels.

The effectiveness of Twinings' marketing mix can be seen in the figures below.

Two years later, Twinings' 2007 sales were still rising and Stephen Fry was fronting the launch of Twinings Coffee. This has proved more than an everyday success.

(Source: A. C. Nielsen quoted in *The Grocer*, 17 December 2005)

Stephen Fry

Twinings' UK annual retail sales, 2004 and 2005

	2004	2005
Tetley	£132.3m	£130.1m
PG Tips	£129.7m	£123.9m
Twinings	£49.8m	£56.3m

Questions

(30 marks; 30 minutes)

1   Outline the marketing mix used by Twinings to launch its new Everyday Tea. (8)

2   (a) Outline two actions the managers of PG Tips might have taken at the time of the Everyday Tea launch. (4)

    (b) Briefly explain the reason for taking those actions. (4)

3   (a) Calculate the percentage sales change between 2004 and 2005 for each of the three tea brands. (6)

    (b) To what extent does this provide proof of the success of Twinings' launch of its Everyday Tea? (8)

Limited versus unlimited liability

As many as half of all new businesses close down within three years. Each year over 12,000 companies go into liquidation (selling off the assets to pay off the debts), and in 2007 over 50,000 individuals were declared **bankrupt**. All business failures are painful, but there is a big difference between a company going into liquidation and an individual being made bankrupt.

When a company goes under, an independent accountant is appointed to try to raise as much cash as possible to repay the firm's debts. If there is a shortfall, the company's owners (the shareholders) do not have to repay the debts. The losses of the shareholders are restricted to the money they invested in the business. This is known as **limited liability**. By investing in shares,

Unpaid business debts could lead to the owner losing his possessions as part of bankruptcy proceedings

they took a risk; but their gamble can only cost them the amount they invested, not a penny more. Their liability is limited.

By contrast, if the business had **unlimited liability**, financial disaster for the business will become a financial disaster for the owner or owners. Unpaid business debts could lead to the owner(s) losing their house, car and other possessions as part of bankruptcy proceedings. Yet this situation is completely unnecessary, as long as a business is run as a limited company.

Limited liability

To achieve limited liability, a business must be started up as a company. This requires an application to Companies House and the payment of around £150. Once the right forms have been filled in the business becomes a company. Small limited companies must put the letters 'Ltd' at the end of the company name. These businesses have **private limited company** status.

The fee of £150 is a small sum to pay for improved financial security of the entrepreneur. There are also various other benefits from becoming a limited company:

● A company has share capital (perhaps 100 £1 shares), which makes it easy to divide up the ownership between different investors. As long as the company's founder keeps hold of 51 per cent of the shares, he/she still has total control.

● If the business needs to raise more capital, it is quite easy to issue more shares for sale to other investors.

- The business continues to exist even if the founder of the business dies. The company develops a life of its own.

- Due to limited liability, the owners/shareholders can be bold about investing in the future of the business. If a bold move goes wrong, the business may suffer, but individual shareholders are not liable for the debts.

Given the advantages of limited liability, it is amazing that most businesses in the UK do not bother to turn into limited companies. Presumably the owners believe either that nothing can possibly go wrong, or that they will be able to cope financially even if something does go wrong. The clearest reason to avoid limited liability is that companies need to have their accounts drawn up by a qualified accountant. This means an annual cost of perhaps £1500 to be paid to an accountant.

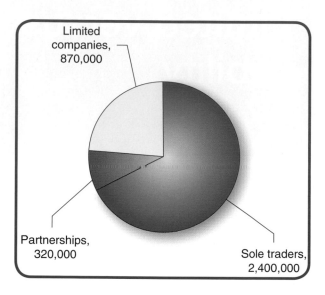

Number of businesses in England and Wales, 2008)

The only logical reason for ignoring limited liability (forming a company) is if there is no realistic possibility of debts building up. For example, if the business is a market stall, and goods are bought for cash in the morning and sold out by the afternoon, it is hard to see how debts could be built up. So why bother with the cost and paperwork involved in setting up a limited company?

Unlimited liability

Anybody can start a business today. All that is needed is to tell Inland Revenue and the National Insurance office. In few countries of the world is it so easy to start up. You would probably need a bank account, but is unlikely to be a problem unless you are trying to borrow large sums from the bank.

However, this business is not a limited company, and is therefore treated in the same way as the individual's own earnings. The business and the person are one and the same for tax and legal purposes. This is why failure by the business leaves the entrepreneur liable in full for any debts.

A person running her/his own business without forming a company is called a **sole trader**. It is also possible to join with others in a partnership. Sole traders and partnerships both have unlimited liability.

A person running his/her own business without forming a company is called a sole trader

Conclusion

Everyone starting a business should think seriously about forming a company and therefore having limited liability. This is especially important if money is being borrowed to finance the business. Individuals with unlimited liability should not take risks with borrowing or with credit.

Revision Essentials

Bankrupt – when an individual is unable to pay his/her debts, even after all personal assets have been sold for cash.

Limited liability – restricting the losses suffered by owners/shareholders to the sum they invested in the business.

Private limited company – a small family business in which shareholders enjoy limited liability.

Sole trader – a business run by one person; that person has unlimited liability for any business debts.

Unlimited liability – treating the business and the individual owner as inseparable, therefore making the individual responsible for all the debts of a failed business.

Exercises

(25 marks; 30 minutes)

Read the unit, then ask yourself:

1 Explain in your own words:

(a) Limited liability. (3)

(b) Bankrupt. (3)

2 Why might an entrepreneur be reluctant to sell more than 50 per cent of the shares in his/her business? (3)

3 (a) Use the figure on page 140 (Number of businesses in England and Wales) to calculate the percentage of businesses in England and Wales that have unlimited liability. (3)

(b) Outline one reason why businesses avoid becoming companies and therefore having limited liability. (2)

4 Explain why it is easier to make bold business decisions if your business is a limited company than if it is a sole trader with unlimited liability. (5)

5   K. V. Builders and Sons is an unlimited liability business that builds houses. It employs five people and borrows up to £150,000 to finance each job. Explain two reasons why it should form a company and therefore provide limited liability to its owners. (6)

Practice Questions

In recent years there has been an increase in the number of people becoming bankrupt. Some get into this state due to overspending on their credit cards, but more than half become bankrupt as a result of a business failure.

The most likely explanation for the increase is the high level of consumer debt. It is also possible that small, unlimited liability businesses are finding it harder to compete with big companies such as Tesco and Primark.

Whichever answer is the right one, the graph gives a clear signal to people starting up a business for the first time: form a limited company.

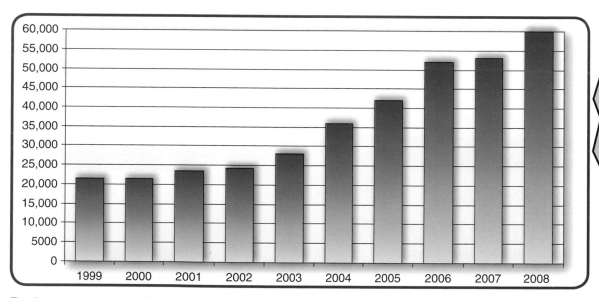

Bankruptcy orders in England and Wales, 1999–2008.

Questions

(20 marks; 20 minutes)

1   What was the approximate increase in bankruptcies between 1999 and 2008? (3)

2   Outline two reasons why a business might end up being unable to continue financially. (4)

3   The biggest category of bankrupt businesses is in the construction sector. Identify and explain two possible reasons why the building trade might have a high rate of business failure. (6)

4   Explain why the graph gives a clear signal to people setting up a business for the first time to form a limited company. (7)

Start-up legal and tax issues

In September 2000 Tamara Girvan opened a hairdresser's in Birmingham. It specialised in Afro-Caribbean hairstyles, and pitched itself as a smart, quite expensive, outlet. It did fantastically well, enabling Tamara to employ three trusted friends and four professional stylists. In 2003 a second shop was opened in the city centre, and it did even better. By 2005 Tamara employed 15 people and had a wage bill of over £180,000 a year. Her 2005 profits were over £85,000.

In mid-2005, however, Inland Revenue started an investigation into her personal tax position. The business had always been run as a sole trader, so the income of the business was the same as Tamara's personal income. The tax inspectors found that Tamara's record-keeping had not been great. Many of the items she claimed as costs had no paper-work/evidence to back them up. For example, in the early days she had paid a friend £500 in cash to install the plumbing. She had no record of this, therefore the tax inspectors refused to accept it as a business cost.

Eventually, with the help of an accountant, Tamara sorted out her tax problems. It cost her £18,000 plus £2200 in fines and £2500 to the accountant! Although the success of the business meant she could afford to pay, she always tells any other potential entrepreneurs to be very careful with the taxman.

The basics

When starting a business, the first rules are to tell Inland Revenue (the taxman) and the **National Insurance** office. You should also make sure that the business you start has a unique trading and business name. After that, just make sure to keep clear accounts of what you are spending (your costs) and what you are receiving in revenues. You need this information for yourself, so that you know what your profit is. Even more, though, there is a legal requirement that you should have this evidence available for the taxman.

The difficulty for someone like Tamara is that there are lots of issues to deal with when running a business – staffing to sort out, customers to keep happy, bills to be paid, and so on. Therefore it is easy to push back tax and accounting-related issues until next week . . . or month.

To make things easier for yourself:

An Afro-Caribbean hairdresser

- Keep a paper record of what you have to pay out for the business; it helps enormously if you use a business credit/debit card to pay for everything, as this creates its own records of how much you paid and to whom. Try not to pay in cash as it is harder to prove what you spent the money on.

- Keep a paper record of sales revenue from customers. If your customers get credit (time to pay), make sure to keep track of who has paid and who has not.

- Keep your own records up to date, probably on a spreadsheet such as Excel.

- Best of all, budget from the start to have a bookkeeper to come in for half a day a week to do the paperwork for you. This will probably pay for itself in reduced stress and lower tax bills.

Talking Point

Should the taxman give a second chance to new entrepreneurs who make mistakes about tax?

When the business starts to grow, there is another tax to consider – VAT (value added tax). As of 2008, firms with an annual turnover of more than £67,000 have to charge 15 per cent VAT to customers, and then pay that money to the government. (This VAT rate is expected to rise to 17.5% from January 2010) Failing to register for VAT can be an expensive mistake.

Taxes do not end there. When the business makes a profit, **corporation tax** has to be paid. This is paid as a percentage of the profit made by the business. In 2009 the small companies' corporation tax rate is 21 per cent, i.e. £21,000 of tax for every £100,000 of profit. An entrepreneur would also have to pay **income tax** on any wages paid by the business.

Every employer is responsible for health and safety

Legal issues

Business organisation

The first legal question is which type of business organisation you want – a limited company or an unlimited firm? Establishing a company creates a separate **legal entity**. In other words, even if Tamara Girvan owned 100 per cent of the shares in Tamara Girvan Ltd, the two would be treated separately in law. If a customer sued after an accident had cut her ear, the customer would be suing the business – Tamara Girvan Ltd. If the courts imposed a fine of £100,000 and the business could not pay, Tamara the person would not be liable for the debts of Tamara Girvan Ltd. Therefore if there is any serious risk of legal action, it is wise to form a limited company.

Employment

Every employer has a number of legal responsibilities. The employer's duty of care requires careful thought about Health and Safety at Work, both mental and physical. There are also a series of other laws that need to be complied with, including the Minimum Wage, the Working Time Directive and laws against **discrimination** on grounds of sex, race and age. Therefore every job advertisement has to be thought about carefully. You cannot advertise for 'attractive young waitresses' or 'mature white men'.

Consumer protection

An employer also has clear responsibilities towards customers. The Sale of Goods Act insists that goods should be 'fit for the purpose for which they are sold'. Therefore, if they do not work, customers are legally entitled to get their money back. It is also a requirement that advertisements and pack labels should tell the truth. In fact, telling the truth in pages of small print (as on most financial products) can be worse than useless for the customer.

Environmental protection

Employers have environmental responsibilities too. They are required to put waste materials in landfill sites instead of dumping them on the roadside. They must conform to laws about clean air and clean waste water (to avoid polluting rivers). For most small service businesses there are no significant issues here, but for manufacturers they may represent some important and expensive concerns.

Conclusion

Starting a business is a massive undertaking. It can lead to a challenging, exciting working life, and can even lead to riches. Yet it is also a massive responsibility. Each year there are more than 100,000 accidents in the workplace. And each year there are people who get food poisoning from restaurants or suffer anxiety from a pension or an investment that was supposed to be safe, but proves not to be. Good businesses look after their staff and their customers because it is the only way to build a successful long-term future. Unfortunately there are also firms that cut corners in their determination to get rich quick. They end up on TV programmes such as *Watchdog* – or in the law courts.

Revision Essentials

Corporation tax – **tax paid as a percentage of a company's profit.**

Discrimination – **treating some types of people worse than others for reasons of prejudice.**

Income tax – **tax paid as a percentage of a person's wage/salary.**

Legal entity – **a person or company that is treated by the law as having its own independent rights and responsibilities.**

National Insurance – **a form of tax that is paid by employers and employees as a contribution towards welfare payments such as unemployment pay. Employers pay around 13 per cent of the employee's salary.**

Exercises

(25 marks; 30 minutes)

Read the unit, then ask yourself:

1 Explain in your own words:

   (a) Limited company. (3)

   (b) Consumer protection. (3)

2 Why does the text advise against using cash to pay bills? (3)

3 (a) What is a bookkeeper for? (2)

   (b) Explain how Tamara might have benefited from using a bookkeeper. (4)

4 Identify four faults in these recruitment advertising statements:

   (a) **Wanted: a recent school-leaver to train as a postman.**

   (b) **Wanted: strong, fit Afro-Caribbean waitress for a new bar in Brixton.** (4)

5 Given Tamara's achievements with her new business, discuss whether she should have been put off by the problems with the taxman. (6)

Practice Questions

Michael Woolsey started a printing franchise business at the age of 21. His parents helped him with the start-up capital, but after that he was largely on his own. His father's only piece of advice was to use the government's Business Link service for small firms. This proved invaluable.

When he contacted Business Link through their website (www.businesslink.gov.uk) Michael was offered a free session with a local business advisor. Their meeting went very well, so Michael paid for another session two weeks later. The advisor was especially helpful about accounting software, showing him how to record costs and revenues and to automatically produce profit statements. Michael was warned about the need to keep evidence of money spent on business costs.

After the second meeting Michael started to use the Business Link website more and more. He found a page entitled 'Find out what taxes you need to pay', which he found helpful. Before hiring his first member of staff he went back to the site to read the pages of advice on 'Employing people'.

Two years after starting up, the business (Creovation Ltd) is doing very well.

Michael has expanded it to include a website design service and is thinking of opening his second franchise. The success is due to hard work and his positive, warm approach to the four staff and many customers. He is quick to acknowledge, though, that his contacts with Business Link helped him avoid unnecessary and costly mistakes.

Michael received a free session with a local Business Link advisor

Questions

(20 marks; 20 minutes)

1   Explain how Michael's business would have been helped by the advice on keeping accurate records. (4)

2   (a) Identify the evidence that Michael set the business up as a limited company. (1)

    (b) Outline two possible benefits of this to Michael. (4)

3   Outline two legal issues Michael should have considered before hiring his first member of staff. (4)

4   To what extent was Michael's success due to Business Link? (7)

Effective, on-time delivery

In 2000 the big business story was the internet. A company called Boo.com received pages of press coverage as its two founders were young and newsworthy. A company called Screwfix.com was hardly mentioned. Yet by 2002 Boo.com had collapsed, while Screwfix sales had risen to over £100 million. There were many differences between the two companies, but the biggest single one was delivery. Screwfix promised to deliver within a day (and did), while Boo.com was famously slack about on-time delivery. Customers felt they came second to the owners' lifestyles, whereas at Screwfix the customer came first.

To deliver on time, every time, is extraordinarily difficult. It requires highly efficient, reliable systems at every stage of the **supply chain**. In November 2005 the Xbox 360 was launched by Microsoft. The publicity suggested that it was a brilliant success. In fact, only 325,000 360s were sold in November in America. In the same number of days after the launch of the original Xbox, 550,000 units had been sold. The 2005 problem was that Microsoft had failed to supply enough product to meet the demand. As Nintendo Wii would be launched by Christmas 2006, this was a serious delivery failure.

Producing the right number of products at the right time requires four main resources:

1 Sufficient physical capacity. In a restaurant there may only be enough space and enough cookers to be able to produce 30–35 meals an hour. And there may only be enough seats and tables to cope with a maximum of 35 customers at any one time. So the restaurant's physical capacity is 35 an hour. If 40 people arrive, some will have to queue.

2 Enough trained staff. A sudden increase in demand may outstrip the company's ability to hire and train extra staff to get the work done. Even if a firm is not growing, a few absences by staff may make it impossible to get an order completed on time.

3 Capital. A sudden big order can strain a firm's cash flow. Cash has to be paid out on supplies and overtime before any cash can come in from the customer. Therefore effective delivery requires extra capital.

The founders of the failed internet start-up Boo.com

4 Effective management. Businesses require different members of staff to work in a coordinated way. It is the job of a manager to establish this coordination and to motivate people to work together.

Together, these four factors are known as land, labour, capital and enterprise.

Even if all four factors are in place, serious problems can still occur. Shocks can disrupt the ability to deliver, and they can come from inside or outside the organisation. A fire at a key supplier can cause chaos. Or bad weather may stop a supplier from being able to deliver to you on time. From inside the business, a strike by your own staff will wreck the ability to supply on time. Machinery breakdowns can cause the same disruption.

Achieving efficient delivery

There are two main requirements:

1 Strong links with customers. A firm needs to be able to forecast the likely level of future demand in order to plan ahead. Close links with consumers should ensure a clear understanding of their purchasing plans (GameBoy or

PSP?). Large firms also use electronic links with retailers to get the most up-to-date idea of consumer demand. The information recorded every minute by Tesco's till scanners can be fed through so that Danone knows exactly how many Actimels are being bought this morning. This gives a warning of whether tomorrow's order from Tesco will be higher or lower than today's.

2 Commitment throughout the staff. If a promise has been made to a customer, all the staff should be determined not to break it. In a large firm it may be hard to get all the staff to really care about each and every customer; this is where small firms have a major opportunity. At a small TV production company in London, four staff came in on Boxing Day (unpaid) to complete a commercial that was to have its first showing on 28 December. If people enjoy their job, they will be willing to make extraordinary efforts.

Talking Point

Asda has just won an award for 'Most Reliable Online Supermarket'. What factors may have helped them to win and how may Asda benefit?

Airline punctuality January to March 2008

	Arrival within 15 minutes	1 hour+ late
Air Berlin	86.2%	1.1%
Ryanair	79.5%	2.4%
easyJet	76.2%	4.1%
Lufthansa	68.6%	6.4%
British Airways	56.3%	10.8%
Virgin Atlantic	55.7%	11.7%

Source: www.flightontime.info based on CAA data

The business benefits

If a firm gets a reputation for reliability and efficiency, it will attract customers. If achieving reliability has required higher-cost production, the higher price of the service will put off some customers. Nevertheless there may be a profitable business targeted at customers willing to pay for reliability. As the table below shows, different airlines perform very differently as regards arriving on time. It looks as if the German airline Air Berlin should emphasise its reliability to busy business passengers.

Most important of all is that reliable, on-time delivery encourages **customer satisfaction**. This, in turn, gives a firm a more confident basis for operating. If costs rise a little, a firm can push its prices up, knowing that loyal customers will keep coming. Confidence in the loyalty of customers also helps a firm take more risks in investing in its future. In 2008 Ryanair was in talks with Boeing and Airbus about 200 aircraft for delivery from 2012 onwards. This might require spending £6000 million. It had the confidence to do this as its passenger numbers had grown by 500 per cent between 2001 and 2008.

Conclusion

Small firms have many disadvantages compared with larger rivals. On-time delivery, though, can be a major area for competitive advantage. Small firms have greater scope to be flexible and adaptable. If Cheryl Cole desperately needs a table-sized birthday cake to be delivered by 5 p.m. tomorrow, a small firm can produce it and make absolutely sure it gets there on time. Mr Kipling would not be able to compete.

Large extravagant-looking birthday cake

Revision Essentials

Customer satisfaction – the degree to which buyers rate the quality of the service they have received.

Repeat purchase – buyers returning regularly to buy from the same supplier.

Supply chain – the links in the chain from the start to the end of the supply process. For a bakery that might be: wheat from farm – ground into flour – delivered to baker – baked into bread – sliced and wrapped – delivered to shops.

Exercises

(25 marks; 30 minutes)

Read the unit, then ask yourself:

1 Why will Nintendo be delighted to hear of Microsoft's supply problems with the Xbox 360? (2)

2 Explain in your own words:

(a) physical capacity (3)

(b) absences by staff. (3)

3 Why may effective, on-time delivery be easier for a business with a clear customer focus? (4)

4 The biggest requirement for on-time delivery in Britain at the moment is to get the Olympic Village ready for 2012. Outline how the managers of the London Olympics should handle the four key factors: land, labour, capital and enterprise. (8)

5 Outline one way in which Air Berlin might make more use of its impressive punctuality figures. (5)

Practice Questions

Food stores in online sales surge

For supermarkets, Christmas is the busiest and the most worrying time of the year. If a store runs out of turkeys on Christmas Eve, customers will be furious. Yet if too many are ordered there will be a lot of marked-down prices. The position is made even worse with online deliveries, as there is the further factor that the deliveries might go wrong. Retail

Consultancy TNS has said that 'cash-rich and time-poor customers do not want to be messed around'. Worse still, stories of people's Christmas being ruined by failure to deliver the groceries would be a publicity disaster.

For Christmas 2007 Sainsbury predicted a 50 per cent increase in online sales and arranged to have 1800 drivers on duty. This estimate proved very accurate so the Christmas deliveries went smoothly. Things proved harder for Morrisons, which enjoyed a 120 per cent increase between Christmas 2006 and 2007. Luckily it had decided in advance not to deliver on Christmas Eve, which gave it an extra day to make up for any delivery delays.

Ocado delivery service

In the run-up to Christmas 2007, Tesco and Ocado, the country's two biggest home-delivery grocers, increased the price of delivery. Ocado's doubled to £8, but it was still fully booked for Christmas Eve. Some people called this 'cashing in', but the company said it was necessary to maintain a good service. Ocado was the only major supermarket to be offering deliveries on 24 December.

In January 2008 Tesco said its online sales had risen 20 per cent to £190 million over Christmas. Across the whole retail sector, online sales for Christmas 2007 rose by 50 per cent. Sainsbury's management could feel very pleased with itself.

Questions

(20 marks; 20 minutes)

1. Outline one way in which the supermarkets coped with the big increases in online grocery sales in the run-up to Christmas 2007. (4)

2. Explain the importance to firms of the statement: 'Cash-rich and time-poor customers do not want to messed around'. (4)

3. Examine two possible effects on a firm of a 'publicity disaster' in relation to Christmas orders. (6)

4. Which do you think is the single most important factor in achieving effective, on-time delivery for groceries ordered online? Explain your reasoning. (6)

Recruiting the right staff

Salvatore Falcone has run a bakery in Wimbledon for nearly 40 years. In that time he has built Panetteria Italiana into a terrific business. People drive 20 miles to buy armfuls of bread for their freezer. His Saturday morning queue is legendary. Yet in all these years he has rarely been able to find and keep staff. His business works because his wife and three children work there. When he tries to recruit someone, he usually finds the person too slow or too unconcerned to be worth having. He says, 'I take them on, I spend weeks training them up, then they decide to go elsewhere.'

For a small firm, recruiting staff is a worrying process. There is a huge amount that could go wrong. And a small business lacks the expertise to avoid some of the pitfalls. Could the job advertisement be accused of **discrimination**? Is the job interview process unbiased? And does the person being interviewed really want the job, or is he/she just planning to use it as a stepping stone to something better?

> *'I don't care if his skills are weak and he's got no experience. Look at that enthusiasm and energy level. He's going to be terrific!'*
> **Edgar Trenner, businessman**

The breakthrough

There are nearly 4 million businesses in Britain, but fewer than 1.2 million have any employees. The vast majority are true sole traders, employing no one. The business is run by one person, helped by family members.

The star businesses are those that break away from being purely family firms. They need the courage to hire staff, despite the problems that may result. Every staff member causes a business to pay extra taxes, give four weeks' holiday pay and meet laws that cover health and safety, job security and conditions of work.

The breakthrough comes when employers gain the commitment and confidence to hire people and start treating them like adults. This requires skills that many entrepreneurs lack. They are often good at bossing people about, but poor at encouraging people to think for themselves.

A true sole trader

An interview enables the boss to judge the applicant's personality and attitude

Often small firms start by recruiting friends or former workmates. This gets round any concerns about whether the new recruit will prove unfriendly or work-shy. As a business grows, however, the boss will soon run out of friends to be brought in. Then the real process starts of judging people who you do not know. The keys to this process are:

● a CV (**curriculum vitae**), which sets out the person's qualifications, experience and any other relevant facts

● **references**, usually in the form of a letter from a named friend, teacher or colleague, who will write about the applicant's qualities

● an interview, which enables the boss to judge the applicant's personality and his/her attitude to the job on offer (enthusiastic? well prepared? scruffy, with a couldn't-care-less attitude?)

● sometimes a test of the person's skills (typing ability and speed, perhaps) or their personality.

Small firms should be especially careful about the personalities of the people they recruit. A quiet, dull person may dampen the atmosphere at work, making it harder for people to enjoy coming to work. The table that follows shows the skills that employers say they are looking for. Usually this is on top of a requirement that candidates should have GCSEs in Maths and English.

> '*Judge a man by his questions, not his answers.*'
> **Voltaire, French philosopher**

Top 10 skills that employers look for

Commercial awareness	Knowing what makes companies tick
Communication	Including presentations and written and verbal communication skills
Teamwork	Proving you're a team player but with the ability to manage others
Negotiation and persuasion	Being able to 'get your way', but also understanding where the other person is coming from
Problem solving	Including analysis and logical thinking
Leadership	Motivating a team and assigning tasks and deadlines
Organisation	Prioritising your workload and time
Ability to meet deadlines	Proving your efficiency and time-management skills
Ability to work under pressure	Keeping calm in a crisis and not becoming too overwhelmed or stressed
Confidence	In yourself, your colleagues and the company

Source: doctorjob.com

More of the same?

Entrepreneurs are inclined to recruit people like themselves. It is comfortable to work with people of the same race, from the same area and of the same age. Yet this may cause serious problems for the business. Firms need staff with different points of view, perhaps stemming from different backgrounds. In 2001 the frozen foods business Iceland decided to drop its buy one get one free promotional campaign and reposition the business as an organic foods company. Prices went up – and sales plunged. Within six months this daft strategy was reversed. How come no middle manager said beforehand that this was a bad idea? The senior management was too wealthy and too middle class to understand the customers. The business needed some different points of view.

Well-run firms like to have a wide range of different ages, classes and races working for them. This ensures that all possible types of customer can be understood by staff working within the business.

Iceland

Conclusion

Firms that aim to grow have no choice but to recruit staff. When they do this they need to be alert to the risks of hiring someone who may be disruptive, yet accept that this is unlikely. Most workers want to do a good job, and should be given the opportunity and encouragement to get on with it.

> 'Hiring and training are costly – but it is infinitely more costly to have a barely average man on the company payroll for 30 years.'
> **Gordon Wheeling, personnel manager**

Revision Essentials

Curriculum vitae – the story of life (i.e. a summary of a person's qualifications, achievements and interests).

Discrimination – choosing one type of person in preference to another, perhaps on the grounds of race, sex or age.

Reference – a letter to support a job application from someone the job applicant has chosen (e.g. a previous boss).

Exercises

(25 marks; 25 minutes)

Read the unit, then ask yourself:

1   Salvatore has had little luck finding staff. Identify two possible reasons why he might be failing to recruit the staff he needs. (2)

2   (a) How many British businesses employ no employees at all? (1)

    (b) Identify two reasons why businesses may be reluctant to hire staff. (2)

3   Reread the explanation of 'reference' (under 'Revision essentials'). Outline one reason why an employer might be cautious about a very positive reference about a job applicant. (2)

4   Explain why a small business should look carefully at the personality of a job applicant. (4)

5   Discuss the importance of recruiting staff from a wide range of social and racial backgrounds to one of the following organisations:

    (a) hospital

    (b) hairdresser

    (c) dress designer. (6)

6   Explain in your own words the meaning of Gordon Wheeling's statement: 'Hiring and training are costly – but it is infinitely more costly to have a barely average man on the company payroll for 30 years.' (3)

Practice Questions

Recruitment 'inhibits small firm growth'

One in five small businesses cannot grow their business because of problems recruiting staff, according to research released today.

A report from the Tenon Forum think tank shows 20 per cent of small businesses feel effective recruitment is the largest barrier to their growth. Larger firms can offer salary and benefit levels which they cannot. Many small businesses are also less likely to have the expertise to find talented staff.

Bigger businesses find recruitment less of an obstacle to growth. Of companies with 5–9 employees, 22 per cent say recruitment is their biggest barrier, compared to 9 per cent of firms with 200–499 employees.

Small firms have a number of distinct benefits that are not always found in larger organisations, said Richard Kennett of the Tenon Foundation. '[Smaller firms offer] earlier opportunities for promotion and career advancement, more job flexibility, more direct personal contact with senior management and a higher profile within the company,' Kennett said. 'By increasing awareness of these benefits, small businesses will start to address the issue of recruitment.'

The survey also identified market conditions, cash flow, competition and attitudes to risk were listed as other leading restrictions on the growth of small firms. (Source: adapted from www.startups.co.uk)

Questions

(20 marks; 20 minutes)

1   Outline two reasons why recruitment may be the largest barrier to the growth of small firms. (4)

2   Explain two possible advantages to employees of taking a job in a small firm rather than a large one. (6)

3   Discuss the restrictions on the growth of small firms caused by any one of the following:

   (a) market conditions

   (b) competition

   (c) attitudes to risk. (10)

Staff training

In 2002 chef Jamie Oliver set up a charity called Fifteen. Its aim was to open a top quality restaurant staffed by young people from difficult backgrounds. One-third of the places on the course would be reserved for teenagers who are homeless or recently out of prison. None would have any previous experience in catering, yet all would be trained to become top-class chefs. It was a dazzlingly ambitious idea.

The Fifteen programme costs the charity £18,000 per trainee, and includes:

- three months at a catering college, learning basic kitchen skills, such as cutting and slicing

- 'sourcing' trips, going to farms in Scotland or vineyards in Italy to learn about the importance of top quality ingredients

- constant emphasis on improving the students' ability to taste the difference between average and delicious foods and wine

- work experience, often at some of London's finest restaurants, such as Le Gavroche, where the standards demanded of the students are incredibly high

- working at Fifteen, spending a week on each section: grill, pasta, pastry, fish, butchery, bakery and as a waiter, to really learn the trade, then a period of time specialising in one section.

Today, Fifteen is a hugely popular restaurant in Hoxton, east London, with all its profits being used to fund the charity. It is working with its fourth group of students, and its graduates are working in great restaurants around the world. There is an equally successful Fifteen in Amsterdam, one in Cornwall and another in Australia. The whole project is based on Jamie Oliver's view that everyone deserves great training. One of the first graduates from Fifteen, Asher Wyborn, has said:

> One of the biggest lessons I'll take with me is that you don't need to treat people badly to get results. I hope none of us become like the old-style breed of chefs that treat people like scum because that's how they were treated on the way up. This place has shown me that respect breeds respect and it's something I'll take with me wherever I go.

Why train?

If a job was so simple that it required no training, it probably could – and would – be

Jamie Oliver's Fifteen restaurant

done by a robot. Yet there is much more to training than telling people how to do a job. Well-run organisations keep investing in staff training because there is no limit to the amount to be learned. Take, for example, the reasons why experienced teachers might need training:

- to know about a new GCSE course, or a change to an existing one;

- to be kept up to date by the chief examiner about the latest thinking in how the exams are to be set and marked;

- to learn about new technology available for teaching, perhaps downloadable from the internet.

In other words, things change, and training is a way to keep people on top of their job. This should ensure high quality staff performance, and also helps staff feel properly looked after by the business, which helps morale and motivation.

'Train everyone – lavishly . . . You can't overspend on training.'
Tom Peters, management guru

Training is a way to keep people on top of a job

For a new, young employee, the length (and therefore cost) of the induction programme is a good indication of how seriously the management treats your appointment. If, as at Fifteen, you are flown off to Italy for part of the programme, you would be right to feel special.

Induction

When you join an organisation, there is always some **induction** training, to ease you into the job. Simple induction tasks include being shown the fire exits and the canteen and being introduced to colleagues. A more ambitious programme will include:

- a presentation by a director on the aims and plans of the business

- a detailed explanation of the role of the department you are working for

- perhaps, as at Fifteen, a programme of spending a week in different departments, to get a broad understanding of the business.

Training

Training can be **on-the-job** or **off-the-job**. Both have an important role to play in most businesses. A new recruit at Tesco might learn to use the till on-the-job, helped by a supervisor. Later, though, if there is a chance of promotion, off-the-job training may take place at a local college. This training might be in people skills, such as persuasion, or in IT skills, such as using the company's spreadsheet system of recording stock wastage (theft plus stock thrown away as it passes its sell-by date).

The most important aspect of training, though, is whether it is aimed at the attitudes and personal skills of the individual, or whether it is solely for a practical purpose. A

'The more a person can do, the more you can motivate them ... that's the point of training.'
Professor Herzberg, academic

Is training always a good thing?

Tesco supervisor might be put on a training course on 'Using the new Tesco stock control system'. This is fine, but it is purely for Tesco's benefit. Well-run companies also encourage staff to pursue training programmes that develop the person. For example, shy people might be encouraged to go on an assertiveness training course. This would teach them to be stronger and firmer when dealing with others (including their boss). Many firms allocate a sum of money per employee, allowing the individual to follow any course they would like (e.g. learning to speak Spanish or play the piano). The companies do this because they want to be seen to invest in their staff. Tesco has long had an excellent reputation for this type of personal development as well as purely business-focused training.

Training, like teaching, is a good thing unless it is boring or seems irrelevant. Large firms are likely to prepare training programmes for all their staff. There may be a section on health and safety that is vital to some and means nothing to others; or a section on equal opportunities at work that many feel is stating the obvious – that there is no place at work for prejudice on grounds of race, age or sex.

To be effective, training programmes need to be tailored to individual needs. A part-time worker wondering about a career may welcome the opportunity to go on a training course on supervisory skills. Another may only be interested in Friday's pay cheque and therefore hate 'boring' training. Good managers know their staff well enough to know who wants what, and why.

'All genuine knowledge originates in direct experience.'
Mao Tse-Tung, Chinese leader

Revision Essentials

Induction – initial training to make newcomers feel comfortable in their new job.

Off-the-job – training that takes place away from the job (e.g. at college or at a company's training centre).

On-the-job – **training that takes place while working at the job (e.g. till training at a supermarket).**

Exercises

(20 marks; 25 minutes)

Read the unit, then ask yourself:

1. When they are finally graded, Jamie Oliver's programme judges each student on four key factors: attendance, skills, effort and attitude. Briefly outline the importance of any two of these factors to an employer. (4)

2. The training programme at Fifteen takes 14 months, whereas a new employee at a fast-food restaurant might get only a day's training before starting work. Discuss how employees at Fifteen are likely to feel about their job compared with those starting at the burger bar. (6)

3. Give two reasons why a firm should run an induction programme. (2)

4. Sam Allardyce, the football manager, has taken a lot of off-the-job training, including a course on management at Warwick University. Outline two ways in which he might benefit from this. (4)

5. 'Staff training would be a waste of money, as half my staff leave within a year.' Explain to this business owner two reasons why he/she should change this attitude to training. (4)

Practice Questions

Training in a RuneScape world

RuneScape is a fantasy world of warring races, ravaged landscapes and sinister powers. It is one of the world's most heavily used online games, with as many as 100,000 people playing at any one time. Behind this huge gaming success are two brothers from Nottingham. Still in their 20s, they have created a multi-million pound business out of one computer game. The 2008 *Sunday Times* 'Rich List' estimated their combined wealth at over £100 million.

RuneScape online game

If you Google 'RuneScape' and then follow through to the website, you are invited to join in a computer adventure game – for free. More than 150 million have already played. During 2007, 5 million played on the free site and a further million paid to get the upgraded version of the game. The RuneScape website also generates income from advertisers. In 2007 the company made a profit of more than £15 million.

In 2008 the 600 staff at parent company Jagex Ltd put the business forward as one of the Top 100 employers in the country. This is partly because of how well staff are treated (no dress code; annual bonus; trips to overseas 5-star hotels; gym membership) and partly because of the excellent team spirit. In the Top 100 survey, 86 per cent of Jagex staff said their teams were fun to work in.

Also important is the training involved. This comes in two ways. First, staff are encouraged to show initiative and be innovative. Therefore the most important training comes from within. Staff push themselves and their teams to find new ways to do things. Therefore they learn on the job. This is informal training.

Jagex also makes use of formal training approaches. In their first year at Jagex, newly qualified graduates get a lot of training from senior programmers. All staff can get huge financial support to follow further degrees, such as a Masters or PhD. Staff might also be sent on specialist software courses. More commonly, training is done in-house. With such a large staff of software developers, it can be helpful to bring in industry experts as trainers.

The effect of the excellent management of staff at Jagex is that the business gets more than 10,000 applications for the 100 graduate jobs it has each year. This enables it to pick the best of the best.

Questions

(20 marks; 25 minutes)

1 From the article, identify two reasons graduates are so keen to get a job at Jagex. (2)

2 Comment on the likely benefits to new staff of the formal training provided at Jagex. (5)

3 Explain why a small business such as Jagex might find it easier to provide good training than a huge firm such as Microsoft. (5)

4 The text mentions informal and formal training. Discuss whether formal or informal training is likely to be the more important in developing staff skills at Jagex. (8)

Motivation

Motivation matters. Motivation matters massively. In January 2006 Burton Albion played Manchester United in the FA Cup third round. Playing at home, the part-timers of Burton outfought and even outplayed United. Even when Wayne Rooney came on with half an hour to go, Burton looked the more motivated side. The game ended nil-nil, providing Burton with a £500,000 jackpot in a replay at Old Trafford. Motivation allows small companies to outperform large ones, and employees of average ability to outperform cleverer ones.

At 3.30 a.m. on a Saturday morning, Salvatore Falcone starts work at his bakery. He makes and bakes bread, pizzas, doughnuts, cakes and pastries until 11.30 a.m., then serves customers until 4.30 in the afternoon. On a Sunday evening he races stock cars at Wimbledon race track, often winning in this fast, dangerous sport. In return for his amazing motivation, he has been able to afford houses in London and Italy, and is now eyeing a soft-top Ferrari Testarossa. He works hard, plays hard and is about as happy a man as you could find.

Entrepreneurs have motivation, but the big question is how to motivate staff who are not getting the direct financial reward from the success of the business.

What exactly *is* motivation?

To most people, motivation simply means having the commitment to do something. Within the home, it may be decorating the bathroom; at work, it may be working late to finish a job. However, Professor Herzberg says that motivation is doing something because you *want* to do it. In other words, motivation is not about whether you do it, it is why and how you do it. Motivation, he says, does not come from money or from threats ('do this, or else'); it only comes from within.

There are many possible ways to motivate staff. Among them are:

- Give them a real sense of purpose. Staff on a hospital maternity ward should be fine, but in a profit-making business it may be harder. Yet high quality standards can motivate people, as can success. Employees of Apple loved seeing iPod

A reward for a motivated entrepreneur

beating Sony and taking 75 per cent of the market for MP3 players.

- Involve them in the decisions made by the business (e.g. getting shop-floor staff involved in deciding how to rearrange the shop to encourage higher sales).

- Give them meaningful, challenging tasks; an American TV station asked its staff to come up with a new schedule of pro-grammes for a Friday night. The man-agement followed the advice of staff and the viewing audience rose 20 per cent. The staff then reorganised the rest of the week's programmes with equal success – and the number of staff days off 'sick' fell by 30 per cent.

Is money not a motivator?

Everyone agrees that pay is a crucial part of staff satisfaction. People work in order to earn money, and if they feel underpaid they leave. That is not the same as saying that pay makes people work harder or better. A head of department may earn 35 per cent more than an ordinary teacher. Does that make him/her work 35 per cent harder? Or even any harder at all? Probably not.

Of course, money can be used to make people work faster. A bricklayer who lays 500 bricks a day could be offered a £30 bonus for laying an extra 100 bricks in the time. Almost certainly the bricklayer will work faster to achieve the bonus. The risk is that this will be at the cost of poorer quality bricklaying.

Professor Herzberg explains that money can get people to work faster or longer, but people produce the best work when they are motivated; and motivation comes from within. Motivation is doing it because you want to.

Talking Point

In which school subject are you the most motivated? Why do you think you have greater motivation towards this subject?

What should managers do to motivate their staff?

In a small firm it should be quite easy to ensure that most staff are well motivated. The boss should:

- Train staff so that they feel confident doing what they are asked to do.

- Give them meaningful jobs to do, with opportunities to show their ability.

- Talk to them regularly to make sure they know what is happening now and what is planned for the future.

- Give them the opportunity to contribute ideas; and then act on the good ones.

- Pay fairly, so that someone who is contrib-uting a lot is given pay rises to reflect his/her achievements and efforts.

A motivated bricklayer may work faster

What are the benefits of a motivated staff?

High morale and motivation rubs off on customers. They feel better about the company and therefore keep coming back. This is especially important in businesses where staff see the customers every day, such as a waiter, a hotel receptionist or a school teacher. High motivation is also likely to lead to:

- lower **absenteeism** (i.e. very few staff taking days off work).

- lower **labour turnover**, with fewer staff looking for other jobs and therefore fewer leaving. As recruiting staff is expensive, it saves a huge amount if staff stay loyal.

- improved teamwork within the business; this encourages more ideas to come from staff discussions that may lead to major business benefits.

> *'In order that people be happy in their work, these three things are needed: they must be fit for it; they must not do too much of it; and they must have a sense of success in it.'*
> **John Ruskin, philosopher**

Conclusion

The most successful companies are usually those with the best motivated staff. People who have started their own business can underestimate the importance of this. They often expect people to find the motivation from within, without doing enough to create a situation in which staff can easily be motivated. If the boss barks out orders and hands over a series of dull tasks, it is no surprise if staff dislike their work. Motivation requires a manager to think how to organise work so that staff can feel that their intelligence is being used properly.

Revision Essentials

Absenteeism – the percentage of the workforce that is absent on the average day. The national average is about 3 per cent, but in some organisations it is as high as 10 per cent.

Labour turnover – the percentage of the workforce that leaves each year and has to be replaced.

Exercises

(20 marks; 25 minutes)

Read the unit, then ask yourself:

Claude Makelele,
Chelsea footballer

1. Why may it be harder for entrepreneurs to motivate their staff than it is to motivate themselves? (3)

2. In 2003 Claude Makelele left the world's most glamorous team, Real Madrid, to join Chelsea. Although he earned over £1 million a year at Real, he felt unfairly treated compared with the star names such as Ronaldo. So he left. For the following two years Madrid won nothing.

   (a) Outline two reasons why firms should treat every member of staff fairly. (4)

   (b) Explain why a firm should be worried if its labour turnover is too high. (4)

3. Why may Professor Herzberg believe that money is not a motivator? (3)

4. Identify two reasons why training staff may improve their motivation. (2)

5. Explain two ways in which a firm might benefit from lower absenteeism. (4)

Practice Questions

Building a building business

Jensens Engineering was founded in 1993. It designs, builds and installs heating, ventilation and air-conditioning equipment throughout the UK. The company has 50 employees. It supplies the building trade, which is one of the most dangerous trades to work in.

The challenge

The company's directors were concerned about a high rate of staff turnover and the effect this was having on projects, availability of skills and profits. Despite being paid competitive salaries, people still moved on and the morale of those who remained was low. The whole company approach had to change in order to maintain its reputation and growth.

The strategy

The directors aimed to give all employees a greater feeling for the company through greater involvement in their day-to-day work. Managers started to meet each member of staff once a fortnight instead of once a year. Identifying and taking action on training and development was supported by generous budgets, especially on health and safety.

The result

Staff turnover has been reduced by over 70 per cent. Similarly, absenteeism has been slashed. Sales turnover doubled in the following three years. Sales and profits improved significantly year on year. The way the organisation now works, and what its people feel about it has changed beyond recognition. 'The pay cheque is important, but it's the job that's the trophy.'

Questions

(20 marks; 25 minutes)

1 How might a high rate of staff turnover affect profits at Jensens Engineering? (4)

2 When morale is bad, it is usually the most highly skilled staff who leave, as they can find another job quite easily. Outline two effects on a firm of losing its most highly skilled staff. (4)

3 Why may Jensens management have decided to meet each staff member once a fortnight? (4)

4 Discuss the causes and effects of Jensen's efforts to improve the motivation of their staff. (8)

Exam-style Questions

DON'T RUSH; check answers carefully

1. Identify three important legal and tax issues when starting up a small business.   (3)

a) To let Inland Revenue know that you are starting a business.

b) To pay Inland Revenue half of the tax you forecast on your first year's profits.

c) To hire an accountant to work for you full-time.

d) To establish a unique business name to trade under.

e) To obtain permission from the government to start the business.

f) Set up a record-keeping system so that there is no doubt how much tax you owe.

g) Show proof to the taxman that you have enough cash to pay your bills.

2. Tim and Nattasja are setting up an Extreme Sports Travel Agency in London. They're aiming at young adults wealthy enough to afford £1000–£4000 on a holiday based on skydiving, mountaineering or jungle-trekking. They need to recruit three staff to work in the front office, selling directly to customers.

   Which three of the following would be the most important things to consider when choosing who to recruit for these jobs?   (3)

a) At least two years' experience within the travel industry.

b) A warm, outgoing personality.

c) A very well presented CV.

d) Enthusiasm for unusual, tailor-made holidays such as these.

e) Full understanding of travel industry computer-booking systems.

f) Family and school background – the wealthier the better.

g) Eager to learn the systems involved in providing customers with what they want.

3. Which of the following is the best definition of unlimited liability?   (1)

a) Provides the entrepreneur with a limitless opportunity to make high profits.

b) Ensures that, if things go wrong, the owners can only lose the money they invested.

c) It's the best way to cheaply start a small business that has low risks.

d) It's the method used by the majority of businesses in Britain.

e) The business owners can be held responsible personally for any debts of the business.

Questions 4 and 5 are based on these sales data for Dave's Drinks Ltd.

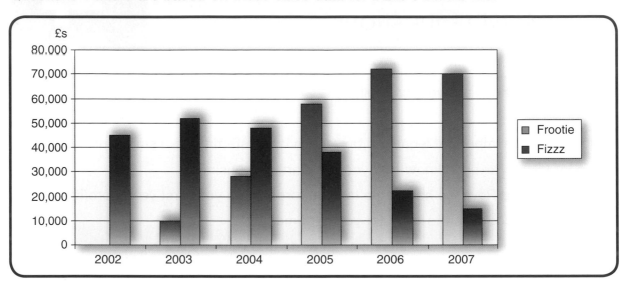

4. Identify two correct statements about sales at Dave's Drinks. (2)

a) Total sales in 2004 were £14,000 higher than in 2003.

b) Frootie outsold Fizzz by £70,000 in 2007.

c) Fizzz sales in 2006 were £20,000 down on the 2003 figure.

d) Total sales in 2007 were £85,000.

e) Frootie sales in 2007 were £32,000 higher than in 2004.

f) Total sales of Dave's Drinks peaked in 2004.

g) Sales of Frootie were 5 times higher in 2007 than in 2003.

5. The boss of Dave's Drinks wants to put £50,000 behind advertising either Frootie or Fizzz in 2008. Identify the strongest argument from these five. (1)

a) It should be Fizzz because without advertising the product will die.

b) It should be Frootie because its sales are higher.

c) It should be Fizzz because its sales decline has only been because of consumer concerns about health issues with sweet fizzy drinks.

d) It should be Frootie because it makes a higher profit per £ of sales than Fizzz.

e) It should be Frootie because the brand was Dave's own idea.

6. Jackson's has a policy of pricing low to attract sales. This forces it to cut a few corners, but owner Tess Jackson is proud that her business has the second highest sales volume in the industry. The industry number one is GFH Ltd. Tess has just hired a new manager who used to work for GFH Ltd. This has allowed her to find out about her rival's customer service figures.

	Jackson's	GFH Ltd
On-time deliveries	88.40%	93.80%
Damaged deliveries	2.40%	0.65%
Customer returns	3.10%	1.05%
Customer satisfaction	78.40%	91.70%

Identify three conclusions that can be taken from these figures:

a) The low-price policy at Jacksons is definitely working.

b) Tess can feel proud that only 3.1 per cent of customers send their goods back.

c) Tess urgently needs to look into why 21.6 per cent of her customers are unsatisfied.

d) Tess should ask her new manager to explain exactly how GFH Ltd handles deliveries.

e) Jacksons has clearly achieved an effective system of on-time delivery.

f) There is a serious risk that repeat purchase levels at GFH Ltd will fall in future.

g) Tess should discuss these figures with all her staff, inviting ideas for improvement.

7. Which element of the marketing mix covers 'distribution'?

UNDERSTANDING THE ECONOMIC CONTEXT

Introduction to the economic context

Even if you make good decisions at every key point, starting up a new business is difficult. Making it harder still are factors outside any manager's control. Many stem from changes to the economy. For instance, a slowdown in the economy may lead to rising unemployment. If people are out of work (or feel the threat of unemployment), they cut back their spending, especially on luxuries. This may lead to a sharp decline in takings at restaurants, jewellers and pricier shops.

Many businesses start up when times are good, and it seems easy to make money from free-spending customers. It is important to remember, though, that hard times can be around the corner. This should be okay as long as you have thought how to respond to an economic downturn. During the 1990–92 **recession**, many commentators suggested that Richard Branson's Virgin group was about to collapse. In fact he came through that period stronger than ever.

In 2008, Britain suffered a sharp economic downturn that looked likely to become the first recession for nearly 20 years. At times such as this, well-run businesses find new ways to appeal to customers.

What is the economy?

The British economy is the collection of business transactions that takes place throughout the country, throughout the year. If you add up the value of all the goods and services produced in Britain in a year, the total figure comes to over £1 trillion (£1,000,000,000,000). 'The economy' is made up of lots of companies buying and selling with each other, lots of firms selling directly to customers (some here and some overseas) and lots of money raised by and spent by the government.

The key to understanding the economy is to see it as a series of connected loops. If I buy a new Mini Cooper in London, I pay £15,000 to the dealer. Yet that triggers a series of payments to: Oxford (where the car was made); Swindon (where the steel body panels were made); Hams Hall, Warwickshire (where the engine was made); Port Talbot, South Wales (where the steel was made); and so on. In fact, over 2000 suppliers are involved in producing every

Mini Cooper

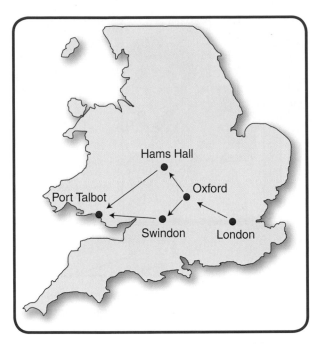

The economy as a series of connected loops

downturn there is a downward spiral of falling confidence and lower spending. Cutbacks by customers in London can have knock-on effects in Oxford, Swindon, Scotland, and so on.

What makes the economy go up and down?

It is important to remember that Britain is one of the world's most open economies. Trade with other countries accounts for more than 30 per cent of the value of all goods and services produced in Britain per year. Therefore if America gets flu, we catch a cold. Cutbacks by American consumers would hurt our large companies in banking, insurance and car production, all of which rely on **exports**. Poor economic conditions in Europe hit us even harder, as more than 50 per cent of all British exports are to European Union countries such as France and Germany.

BMW Mini, and they come from Scotland and the North-East as well as in the areas immediately around Oxford. The higher the demand for Minis, the greater the injection of money and jobs into the veins of the national economy. As workers become more confident of their future prospects (secure job, good income, etc.), they become more willing to spend – perhaps on a new Mini. Greater prosperity feeds on itself, creating an upward spiral.

Needless to say, if things start to go wrong, the reverse happens. During an economic

Talking Point

From your general knowledge, how well or badly is the British economy doing at the moment?

Problems can also hit the economy from within the country. In 2008, falls in house prices led to a series of banking failures. This led to dramatic falls in consumer confidence. Solid businesses such as John Lewis saw falls in sales as high as 20 per cent. Weaker firms such as Woolworths and MFI collapsed. Job losses led to rising unemployment and the start of a major recession.

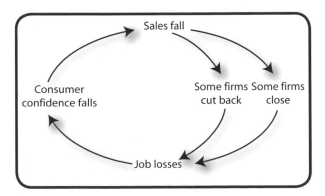

Recession – the downward spiral

What do business-people most need to know about the economy?

The way interest rates can change

The interest rate is the amount a lender charges per year to someone who has borrowed money. It is measured as a percentage, for example 8 per cent – in other words, the borrower has to pay the lender £8 per year for every £100 borrowed. In addition, the lender must pay the £100 back, perhaps on a monthly basis.

In early 2008 banks charged between 8 and 10 per cent for money borrowed to finance a business start-up. There have been times before when the rate has risen as high as 15 or even 20 per cent, making it very hard to afford the repayments. Whenever possible it is wise to get the bank to agree to a fixed interest rate, so there are no nasty surprises.

The way exchange rates can change

The exchange rate is the value of the £, measured by how much foreign currency can be bought per £. For instance, in March 2008, £1 could be exchanged for $2.00 when travelling to America. By September 2008 the £ had fallen, so that it was worth just $1.75. For a British tourist, the lower exchange rate would dampen the shopping thrills of New York. For Rolls-Royce, selling a £50 million aero-engine to an American airline, the stakes are higher. A falling £ makes UK exports more profitable.

The firms who would be most concerned about changes to the £'s exchange rate are:

For a British tourist, lower exchange rates dampen the shopping thrills of New York

- Big importers, such as electrical goods companies or car showrooms.

- Big exporters, such as Rolls-Royce, who export more than 90 per cent of the products they make; for Rolls-Royce, a higher £ squeezes the profitability of their exports.

- UK producers competing in the UK against foreign companies (e.g. JCB excavators, which has to compete directly against the Japanese Komatsu and the US firm Caterpillar).

The threat of recession

During the sharp economic downturn in 2008, thousands of people were put out of work. Some businesses cut back on staffing levels; others, such as the airlines Zoom and XL, collapsed altogether. A few firms succeeded despite the difficulties, such as the discount shops Matalan, Lidl and Aldi. For most, though, it was a nightmare.

A recession is a severe downturn in the economy, often described as when economic activity falls for two successive quarters of the year. Firms can usually expect that **consumer spending** will grow a little each year, perhaps about 2.5 per cent. When spending actually falls, companies struggle to cope with falling revenues and cash inflows.

Well-run companies look ahead, both to check that no recession is looming and to make sure that they can cope if one arrives. For instance, when the 2008 consumer slow-down hit John Lewis department stores, the company was helped out by the strong showing of Waitrose, its supermarket chain.

Revision Essentials

Consumer spending – the total spent by all shoppers throughout the country.

Exports – goods produced in one country but sold overseas (e.g. a British-made Mini sold in France).

Recession – a downturn in sales and output throughout the economy, often leading to rising unemployment.

Exercises

(A and B: 22 marks; 30 minutes)

A. Read the unit, then ask yourself:

1   Give two examples of transactions where one business would sell to another business. (2)

2   Explain what the text means by 'an upward spiral'. (3)

3   If a small British firm wanted to start exporting for the first time, would it prefer the £ to be high and rising or weak and falling? Briefly explain your answer. (5)

B. Exports smash through £11 billion barrier

Students often ask: what does Britain export? A surprising answer is food. In 2007, for the first time, British exports of food and drink exceeded £11,000 million. Many of the success stories were small firms such as Walkers Shortbread and Welsh Exporter of the Year: Llanllyr Water. 2007 was a good year partly because the value of the £ was lower against the euro. This meant that it was easier for British firms to sell goods to countries in the Eurozone such as Italy, Spain and France. Exports were also helped by higher consumer spending in much of Europe.

1   Outline two possible benefits to small firms of finding export markets for their goods. (4)

2   Outline two reasons why British food exports rose in 2007. (4)

3   Small firms usually charge higher prices in export markets than in Britain. Explain why that might be necessary in order to make exporting profitable. (4)

Practice Questions

Tough times in car manufacturing

March 11th 2007 was a proud day for David Richards. He had just bought the Aston Martin luxury car business from its owner, Ford. He put together a deal to buy the Aston Martin factory, brand names and distribution system – for £480 million. This is a lot of money, but what he was buying was a very small part of the car market. In 2007 Aston Martin's sales of 2190 cars gave the company a 0.1 per cent share of the UK car market.

In the previous years of economic boom, Aston Martin sales raced ahead. On 11 March Richards announced that Aston Martin would soon be looking to hire 200 more UK staff. Yet within three months of buying the business, the August 2007 'credit crunch' changed the picture. Bankers and estate agents had been among the new Aston Martin buyers in 2006 and early 2007. Quite suddenly they disappeared from the showrooms.

Early 2008 saw a serious worsening of the position for car companies. Oil prices were shooting ahead, causing petrol pump prices to rise. Car buyers might have wanted a Lexus or an Aston Martin, but the thought of £80 to fill the tank was very off-putting. And then there was the gloom – the drip-drip of news stories about the economic 'downturn' and rising unemployment. In August 2008, the Chancellor of the Exchequer, Alistair Darling, made headlines such as this in *The Guardian*: 'Economy at 60-year low, and it will get worse'. No surprise, then, that sales of new cars fell by 18 per cent in August 2008. And, as you can see in the graph below, sales of bigger, thirstier cars fell far more dramatically than this.

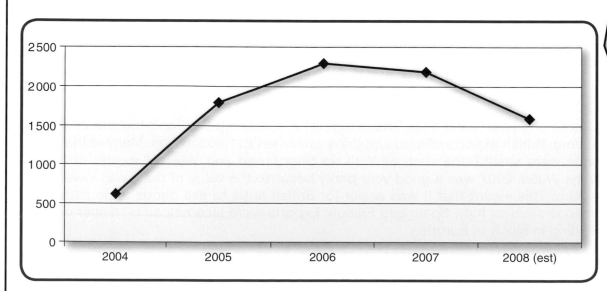

UK 12-month sales of Aston Martin cars

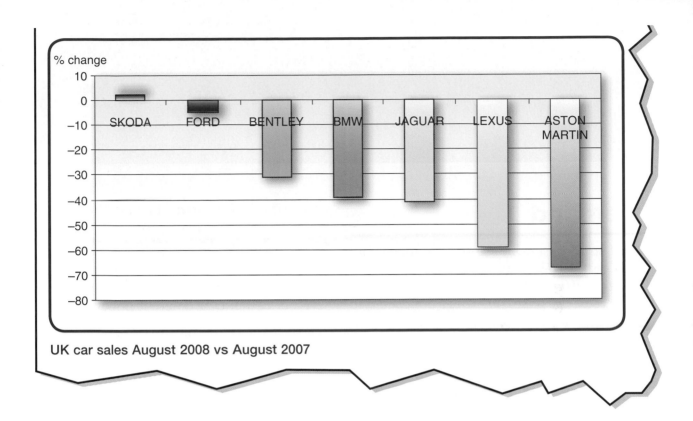

% change

UK car sales August 2008 vs August 2007

Questions

(20 marks; 25 minutes)

1 Explain two possible reasons why sales of Skoda cars rose in August 2008. (4)

2 Outline two factors that might make Aston Martin a riskier business to run than, for example, Tesco or Sainsbury's. (4)

3 Mr Richards announced a plan to hire 200 more production staff in March 2007. What would have been the effect on the business if this plan had gone ahead? (4)

4 Outline how a general fall in UK consumer spending might affect:

(a) Rococo, a small business making and selling luxury chocolates. (4)

(b) T. Hughes, a small bakery with loyal, local customers. (4)

Demand and supply

Demand

Most small business decisions are made with little real certainty about the circumstances and the effects. When a minicab firm decides to increase the price it charges from Oxford to Heathrow Airport to £36, it may not know all the prices charged by all its rivals; and will certainly not know how the rivals will respond. Will they increase their prices as well? Or will they fight rough by holding prices down (making it hard for the firm to get business)?

For a **market** trader the situation is easier. If he/she starts the day with strawberries priced at £2.50 a kilo and they are not selling, he/she cuts the price to £1.50 and sees what happens. If sales jump ahead, creating a threat that they will be sold out by lunchtime, the trader can quietly slip the price up to £2.20. In this way, the trader can end up creating what is called a demand curve. This is a diagram showing the level of customer demand for a product at different price levels. (See figure below.)

Drawn out on a piece of graph paper, a demand curve shows not only the known levels of demand at different prices, but also gives an idea about the likely sales at other price points. In the figure on this page, for example, if the trader had 150 punnets left and just an hour before the market closes, he/she would know that a price cut to £1 per kilo would be needed.

How useful are demand curves?

They are useful whenever they can be drawn up. The problem is finding out the information. A market stall trader can experiment every hour of every day. It is not possible for BMW, though, to offer their 5-Series for £40,000 one month and £30,000 the next (to find out the effect on demand). Customers would not understand what is going on, and there would be a risk of damage to BMW's image.

The most important type of demand curve is one for a **commodity** such as oil. Every day, hundreds of millions of £s are spent on oil. The lower the price being charged, the higher the level of demand. In the City of London many businesses make a living from buying at a low price one day and selling at a higher price the day after. They need a clear idea of the link between price and demand.

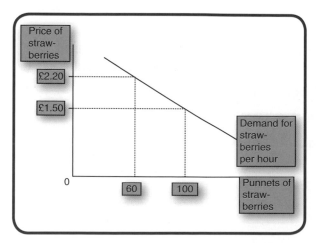

Demand curve for strawberries on a market stall

Supply

In markets, price is not only affected by demand, but also by supply. In a street market, if there was a day when only one stall sold strawberries, that stall would have a local **monopoly**. It would be the only supplier of the fruit. If there were not many strawberries available to the market shoppers, the one seller would soon start to sell out. The natural reaction would therefore be to put the price up. If an increase from £1.50 to £2.20 still did not stop customers coming, the trader would push prices up further. In other words, the lower the supply the higher prices will rise.

For a large firm such as Mars, an increase in demand for Maltesers would lead the company to produce more, perhaps by getting staff to work overtime. In some circumstances, though, it is impossible to increase supply in the short term. Chelsea season tickets are in great demand, but the supply is limited by the 40,000 capacity of Stamford Bridge. This limited level of supply enables Chelsea to charge some of the world's highest prices for watching football. In a street market, the day's fruit is bought **wholesale** in the early hours of the morning, so there is no possibil-

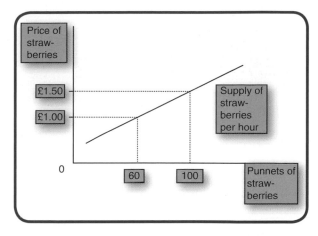

Supply curve for strawberries on a market stall

ity of getting extra supply within the day's market trading.

The overall message is simple: a supply shortage leads to high prices; plentiful supply causes prices to fall. Nevertheless, what every supplier wants is high prices. The higher the price, the more enthusiastic he/she will be to supply. This is shown in the figure above, in which a supplier will happily supply 100 punnets when the price is £1.50, but only 60 punnets if the price is £1.

When supply and demand are in balance

Day by day the prices of many commodities change relatively little. This is because supply and demand are broadly in balance. In other words, the demand for the item is in line with the amount available. In a situation where demand and supply are matched, the price of the item should be quite stable. Heinz can forecast sales of baked beans with some accuracy, and therefore produces enough to meet the demand. Shop shelves are neither overloaded with beans, nor short of them.

A situation of balance between demand and supply is shown in the figure on page

On a day when only one stall sold strawberries, that stall would have a local monopoly

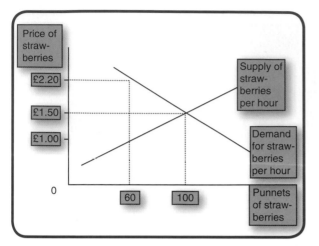

Supply and demand curves for strawberries on a market stall

The price of Maltesers is set by Mars

182. Note that the diagram suggests that a selling price of £1.50 is about right. If the price were less than £1.50 there would be plenty of demand, but too few sellers would be willing to supply. If the price was higher than £1.50 the demand would be lower than the amount supplied, leading to rotting, unsold fruit.

What if supply and demand are not in balance?

Small firms need to understand that the prices of key products may vary dramatically with changes in supply and demand. In late 2005 the price of copper was $4000 per tonne. By April 2008 it was $8500. The price difference was due to rising demand at a time when copper mines were struggling to increase output. Many a plumber could have been caught out by unexpectedly high prices for copper pipes. (Source: www.indexmundi. com)

Conclusion

Supply and demand determine price in a series of markets, especially those where there are no real differences between the products supplied. The price of Maltesers is decided on by Mars. Yet for a commodity such as copper, high demand can cause prices to shoot ahead, as can a shortage of supply. Clever entrepreneurs make sure they understand what influences the price of everything they buy, to avoid being caught out.

Revision Essentials

Commodity – a product in which all supplies are the same, such as a pound of sugar. By contrast, types of jam have different flavours and different brand names.

Market – where buyers and sellers come together; it could be in a particular street, or at an internet location (such as eBay).

Monopoly – where sales in the market are dominated by a single supplier.

Wholesale – **the middleman between producers and retailers; retailers can buy at discounts when they buy wholesale, and may pass that discount on to the public.**

Exercises

(20 marks; 25 minutes)

Read the unit, then ask yourself:

1 In the figure on page 180 (Demand curve for strawberries on a market stall), how much revenue would be made per hour by selling at £1.50? And how much at £2.20? (4)

2 Outline two ways in which a firm might use the information found in a demand curve for their key product. (4)

3 In 2012 Liverpool FC plans to increase its seat capacity from 45,000 to 60,000. Outline two possible disadvantages of this to the club. (4)

4 Explain what would happen to a commodity if its demand were higher than its supply. (4)

5 Firms love to lead a predictable life. Why would that be easier for a monopoly supplier than for one operating in a competitive market? (4)

Practice Questions

2007 saw some big shifts in sales of juices and drinks. Most were influenced by the strong desire by consumers for healthier choices. But some changes in demand were purely a result of good – or bad – marketing.

Tropicana juices had a good 2007, with sales rising by £26m (million) to £238m. This switch to pure fruit juice was at the expense of sugared fruit drinks such as Tango: sales fell sharply from £38m in 2006 to £28m a year later. The biggest percentage increase was achieved by Innocent, with sales rising from £82m in

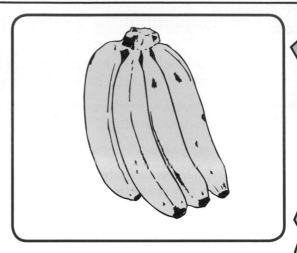

Bananas are a key ingredient in Innocent Drinks' fruit smoothies

2006 to £131m in 2007. But Coca-Cola remained the daddy. In 2007, its total retail sales were worth £940m.

Questions

(20 marks; 25 minutes)

1   (a) Calculate the percentage decline in sales of Tango in 2007. (3)

   (b) Outline two possible ways in which Tango might respond to this fall in demand. (4)

2   Bananas are a key ingredient in Innocent Drinks' fruit smoothies. In the first half of 2007, the price of bananas increased by 25 per cent. What changes to the supply and demand for bananas might have caused this sharp price rise? (4)

3   (a) By what percentage did Innocent's sales rise in 2007? (3)

   (b) Examine two possible causes of this sales increase. (6)

Prices in commodity markets

The prices of many of the goods sold in the high street are set by producers and shop-keepers. The latest Nokia model is priced by Nokia, not by 'the market'. Yet there are many markets where the producers have no control over the prices. If an oil producer sets the price of its oil at 10 per cent more than the market price, it will not sell any. So the sellers of commodities such as oil have to understand – and respond to – the market.

Commodities include:

- metals such as steel (cars), copper (housing and electronics) and aluminium (cans and also for making aircraft)

- clothing materials, such as cotton, wool and man-made products such as nylon

- food, such as coffee, cocoa and sugar.

Commodities include coffee, cocoa and sugar

The key characteristic of a commodity is that the products are interchangeable. In other words, you can swap one pound of sugar for another, without noticing any difference. Therefore it does not matter who you buy from. Contrast this with football season tickets. Are Manchester United and Manchester City tickets interchangeable? Not according to the customers – the fans. So sugar is a commodity, but season tickets are not.

Supply and demand

The price of a commodity depends on supply and demand. As shown in the figure on page 196, the price will be where supply and demand are in balance. In this case, it is at a figure of $90 per barrel of oil and a sales volume of 70 million barrels per day.

If oil companies want to buy more than 70 million barrels a day the price of oil will rise, possibly quite sharply. In the longer term that may put people off buying oil-based products such as petrol and plastic. Therefore demand will fall back towards its starting point.

Causes of changes in demand for a commodity are:

- a change in the rate of **economic growth**. If the world economy is growing more rapidly than before, demand will rise for almost every commodity. For example, more steel will be bought in order to build more cars. This, in turn, will push up the price of steel.

- a change in technology may change demand. For example, the new Boeing 'Dreamliner' plane will be made with a new, super-strong carbon fibre instead of aluminium. So demand will fall for aluminium.

- a change in buying behaviour. Current consumer attitudes to diet have meant a big drop in demand for sugar, as manufacturers switch to artificial sweeteners such as Splenda. In Britain, Diet Coke now outsells Coke. This has cut the demand for raw sugar – hitting the price obtained by sugar farmers in many developing countries.

Causes of change in the supply of a commodity are:

- if the price of a commodity has been low for some time, suppliers will stop investing in it. For instance, copper prices were low during the 1990s, so the owners of copper mines stopped developing new mines, even when old ones were running out of copper. Then, when the rapid growth of China pushed up the demand for copper between 2004 and 2008, it was impossible to respond quickly by increasing supply. Therefore prices rose sharply.

- changes in technology can also affect supply. New types of seed, perhaps backed by new fertilisers, may boost the level of supply per acre of land. Chemicals have also been used to boost milk yields. The average cow gave 3000 litres of milk a year in the 1940s. Today it is around 7500 litres (to the concern of many animal welfare groups). Rising supply pushes milk prices down, especially as consumer demand for milk (and cream) is weak.

Changes in technology can affect supply

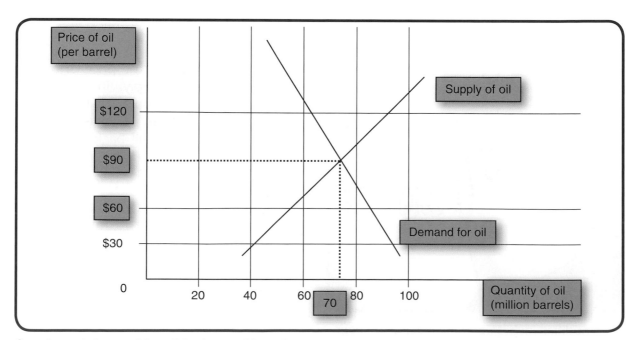

Supply and demand for oil in the world market

Is money a commodity?

In the **foreign exchange markets** money is a commodity. In other words, the £ is bought and sold, just as copper is bought and sold. The 'price' of a £ is measured in terms of foreign currency; for example, in September 2008 £1 could be bought for $1.75.

Given that £s can be bought and sold, the market price depends on supply and demand. If lots of Americans want £s in order to travel to Britain for the 2012 Olympics, demand for the £ will rise. Therefore the £ will rise in value. Perhaps it might rise to $1.85 per £. This higher price will make it more expensive for Americans to stay in Britain. It might even put people off coming, which will allow the £'s value to slip back.

The graph below shows the ups and downs of the £ against the $ over the period 1990 to 2009. Where the line goes up, the £ is rising against the $. This will be because of rising demand for the £ in the foreign exchange markets.

Effect on small firms

Changes in commodity prices have an impact on every business. Whereas large firms may have long-term deals with suppliers, small firms are likely to be hit straight away by changes in the cost of materials. Only manufacturers will be affected directly by changes in the cost of commodities such as iron ore or tin. But every business will be affected by changes in the oil price. This will affect the cost of heating and lighting plus the cost of transport and delivery.

When commodity and energy prices rise, small firms may find it hard to pass on the extra costs in the form of higher prices. If so, their profits will be squeezed. Small firms may find it hard to increase their prices because:

● They may have tough competitors

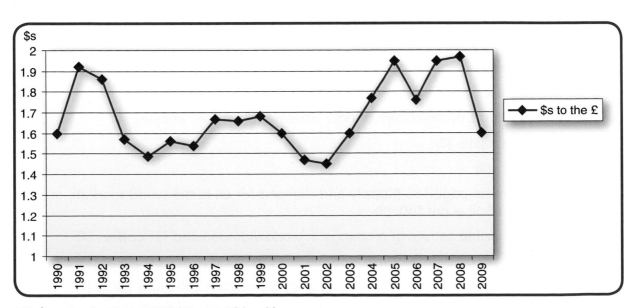

US $ to the £, 1990–2009 (as at 31 March)

- Their competitors may be large firms that have long-term, fixed-price supply contracts

- They may be worried that the loss of one large contract might switch the business from profit into losses

Conclusion

Prices of commodities can be very erratic, jumping around due to changes in demand and supply. Firms that use commodities, such as car manufacturers and food producers, need to plan for the worst. Even if the world price of coffee is low at the moment, producers of instant coffee should prepare for it rising in future (perhaps by buying extra supplies when the prices are low). For businesses that produce commodities, such as farmers, erratic prices are scary. If the price of wheat fell by 40 per cent next year, a specialist wheat farmer might struggle to survive. This is why systems exist such as Europe's Common Agricultural Policy (CAP). The CAP controls the price of many agricultural products within the **European Union** so that the farmers know the prices they will receive for their sugar, milk or wheat.

Revision Essentials

Economic growth – the rate of rise in total output per year within an economy. This rate will determine how wealthy the country becomes in the future.

European Union – the group of 27 European countries that trade freely with one another and have agreements on many areas of social and economic policy.

Foreign exchange markets – the places where currencies are bought and sold. The City of London is a major centre for the massive daily trade in foreign exchange.

Exercises

(20 marks; 25 minutes)

Read the unit, then ask yourself:

1 Give two reasons why the price of a commodity might fall. (2)

2 Are these products commodities or not? Briefly explain your answer.

   (a) Galaxy chocolate. (3)

   (b) Large eggs. (3)

3 From the figure on page 186 (Supply and demand for oil in the world market), explain why the price of oil is not $40. (3)

4 Outline two possible causes of a change in worldwide demand for coffee. (4)

5 Look at the figure on page 187 (US $ to the £, 1990–2006).

   (a) Describe what happened to the value of the £ between 2002 and 2005. (2)

   (b) Explain one possible reason for this change. (3)

Practice Questions

Oil price surge on hurricane threat

After some weeks of falling prices from the level of $140 reached in June, oil prices jumped back towards $120 a barrel today as tropical storm Gustav looked set to hit US oil rigs in the Gulf of Mexico.

Crude oil rose $2.98 to $119.25 a barrel after adding $1.16 yesterday. Fears about the possible impact on production could

Rising US petrol prices

see oil hit a three-week high of $122 over the coming days. The price hikes arise due to an expected cut in supply combined with extra demand due to panic-buying by customers.

BP, the UK oil giant, confirmed today that it had begun evacuating non-essential workers from the Gulf of Mexico ahead of the storm. Traders attributed oil's surge to fears that Gustav could cripple production in the Gulf region if it follows the same path as Hurricane Katrina three years ago. Those storms cost the US $100 billion in damage and cut oil production by 90 per cent, adding pressure to prices.

In the four weeks leading up to Katrina – part of the worst Atlantic storm season in recorded history – oil prices soared. Crude rose $7.76 a barrel on 19 August 2005, two days before Katrina hit New Orleans and Louisiana.

The fall from $140 to $120 a barrel between June and August was a result of figures showing falling demand for oil, especially in America. US drivers had reacted to the shocking rise in the price of petrol at the pumps. Industry experts had been surprised by US drivers' willingness to cut their car usage – and switch from gas-guzzlers to small cars.

(Source: Adapted from *Times Online*, 27 August 2008)

Questions

(20 marks; 25 minutes)

1   (a) Explain the effect of Hurricane Katrina on the supply and demand for oil. (4)

    (b) Why did this, in turn, affect the world market price for oil? (3)

2   This article was written before storm Gustav hit America. Outline the likely effect on the price of oil of Gustav missing the oil rigs altogether. (5)

3   Discuss the possible longer-term effect on the motor industry of the shocking rise in the price of petrol at the pumps. (8)

Interest rates

The interest rate is the annual percentage charge made for borrowing money. For example, a bank may lend a business £5000 for a three-year period at a rate of 10 per cent. Therefore the business must pay £500 a year in interest, and also repay the £5000. So the borrower pays a total of £1500 for three years' use of £5000.

There are two ways in which this arrangement may cause problems for a business:

1 **When too much money is borrowed**. This is often a problem during a business start-up. The owners put in their life savings of £80,000 and borrow a further £60,000 from the bank. The £6000 a year of interest payments prove higher than the business can afford and within two years it closes down.

The bank rate is set by an independent committee of the Bank of England

2 **When the interest rate rises**. In early 2004 the rate of interest in America was as low as 1 per cent a year. It then went up steadily, reaching 4 per cent by early 2006. A business that borrowed a lot of money in 2004 might struggle to pay four times as much interest as expected, just two years later.

What makes the interest rate rise or fall?

Bank profits come from lending money at a higher interest rate than they pay to get hold of money. Best of all for the banks is when you have money in your current account. They pay you 0 per cent, but use your money to lend to others at perhaps 9 per cent a year. But banks cannot get all the money they want from their customers. Sometimes they need to borrow from the **Bank of England**. Then they have to pay the **bank rate**, which is set every month by an independent committee of the Bank of England. If the bank rate is pushed up, the high street banks such as Barclays push up the interest rates they charge people or businesses.

Each month the committee decides what rate to set. If the members are worried that the economy may be slowing down, they might cut the bank rate, in order to encourage people and businesses to borrow more and spend more.

What are the effects of lower interest rates?

A cut in interest rates has two main effects on firms:

- more than half of British families have mortgages; a cut in interest rates cuts their monthly payments, leaving them with more spending power; so lower interest rates mean more spending in the shops, especially on luxuries such as leisure, holidays and entertainment. Higher spending means more revenue for businesses, and therefore higher profits (and more jobs).

- lower interest rates mean lower interest charges on firms' borrowings. As most small firms are financed largely through overdrafts, lower interest rates provide an important reduction in fixed overhead costs.

There is therefore a double benefit from lower interest rates: revenues go up and costs go down.

What are the effects of higher interest rates on firms?

Simply, the opposite:

- Households with mortgages need to cut back on spending because they are paying more to the bank/building society.

- Firms have higher fixed overhead costs, which squeezes their profits.

- Both factors may force firms to cut back on investment spending and, perhaps, on staffing.

Do interest rates change much?

In the period 1997–2007 the **Chancellor of the Exchequer** (Gordon Brown) managed the economy very carefully. In this period interest rates were quite stable – and generally falling. The graph below shows clearly how high interest rates have risen in the past.

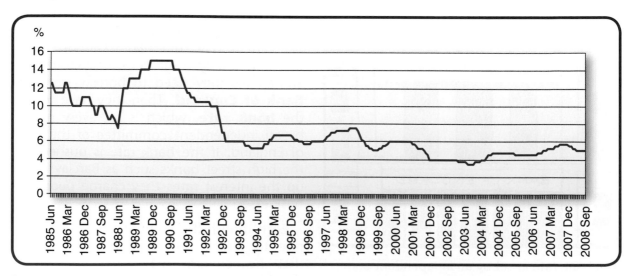

UK bank rate, June 1985 to September 2008 (source: www.bankofengland.co.uk)

In 1989 and 1990 the bank rate reached a high of 15 per cent. It seems extremely unlikely that this will happen again in the next few years, but it should not be ruled out.

Conclusion

Rising interest rates make life hard for all firms, but especially for new, small ones.

New firms are likely to have big debts, and are often struggling to make a profit in the early stages. Even business giants such as Honda can struggle early on. Honda UK's Swindon factories took more than five years to start making a profit. The combination of large borrowings and low profits is tough on small new firms – especially if the Bank of England starts putting interest rates up.

Revision Essentials

Bank of England – the state-owned bank that lends to – and regulates – the high street banks such as Barclays and Lloyds TSB.

Bank rate – the interest rate set by the Bank of England, from which the high street banks decide the rates they will charge.

Chancellor of the Exchequer – the government minister responsible for decisions about the economy. The second most powerful politician in the country, after the Prime Minister.

Exercises

(20 marks; 25 minutes)

Read the unit, then ask yourself:

1   Explain the term 'interest rate' in your own words. (3)

2   Why might an American business that borrowed a lot of money in 2004 struggle when the interest rate rose from 1 to 4 per cent? (4)

3   Briefly explain the likely impact of a sharp rise in interest rates on:

 (a) Tesco plc (3)

 (b) a car sales business specialising in new Porsche car models (3)

 (c) a new restaurant, due to open in three months' time. (3)

4   Business leaders often tell the media they think interest rates should fall. Why are they always likely to want this? (4)

Practice Questions

Store cards 'need rate warning'

Store card statements should carry warnings to alert consumers to the high interest rates charged by lenders, the Competition Commission has said. If the card's interest rate is higher than 25 per cent then the statement should have a 'wealth warning', the Commission said. Statements should also outline late payment charges and the consequences of only making minimum monthly repayments.

In September the Commission said consumers are being overcharged £100 million a year due to high interest rates. The Commission provisionally concluded that the market for offering consumer credit through retail store cards was uncompetitive.

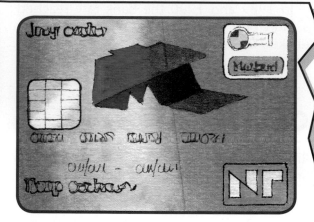

The Competition Commission says consumers are being overcharged for using store cards

The body said retailers and lenders were protected from competitive pressures and there was little incentive to reduce annual percentage rates (APRs) on store cards, which currently average about 30 per cent.

This compares unfavourably to credit cards, which commonly charge between 15 and 20 per cent, and the Bank of England base rate, which is currently 4.5 per cent.

(Source: adapted from www.bbc.co.uk, 21 December 2005)

Questions

(20 marks; 25 minutes)

1   Why should customers be wary of buying goods with store credit cards costing 30 per cent a year? (4)

2   (a) Explain what is meant by the phrase 'protected from competitive pressures'. (4)

    (b) At a time when the Bank of England base rate was 4.5 per cent, why might stores be charging an average of 30 per cent on their own credit cards? (4)

3   Discuss whether consumers would act more responsibly with credit cards if there was a 'wealth warning' on any card with an interest rate higher than 25 per cent. (8)

Exchange rates

In January 2004 Ted Rahman started importing Pink iPod Minis from America. He found an American supplier who charged him $225, including delivery to London. With an exchange rate of $1.80 to the £, this meant paying $225/1.80 = £125 per iPod. As the product had not yet been launched in Britain, it was easy to sell these Pink iPods for £200 each. Ted sold 1000 of them in February alone, making an astonishing £75,000.

What Ted noticed was that iPods could be sold in London for £200 while they sold for $225 in America. Yet because the exchange rate allowed him to exchange £1 for $1.80, the price for buying the products in America was just £125. He grabbed the opportunity.

By late 2005 iPods were selling in England at much lower prices, and the fall in the value of the £ (to $1.70 per £) made it less attractive to import the products.

The exchange rate allowed Ted to profit on the sale of iPods imported from America

price you see in an American shop can be halved to work out the British equivalent. For example, a $1 bottle of Coke is costing 50p in our money (with $2 to the £, you can buy 2 Cokes for £1).

What does it mean?

The rate of exchange shows the value of one currency measured by how much it will buy of other currencies. If £1 buys $1.70 in March and $1.75 in April, the £ has risen in value because it buys more $s. The £ is therefore worth more $s.

If the £ buys more $s it makes it cheaper for us to buy American goods. Over the past 15 years the value of the £ has varied from £1= $1 to £1 = $2. If £1 buys $2, then every

What changes the exchange value of the £?

The answer is simply supply and demand. If lots of Americans want to buy £s, the high demand for the £ will push up its value (e.g. from $1.70 to $1.75). If lots of British people buy US $s to go on holiday, the price of the $ will rise.

There are many possible causes of higher supply or demand for £s, but the key thing to remember is that it is the balance between supply and demand that determines the price. Demand up, price up; supply up, price down.

Why does a strong £ matter?

It matters because a strong £ (lots of $s to the £) makes it cheaper to import goods from America. This is great for us as consumers because American goods will seem great value. Yet it is tough on British firms that are trying to compete with cheap imports from America. A British shopper is happy if the price of an American computer has fallen from £350 to £290; but a British computer company with production costs of £320 can make a profit at £350, but will make a loss at £290.

So a strong £ is good for British shoppers, but bad for British producers.

The knock-on effects could be even greater. A British producer that cannot compete with American imports may find it has to cut its staffing levels. So British jobs may be lost.

Talking Point

Can you think of any businesses that should do well during a recession?

A British shopper is happy if the price of an American computer falls from £350 to £290

What if the £ is weak?

If the value of the £ is falling against foreign currencies, it is said to be weak. That means the £ buys less of any foreign currency (e.g. £1 used to equal $1.80, but now only buys $1.50). When the £ is weak it costs a British buyer more to buy from overseas. So imports become more expensive, which makes people buy fewer of them. A computer game that sells for $54 in America and used to sell in Britain for $54/$1.80 = £30, is now priced in Britain at $54/$1.50 = £36.

Yet this increase in the price of imports is great for UK producers. Suddenly they find it easier to compete with the higher-priced imported goods. They will also find it far easier to sell overseas, because a weak £ makes our exports better value to foreign buyers.

So a weak £ is bad for British shoppers, but good for British producers.

Other questions about exchange rates

1 **What about the £ against other currencies?** Britain's two biggest foreign markets are Europe and America. Therefore the most important currencies are the euro and the US $. Since it began in 1999, there have usually been about €1.50 to the £. By contrast, there have usually been about 200 Japanese yen to the £.

2 **Can other currencies be worth more than £1?** The answer is yes, they can. Strangely, the £ is worth more than 1 of every other major currency in the world, but that will not necessarily last. If the £ weakened against the US $, it could easily be that £1 might only buy $0.95.

3 When I go on a foreign holiday, do I want the £ to be high or low? You definitely want the £ to be strong and therefore allow your £s to buy lots of the foreign currency you need to buy. When £1 gets close to $2, most things seem a bargain to British tourists in America.

Exchange rate calculations

- Rule 1: when exchanging from £s to a foreign currency, MULTIPLY.

- Rule 2: when exchanging from a foreign currency to £s, DIVIDE.

For example, when £1 = $1.80, a £200 Burberry jacket should sell in New York for £200 x $1.80 = $360. At the same time, a $900 Calvin Klein suit should sell in Britain for $900/$1.80 = £500.

Think: if £1 = $1.40, what price should be charged in Britain for a $21,000 Audi?

Conclusion

Companies can be affected greatly by the exchange rate. Manufacturers like the £ to be low so that they can sell goods cheaply overseas and do not face tough competition from imports, as imported goods will be quite expensive. Even more, though, firms like the £ to be stable and therefore predictable in its value. It is hard to trade between America and Britain if the US $'s value is jumping between £1 = $1.20 and £1 = $1.95. This is why some firms have always liked the idea of fixed currency systems such as the euro.

Exercises

(20 marks; 25 minutes)

Read the unit, then ask yourself:

1 What price could be charged in London for $225 iPods when £1 = $1.70? (Answer to the nearest 5p) (3)

2 (a) If £1 equalled €1.50 last month, but €1.35 this month, has the £ risen in value or fallen in value? (1)

(b) What would be the effect of this on the export price to Europe of a £200 UK-made coat? (3)

3 Briefly explain why a strong £ is bad for British producers. (4)

4 Outline why a weak £ is bad for British shoppers. (4)

5 Between March 2005 and January 2006 unemployment rose every month. Explain how a falling £ might help to reduce the level of unemployment in the UK. (5)

Practice Questions

On 1 January 2003 Sean Blake struck his first ever export deal. It was for £20,000 worth of computer software, sold to an Australian bank. As the sales revenue of his whole business had only amounted to £65,000 in 2002, this was a real boost. The only problem was that the £ was very high against the Australian $, making it hard to make a profit on the deal. With the £ valued at A$2.85, Sean had to offer a lot of software for the money. In fact, his profit on the £20,000 deal proved to be no more than £450.

Fortunately, the bank was delighted with the software, which helped to keep up-to-date accounts of all the share dealing done by the bank. So when, in January 2006, Sean went to Australia with a brand new, improved piece of software, the bank was very interested. As the £ had fallen to A$2.35, he saw the opportunity to make far more profit from the new order.

He suggested a price of A$70,500 for his new product and was amazed when the bank accepted, without negotiation.

Seeing the opportunity provided by the falling £, Sean also contacted several other banks in Australia, and found three other buyers. He expects exports to comprise 50 per cent of his 2006/7 turnover of £340,000.

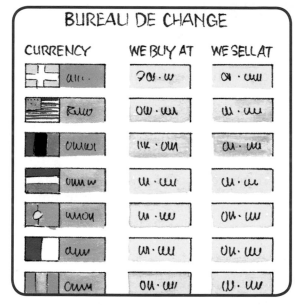

Currency listing board showing exchange rates

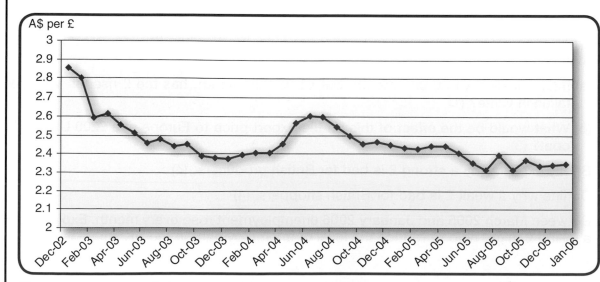

Exchange rate, £ v. A$, December 2002 to January 2006

Questions

(20 marks; 20 minutes)

1   When £1 = A$2.85 Sean Blake sold £20,000 of software in Australia. What price did he charge in Australian dollars? (2)

2   Why was it so difficult for Sean to make a profit when the £ was high against the A$? (5)

3   (a) Use the graph to identify the £ to A$ exchange rate in July 2004. (1)

    (b) At that rate, was the £'s value higher or lower than in December 2002? (1)

    (c) Would a British tourist visiting Australia be better off in December 2002 or July 2004? Briefly explain your answer. (4)

4   (a) How much did Sean receive in £s from the January 2006 sale to the Australian bank? (2)

    (b) Given the ups and downs of the exchange rate shown in the graph, is Sean right to push for three more sales to Australian banks? (5)

Changes in economic activity

A well-run business keeps one step ahead of its competitors. It anticipates changes in customer tastes or buying habits. Therefore it comes up with new products or services just when they are needed. It also makes sure to keep costs under control so that its prices never seem bad value for money. Businesses such as this include Tesco, Primark and Toyota.

Risk of economic downturn

However well-run a business is, it cannot control the economy. In late 1990 the British economy fell back, causing sales to fall month after month for more than two years. Firms that had financed expansion by heavy bor-rowings could not afford the interest pay-ments – and collapsed. By 1992 high streets were full of closing-down sales and boarded-up shops. In Hatfield, just north of London, a shopping centre on the A1 motorway went into **liquidation** before it had opened up! Worst of all, many families lost their homes because they could not keep up with the mortgage payments.

During a period of recession such as this, falling sales cause job losses that eat away at people's confidence. The threat of unemploy-ment makes people cautious about spending money. Sales of 'big ticket' items are hit especially hard; these include cars, carpets, houses and holidays. Even worse hit are the sales of luxuries such as boats, expensive jew-ellery and first-class travel.

At the start of 2006, businesses were able to look back on more than ten years of con-tinuous economic growth, with no **recession** since 1990–92 (see the figure on page 211). Yet good managers were wondering when the next recession would strike and making sure that the business would be capable of surviving it. Firms such as Woolworths failed to do this. Therefore they collapsed when the 2008 recession started to hit their cash flow.

Sales of luxury items are hit especially hard during a recession

Can difficult times be spotted?

The broad answer is no. Recessions always come as a surprise to most economists and business people. Of course, during the house price bubble of 2003–2007 a wise person

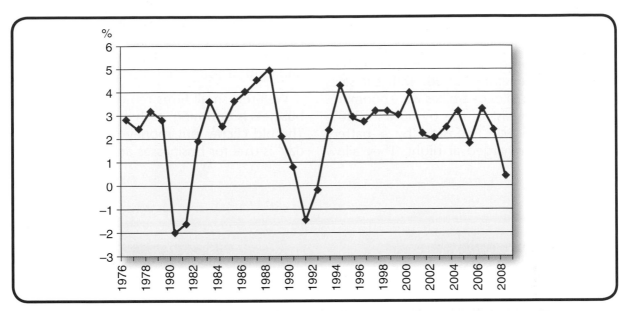

Percentage change in UK economic output, 1976–2008 (source: www.statistics.gov.uk)

would stop to wonder: how can house prices keep rising when they are becoming less and less affordable to the majority of people? Yet although it was clear that the housing boom would burst, no-one could be sure that the result would be the collapse of major banks throughout Britain and America.

If there are warning signs, though, they come in three parts:

● When politicians or bankers say that they have ended the trade cycle, beware

● When everyone is getting desperate to jump on a bandwagon (housing or shares), it's time to get off

● When people say that 'this time it's different', they are usually wrong

Do governments know how to prevent recessions?

In 1997 the new Labour government made the Bank of England responsible for setting interest rates. Since then, it has tried to use this power to dampen down the economy before boom conditions got out of hand. This seemed to have helped in preventing recessions. Yet a severe recession hitting America would always make Britain suffer. Falling sales in America hit our exporting companies. This has knock-on effects throughout the British economy. Therefore the US property and banking crisis of 2007 and 2008 hit Britain hard. Governments may think they know how to prevent recessions, but it does not mean that they always succeed.

Business cycles and small business

Changes in the rate of economic growth can have big effects on small businesses, especially if their products are those that customers love in good times, but ignore when times are tough. In late 2008, jewellery chain Signet reported that sales had fallen by 15% in the UK. Small, independent jewellers may have suffered even more from consumer cutbacks. Just two years before, sales of gold and platinum rings and bracelets had been booming.

But not all products have the same pattern of sales. In November 2008, with car sales down by 33%, sales of e-bikes were booming. They were forecast to rise by 50% in 2009. E-bikes are bicycles boosted by a battery that can be recharged at night. They allow you to ride around town at a cost equivalent of 1,000 miles per gallon of petrol. So bike retailers who specialise in e-bikes were finding that tough times equal boom times!

Well-run small firms remember that when business is booming, cash must be put aside. The old cliché 'put money away for a rainy day' is true for businesses and families alike.

Revision Essentials

Booming – an economy that is growing much faster than it usually does. The term 'boom' implies that it probably will not last (i.e. that the economy is heading for a bit of an explosion).

Liquidation – closing the business down – selling off its assets to raise the cash to pay its debts.

Recession – **downturn in sales and output throughout the economy. The strict definition is 'falling output for two successive quarters of the year' (i.e. for six months in a row).**

Exercises

(20 marks; 25 minutes)

Read the unit, then ask yourself:

1   Explain why a discount retailer such as Lidl might cope better with a recession than a luxury goods retailer such as Selfridges. (4)

2   How may consumers behave if they are feeling confident about their future? (3)

3   Look at the figure on page 201 (Percentage change in UK economic output, 1976–2008). Outline one impressive feature and one disappointment in the government's handling of the economy between 1997 and 2008. (4)

4   Examine one approach that could be taken by British Airways to ensure that it does not suffer too severely when the next recession arrives. (4)

5   Explain why governments should try to prevent economic booms from occurring. (5)

Practice Questions

Steve launched his hi-fi business four years ago. Steve won the contract for selling Bang & Olufsen equipment, selling at prices from £500 up to £8000. At the time, customers and businesses were feeling very optimistic about the economy, so sales were rising sharply. In the run-up to Christmas last year, he sold a £24,000 home cinema and an £8000 music system on the same day!

Steve has been clever to set up his store in the Wirral, where many of the north's best-paid footballers live. They love the unique style of 'B&O' and think nothing of paying half a week's wages for the latest hi-fi equipment. One famous player gave away a six-month-old, £6000 hi-fi to the

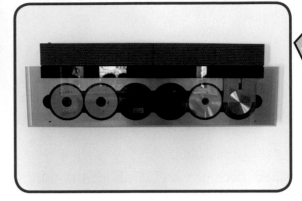

Bang & Olufsen stereo equipment

club's kitman, because he'd just bought a newer model.

Despite this, Steve is aware that only half his sales come from the super-rich; he wonders whether other buyers would keep coming if the economy entered a recession. His first business (a restaurant) collapsed in the 1991 recession, so he does not want to suffer twice over.

Questions

(20 marks; 25 minutes)

1 Explain two impressive features of the way Steve has set up his business. (4)

2 (a) Outline why Steve may be worried about the impact of a recession. (4)

   (b) Outline one other problem outside Steve's control that might affect the business. (6)

3 Discuss how Steve might prepare for the possibility of an economic downturn in the future. (6)

Forecasting economic activity

Business decisions are all about the future. If you are to open a new restaurant in six months' time, you would love to know the future level of interest rates, consumer confidence and consumer spending. A **forecast** could try to do this. The problem is that economic forecasts may not be accurate.

In February 2006 a famous Cambridge University professor, Wynne Godley, predicted that the American and British economies were vulnerable to a 'prolonged' shortfall in demand. In other words, there could be a severe **recession** lasting a number of years. British and American households had been spending too much and saving too little. Therefore, US and UK consumers were sucking in far too many imports, and needing to cut back their spending to lower their credit card bills.

Reading Professor Godley's predictions might lead any business owner to think hard about risking further expansion. After all, if the economy is due to turn downwards, who would want to spend money to expand a factory or develop new markets?

Yet if you enter 'Wynne Godley' into Google, you quickly find that the professor has been saying very similar things for many, many years. There is an article by him from 2002 which tells a broadly similar story. In 2008 his forecast proved correct, but accurate forecasting requires getting the timing right.

Quite simply, forecasting the economy is extremely difficult. Therefore every business should take every forecast with a pinch of salt. Forecasts are worth thinking about, and even planning for, but no business should change gear just because of a forecast.

Talking Point

Can you think of any imports that could be made in Britain? And any that could not be made here?

Why bother?

If forecasts cannot be relied on, why do them? Simply because economic changes can be very damaging for firms, so businesspeople need to think about how the future might look. At the time of writing, shop prices in Britain have risen 2 per cent in the past 12 months. Yet the prices factories are paying for their materials have risen 16 per cent in the past year. So the factory owners must be desperate to push their prices up. However, if Cadbury put up its prices by 16 per cent, while Mars kept to a 2 per cent price rise, Cadbury would lose market share dramatically. Therefore Cadbury has to be able to forecast future consumer price inflation to have a clearer idea about what competitors will do.

Why is it so hard to get right?

One answer is to look at the problems other 'experts' have in forecasting. Every week

Forecasting the economy is extremely difficult

the BBC website features 'expert' Mark Lawrenson predicting the weekend's football scores. If he gets three out of ten right, the BBC boasts about it! For economists, there are two main problems:

1 It is often hard to be sure what is happening to the economy right now. On any day, some firms moan about tough times on the high street while others sound positive. This is crucial because if you are not sure whether things are getting better or worse today, it is hard to predict the position in 6 or 12 months' time.

2 There are so many variables that can affect the economy: some are economic variables, such as a rise in the interest rate or the exchange rate; others are human variables, such as rising consumer confidence – 1966 proved a better year for the economy than was expected because consumers felt better about life after England won the football World Cup!

> *'I'd rather be vaguely right than precisely wrong.'*
> **J.M. Keynes, world-famous economist**

So what should firms do?

The answer is to be prepared. When times are good and consumer spending is rising, it is time to think: what if things turned downwards? Do we have products that people would want or need to buy when times are hard? If the £ is weak against the $ (making exports from Britain very profitable), it is time to ask: what if the £ became stronger? What would we do then?

Well-run firms think ahead. Economic forecasts can help in that process, even if they often turn out to be wrong.

1966 proved a better year for the economy than expected after England won the World Cup

Revision Essentials

Forecast – a prediction of the future based on evidence (e.g. forecasting what UK interest rates will be in six months' time).

Recession – a downturn in economic activity (e.g. a fall in consumer spending and therefore in company sales and production).

Exercises

(20 marks; 25 minutes)

Read the unit, then ask yourself:

1 Outline one reason why:

(a) A house-building firm would love to know the interest rate in six months' time. (3)

(b) Honda UK, exporting more than half its output to Europe, would love to know the £/€ exchange rate in six months' time. (4)

2 Briefly explain why it is hard to make accurate economic forecasts. (4)

3 Rolls-Royce luxury cars are made in Sussex, and sell for more than £200,000 each. More than 75 per cent are exported. What might Rolls-Royce do about:

(a) A forecast that interest rates are to rise sharply in the next nine months? (3)

(b) A forecast that the £ is set to fall sharply in the coming weeks? (3)

(c) A forecast that inflation is to rise from around 2 per cent to around 3.5 per cent? (3)

Practice Questions

Household numbers and projections

	Household numbers (millions)			Household projections (millions)			Percentage increase
	2000	2001	2006	2011	2016	2021	2006–21
North-east	1.09	1.1	1.12	1.14	1.15	1.17	4.50
North-west	2.87	2.88	2.93	3	3.06	3.11	6.10
Yorkshire and the Humber	2.12	2.14	2.2	2.26	2.32	2.37	7.70
East Midlands	1.75	1.76	1.83	1.9	1.97	2.03	10.90
West Midlands	2.18	2.19	2.24	2.3	2.35	2.4	7.10
East	2.28	2.28	2.39	2.49	2.6	2.7	13
London	3.19	3.13	3.25	3.38	3.52	3.65	?
South-east	3.38	3.4	3.57	3.74	3.91	4.06	13.70
South-west	2.1	2.12	2.21	2.32	2.42	2.52	14
England	20.97	20.99	21.73	22.52	23.31	24	?
Wales	1.2	1.21	1.24	1.28	1.31	1.34	8.10

Source: Office of the Deputy Prime Minister; National Assembly for Wales

Questions

(20 marks; 25 minutes)

1   (a) Calculate the forecast percentage increases for London and England as a whole, between 2006 and 2021. Show your workings. (5)

   (b) Outline two possible effects on Londoners of this increase in the number of households between 2006 and 2021. (4)

2   What business opportunities may there be in England as a result of the increase in the number of households? (5)

3   Discuss the possible impact of the forecast proving inaccurate. (6)

The number of households in the south-east is projected to increase by 13.7 percent between 2006 and 2021

Stakeholders

Stakeholders are the people or groups with an interest in the success or failure of an organisation. A business will want to look after those who can help it succeed, which might include the press or the government. These are the **primary stakeholders**. There may also be outsiders who think of themselves as stakeholders, whether or not the organisation wants them to. These are the **secondary stakeholders**. For example, animal rights activists might become concerned at the way a cosmetics business tests new products on animals.

Primary stakeholders

Greggs plc (Britain's biggest chain of bakeries) has always been proud to say that its two key stakeholders are its customers and staff. It places its shareholders in third place, on the grounds that as long as staff and customers are happy, the business will be a financial

Greggs bakery

success. Other companies take a different view. Cadbury, for example, declares that its main priority is to maximise returns for its shareholders.

Staff, customers and shareholders are by no means the only stakeholders a business may have to consider. The owner of a good restaurant may consider suppliers to be massively important. He/she may buy steak from a local farmer who produces tender, organic meat. The restaurant's reputation depends on the quality of the farmer's deliveries. Therefore the supplier becomes a primary stakeholder.

For all organisations, the key primary stakeholders are:

- the owners/shareholders
- the staff/managers
- the customers.

In addition, some will also regard suppliers as vital stakeholders.

Secondary stakeholders

Among other possible stakeholders are:

- local residents, who may be affected by traffic noise from deliveries or by pollution from a smelly or smoky factory or farm
- local government, which is the organisation that will give a yes or no to future planning permission, for example on

whether the business is allowed to build a larger warehouse

- pressure groups, such as Greenpeace, who may organise protests if they feel that an organisation's activities damage the environment.

These would all be regarded as secondary stakeholders, though it is possible to imagine that any one of these (or others) may become very important for a particular business. For example, a football club might regard the police as a primary stakeholder.

Small business stakeholders

For most small firms, the keys to success are customers, staff and suppliers. Treating them well and using them well are essential, partly because you never know when you may need them to help you. A really committed restaurant supplier would drop everything and rush to a client that had run out of chicken half way through the evening. A really committed customer may help out when needed (e.g. paying in cash to help a supplier with cash flow problems). Most important of all are the staff, because if they are well motivated, their enthusiasm will rub off onto customers and suppliers.

Pressure groups may be regarded as stakeholders in a business

Are shareholders number one?

The directors of most public limited companies have little choice but to treat shareholders as the most important stakeholder. This is because the shareholders have the right to vote the directors out of office if they believe the business is badly run. Companies such as Dixons are open about the priority given to profit and, therefore, shareholder returns. Others prefer to suggest that they treat all stakeholders equally.

Organisations and stake holders

Organisation	Ownership	Three most important stakeholders
Manchester United	Family-owned	Supporters Owners Staff
Marks & Spencer plc	Thousands of individual shareholders	Shareholders Customers Staff
Altrincham Bridal Wear Ltd	Family-owned	Customers Suppliers of wedding dresses Shareholders

British company law sets out that the primary duty of company directors is to the shareholders. This weights the issue clearly in favour of suggesting that most companies will treat the shareholders as the single most important stakeholder.

> 'He who pays the piper plays the tune.'
> **Traditional English saying**

Conclusion

Companies need to think about their public image. Therefore it is important for managers to think about their wider responsibilities. If they fail to do so, the result might be a bad press, with local residents or national pressure groups making complaints. Nike has suffered a bad press in the past from the use of low-cost (even child) labour in making its (very pricey) trainers. Pressure groups (and customers) blamed Nike for ignoring its responsibility to its suppliers.

The issue of stakeholders simply urges firms to think more widely about the effects of their business activities. Well-managed firms have always done this. The risk today is that every firm may claim to care about its stakeholders, whereas day-to-day business decisions may continue to make profit the top priority.

Revision Essentials

Primary stakeholders – people or groups seen by the business to be fundamental to the organisation's success or failure.

Secondary stakeholders – people or groups who feel involved in the organisation's success or failure, whether or not the management agrees.

Exercises

(15 marks; 20 minutes)

Read the unit, then ask yourself:

1 Why are employees regarded as primary stakeholders? (2)

2 What is the difference between a shareholder and a stakeholder? (3)

3 Which do you think are the three most important stakeholders for:

(a) your school/college. (3)

(b) your nearest sweetshop or grocer's. (3)

4 Outline two possible disadvantages for staff who work for a business that only focuses on the needs of shareholders, not stakeholders. (4)

What are the most important stakeholders for your school?

Practice Questions

Extract 1: Working with our stakeholders – Lloyds TSB

Our customers, shareholders and employees are our key stakeholders.

Customers: understanding our customers' needs and providing products and services that meet these needs is crucial to our business.

Shareholders: we respond to surveys and enquiries from the socially responsible investment indices.

Employees: we include regular features and articles on corporate responsibility issues in our staff magazine.

(Source: extracts from Lloyds TSB's Corporate Responsibility Report, www.lloydstsb.com)

Extract 2: Fifty thousand people who put over £1bn into Lloyds TSB's Extra Income and Growth Plan (EIGP) are being advised not to accept the bank's compensation deal for any losses

The Financial Ombudsman has written to warn investors that if they accept the bank's offer to reimburse them, they could lose out substantially.

The plan – a Scottish Widows product sold by Lloyds TSB between October 2000 and May 2001 – offered a fixed income payout of over 10 per cent a year, or guaranteed growth if the cash was kept invested for the whole three years.

But the capital was at risk, something many people say they were never told.

(Source: BBC Money Box, news.bbc.co.uk)

Questions

(20 marks; 25 minutes)

1   (a) Outline what Lloyds TSB says are its responsibilities to its customer stakeholders. (4)

(b) Read extract 2, then decide whether Lloyds TSB is living up to these responsibilities. Explain your answer. (6)

2   Outline one reason why a firm might find it hard to always act in the best interests of its customers. (4)

3   Discuss why a firm such as Lloyds TSB might put its Corporate Responsibility Report on its website, instead of just sending a copy to its staff. (6)

The effect of business decisions on stakeholders

In 1989 the Ford Motor Company made one of the worst business decisions in history: it paid £1600 million for the Jaguar car business. At the time of the purchase the exchange rate was $1.58 to the £. At that rate, Jaguar could produce cars in Britain and sell them for a good profit in America. Shortly after the purchase went through, the £ rose in value, making it much harder to export profitably to America. Jaguar started losing money. Fifteen years later it was still losing amazing sums. In 2003/4 it lost £600 million and in 2004/5 its losses were nearly £430 million. For Ford, it has been like throwing hundreds of millions down the drain, year after year.

Ford's decision to buy Jaguar was made in the belief that the £ was only likely to get weaker in future against the $. This would have made exporting to America more profitable – and 60 per cent of Jaguars were exported from Britain to America. The fact that the £ strengthened shows how difficult and how important economic factors can be. If Ford knew then what they know now, they would not have paid a penny for Jaguar, let alone £1600 million.

Effect on stakeholders

On employees

Since Ford's purchase, Jaguar has had to cut staffing levels dramatically. In 2004 the closure was announced of its factory in Coventry, with the loss of thousands of jobs in the Midlands. Many factors contributed, but the main ones were the strong £ and an economic slowdown in America. Not only did the Coventry factory closure hit the staff, but also the companies and staff at dozens of small-scale suppliers working close by the Jaguar factory.

On suppliers

Ending production in Coventry will have an immediate effect on many local suppliers of goods and services. The goods might include spark plugs or car tyres – used to manufacture the cars. The services would be from local cleaning and catering companies, taxis and business travel agencies. In addition, local job losses would hit takings at local shops, pubs and clubs.

Jaguar employees protesting the closure of the company's factory in Coventry

On shareholders

In 2004 Ford paid out more than $1200 million in interest charges on its bank borrowings. It was lucky that interest rates in America were very low at the time. But rising interest rates – plus the drain caused by Jaguar's losses – led to a 50 per cent drop in Ford's share price in 2005.

Conclusion

At the beginning, it is hard to tell the difference between change that is temporary and change that is fundamental. For years people had pointed the finger at the fat content in McDonald's menu, but only in the past few years has it had a serious effect on sales. Stakeholders will only be affected if major changes are taking place. Will Google – as many expect – take on Microsoft and create real competition in computer software? This would affect Microsoft staff (job losses) and suppliers as well as customers. But perhaps Google will choose to avoid tackling super-rich Microsoft head-on. If so, the changes may not look important in the longer term.

Exercises

(15 marks; 15 minutes)

Read the unit, then ask yourself:

1   Outline two reasons why Ford should regret having bought Jaguar. (4)

2   (a) Briefly explain your own attitude to eating at McDonald's. (4)

    (b) Discuss what McDonald's managers should do to bring the customers back. (7)

Practice Questions

Yakult was the originator of the market for 'healthy' yogurt drinks, more than 30 years ago. It was designed to be healthy rather than to taste good. This was also a feature of the advertising, which used the slightly scary claim that the product contained 'good bacteria'.

The market grew steadily but slowly, until the French company Danone entered the market with Actimel. Heavily advertised, and with various sweetened fruit flavours,

Actimel was promoted as a fun, enjoyable product rather than a serious one. At first the advertisements for Actimel helped sales of Yakult, but by 2005 sales started to slip. Consumers wanted the fun, healthy lifestyle promoted by Danone. Also, in 2005, Yakult sales were hit by a new Müller product, Vitality, featuring the 'brain-food' Omega 3. All the clever new products were pushing Yakult to one side.

The bar chart shows the changes in the sales of these three products in 2005 compared with 2004. They are the top three brands in a market with sales worth £260 million a year.

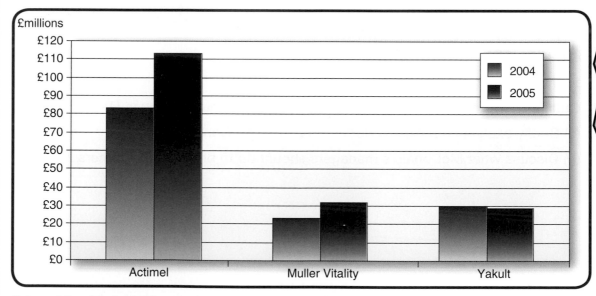

Sales of 'healthy' drinking yoghurts (source: A.C. Nielsen quoted in *The Grocer*, 17 December 2005)

Questions

(20 marks; 25 minutes)

1   Outline one good and one bad thing about the determination of Yakult's managers to stick to the product they believe in. (6)

2   Look carefully at the bar chart, then decide whether the following statements are true or false.

   (a) Actimel's sales in 2005 grew by more than the total sales of Yakult. (2)

   (b) Müller Vitality went from third place in 2004 to second place in 2005. (2)

   (c) Actimel's 2005 sales were more than 50 per cent of the total market size of £260 million. (2)

   (d) Actimel's sales were £83 million in 2004 and £113 million in 2005, so they rose by 26.5 per cent. (2)

3   Sales of healthy lifestyle products such as these provide big opportunities for large companies such as Danone. Discuss whether companies should be allowed to use advertising to worry people into making purchases. (6)

SECTION 5

Exam-style Questions

DON'T RUSH; check answers carefully

1. Identify three likely effects of a cut in interest rates by the Bank of England. (3)
   a) The value of the £ may start to rise against other currencies.
   b) Banks may feel more willing to offer mortgages to customers.
   c) Furniture shops may find it easier to sell goods on credit.
   d) It may help the price of oil to fall.
   e) New small firms with big overdrafts will enjoy falling interest charges.
   f) New small firms will have less tax taken from the company profits.

Questions 2 and 3 are based on this supply and demand diagram.

2. What is the total $ value of sales of Jamaican coffee within the market indicated in the above graph?

   $_____ (2)

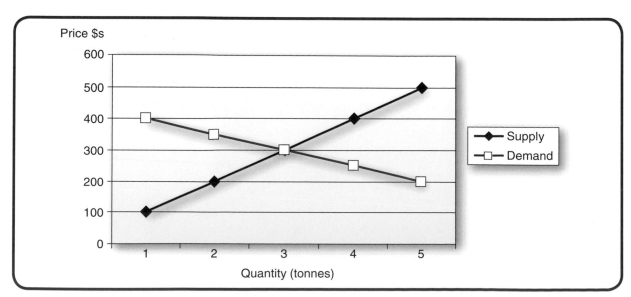

3. Why would the Jamaican producers be unwise to charge $400 a tonne for their coffee? Pick two correct reasons from the following. (2)

a) Because they may struggle to meet the demand for 4 tonnes of coffee.

b) Because they would end up with 1 tonne of unsold coffee.

c) Because sales would crash from 3 tonnes to just 1 tonne.

d) Because there's more profit to be made at $500 than $400 per tonne.

e) Because their income would slump to just $400.

4. What is the term that means a sustained fall in the level of output within a country's economy? (1)

_____

5. In February 2008 Barclays Bank forecast these interest rates for Britain:

November 2007: 5.75%

February 2008: 5.25%

May 2008: 5.0%

August 2008: 4.50%

February 2009: 4.25%

Which of the following businesses would have been the happiest if that forecast proved true? (1)

a) A business that imports low-cost clothes from Sri Lanka and sells them on to street markets.

b) A new house-building business financed 50/50 by shares and loans.

c) A new sweetshop located in the soon-to-be-renovated Birmingham New Street station.

d) A newly opened, posh clothes shop financed by the owner's savings.

e) A funeral service that has operated in Preston for the past 52 years.

6. Barclays Bank's February 2008 exchange rate forecast for the £ against the US$ was as follows:

November 2007: $2.07 to the £

February 2008: $1.97

May 2008: $1.94

August 2008: $1.92

February 2009: $1.90

Which two of the following would have been probable effects on British firms, if the forecast proved accurate? (2)

a) UK importers of US computers would find that the cost of imports would rise.

b) Businesses such as Toyota UK would be unaffected by the changes.

c) Importers of US computers would find that the cost of imports would fall.

d) Exporters to America such as Wedgwood (pottery) would be better off.

e) All British firms would suffer as a result of this fall in the $.

f) Exporters to America such as Wedgwood (pottery) would be worse off.

7. Boeing has just upset the Virgin Atlantic airline by announcing an 18-month delay to the delivery of its 15 new 'Dreamliner' planes. This caused the price of Boeing shares to fall. Boeing staff are worried about their job security now that the Dreamliner programme seems out of control. Identify three Boeing stakeholders identified in this passage of text. (3)

a) Local residents

b) Shareholders

c) The government

d) Staff

e) Customers

f) Suppliers

MARKETING

Marketing and market research

> 'The trouble with research is that it tells you what people were thinking about yester-day, not tomorrow. It's like driving using a rearview mirror.'
> **Bernard Loomis, American toy developer**

While small firms usually focus on sales, building a business requires **marketing**. This means thinking through every aspect of what customers really want and why, and then providing the right balance between product, price, promotion and place. In some cases, all four 'Ps' may be equally important. For example, Coca-Cola has succeeded for 125 years because it pays as much importance to Place (high availability and great display) and Promotion (all those great TV advertisements) as it does to its Product and Price.

More commonly, companies learn that one 'P' is more important to them than any other. Chanel No 5 perfume is all about glamour, so its promotion is crucial. It spends millions on producing exceptional TV adver-tisements for each Christmas. By contrast, for magazines such as *Look*, getting the product right is the most important factor. The table below gives other examples.

Coca Cola's advertising reflects the emphasis that it places on promotion

Examples of where the business focuses on one marketing 'P'

Company	Market	What customers want	Main marketing focus
Apple	Personal music	Stylish, easy-to-use player	Product – the iPod design made it easy to market
L'Oréal	Hair and beauty	To feel confident and stylish	Promotion, using glamorous women on TV
Innocent	Vegetables	Easy-to-prepare but healthy veg	Place: getting distribution for Innocent Veg Pots
Ryanair	Short-haul air travel	Efficient, cheap flights	Price: making sure people think Ryanair is cheapest

Learning where to focus your marketing effort is crucial. It depends hugely on market research.

What is market research?

Market research involves each company getting the information it needs about its own particular market. The company might want to know:

- How many people are in the market for my new breakfast cereal?
- How much would they be willing to pay?
- How often would they buy?
- Does the packaging give the right image for the brand?

In primary market research, customers are asked directly for their opinions

Primary research asks customers direct questions about their opinions or buying habits. For example someone thinking of opening a Subway might ask passers-by how often they would use the service. Secondary research uncovers facts that someone else has already found out, perhaps by using Google.

How does a business use market research?

'Research is the act of going up alleys to see if they are blind.'
Anon

In 2005, after years of sales growth, Walkers suffered from a decline in the sale of their crisps. Market research quickly showed that the problem was for the market as a whole – Walkers' market share was unchanged. Further research showed that the explanation was customers' increasing concern about health.

Walkers' executives decided that the only solution was to take a huge initiative – to make customers see Walkers as the company at the forefront of health concerns. They would come up with a new recipe to cut the amount of saturated fat in their crisps by 80 per cent. This was done in 2006, and Gary Lineker fronted a new advertising campaign emphasising health. In 2007 Walkers' sales were growing again and in 2008 sales rose by five per cent. Helped by market research, the company had identified the problem and the solution.

What is market research?

Primary	Explanation	Advantage	Disadvantage
Questionnaire	A business will carry out a questionnaire assessing potential demand for a product/service.	A firm can identify its target customers (age, job, etc.) – this can help with promotion and also establish the likely selling price and sales level.	Can be very time consuming – taking time to carry out the research is expensive and may not be helpful. Questions can be biased, giving misleading results.
Focus group	This allows for more in-depth answers than a questionnaire and allows more open questions.	Interviews give firms an insight into customer perceptions and behaviour. This can help a firm decide on branding and advertising images.	Time consuming and expensive. The interviewer can sometimes affect the results, e.g. some interviewees may be too embarrassed to admit how much they really spend on chocolate.
Product testing	New products are tested on the public before they are launched.	Very useful to get consumer feedback prior to a product launch to establish likely demand and price customers are willing to pay – can stop a firm launching a product people don't like.	Time consuming and expensive. People will often say what the tester would like them to say, rather than appear rude if they don't like the product.
Secondary			
Mintel report	The Marketing Intelligence reports are put together on more than 600 subjects, ranging from fast-food restaurants to fashion footwear.	The research has already been carried out so it is far quicker to gain market information without collecting the data yourself. It is much cheaper than primary research.	A report costs £600 (but commercial libraries have reference copies you can access for free). The research is about the market in general and won't have local information or have data relating to a new product that has not yet been launched.
Web research	Searches on the web can help identify competitors and allow a business to check on their prices and product range. Web searches will also be useful to source secondary data.	Cheap! Probably costs only the time it takes. Easy to carry out. Quicker than street interviewing.	There is a lot of rubbish on the web and care needs to be taken to ensure reliability and validity of information.

'Advertising people who ignore research are as dangerous as generals who ignore decodes of enemy signals.'
David Ogilvy, advertising executive

Market research at Chester Zoo

Chester Zoo carries out exit interviews with visitors, to establish how long they have spent at the zoo, where they have travelled from, which animals they liked best and how satisfied they were with the facilities.

Personnel at the zoo's marketing department state they can effectively advertise to people only when they know how old they are, where they come from, when they visit the zoo, their **socio-economic group**, how long they stay and whether they will come back. So the research helps in targeting the advertising effectively.

Establishing customer satisfaction allows the zoo to improve its services and encourage repeat visits.

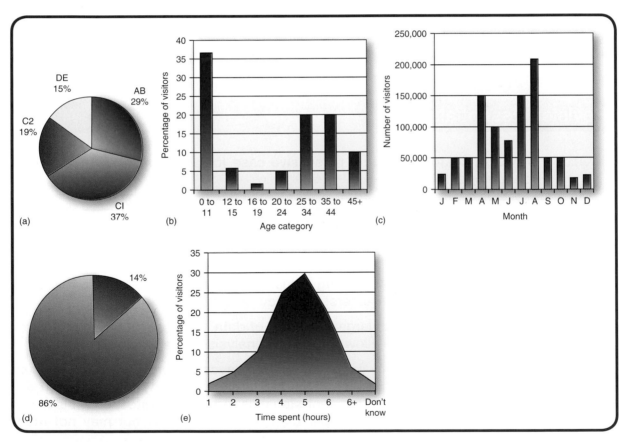

Market research data collected by Chester Zoo: visitors by
(a) socio-economic group
(b) age
(c) date of visit
(d) whether they've visited before
(e) length of visit

Qualitative and quantitative research

There are two things every business wants to know about customers:

1 What do they *really* think (deep down)?

2 What percentage of people think what?

The first of these two is found out by using **qualitative research**. This usually involves psychologists who try to get inside the heads of consumers. Do people buy BMWs because they are faster, or more reliable; or because a BMW gives the owner the image of being a success? Qualitative surveys are in-depth research among quite small numbers of people. The company wants insights, not to find out that 40% like red and 60% like blue.

The second type is called **quantitative research**. This uses questionnaires to ask enough people to find out what percentage think what. For example, should a new Cadbury chocolate bar be called 'Stamp' or 'Coco'? Quantitative research among 200 chocolate buyers might find that:

- 39% choose Stamp
- 51% choose Coco
- 10% have no preference.

From this type of evidence, Cadbury would probably go ahead with the name 'Coco'.

Well-run companies usually use both types of market research, as both can be helpful.

Revision Essentials

Marketing – **providing customers with a persuasive case for preferring your products to your competitors'.**

Primary research – **when a firm carries out first-hand research by field work, e.g. a questionnaire about consumer perceptions of its products. This is usually more useful than secondary research because it is 'tailor-made' to the firm's requirements.**

Qualitative research – **in-depth research using focus groups or depth interviews. It is used to find out consumers' behaviour and attitudes.**

Quantitative research: **This deals with large quantities of data, e.g. a sample size of 500 for a survey. This allows statistical analysis of the results.**

Secondary research (or desk research) – **information from 'second-hand sources'. It could be survey results carried out by another firm, government statistics, books, websites, etc. It is much cheaper than primary research but may not meet the firm's needs.**

Socio-economic group – **the customers' social class. For example, people in the AB group are professionals and managers.**

Exercises

(25 marks; 30 minutes)

Read the unit, then ask yourself:

1   Which months are the busiest at Chester Zoo? (1)

2   Why do you think these months are busiest? (4)

3   How can Chester Zoo increase visitor numbers during winter months? (6)

4   Why do you think such low numbers of teenagers visit the zoo? (4)

5   How can the zoo increase teenage visitor numbers? (6)

6   Why will knowing a visitor's socio-economic group help the zoo plan its marketing campaign? (4)

Practice Questions

'How often, on average, do you send your clothes to the dry cleaners?' was a question asked of a sample of people for a Mintel report about trends in laundry. (There are Mintel reports about almost everything.) Of those interviewed, 48 per cent never take their clothes to the dry cleaners.

The report claims that changing consumer lifestyles mean the dry cleaning market will stagnate. Factors such as home dry cleaning kits, improved fabric technology allowing more items to be machine washed and the increase in the number of people who work from home (who don't need to wear suits that need to be dry-cleaned) have all had an impact on the market.

Questions

(20 marks; 25 minutes)

1   Your friend is considering buying a dry-cleaning business. Explain to your friend whether you consider this to be a good idea or not. (8)

According to a recent Mintel report, more shoes are sold in the UK than anywhere else in Europe – since 2001 spending on shoes has increased by 38 per cent. In fact, one in ten British women own over 30 pairs of shoes, while 20 per cent own between 16 and 30 pairs. In 2008 we spent over £6.7 billion on shoes. However, the Italians still buy the most shoes (£9.8 billion)

One in ten British women owns over 30 pairs of shoes

2   a The research above was carried out by Mintel. What are the drawbacks of this kind of research? (4)

    b This research looks very positive, but what further research would you carry out before deciding whether to open a shoe shop in your home town? (4)

    c Why? (4)

Product trial and repeat purchase

Have you ever seen an advert for something on the TV, thought to yourself 'that looks great', rushed out and bought the product and been really disappointed? You have bought it once but never again.

All businesses try to persuade us that their product is the best there is. Have you seen the advertisement for Cillit Bang? Wouldn't you be disappointed if you bought a bottle only to discover that bang, and the dirt wasn't gone? Cillit Bang claims to be the most powerful cleaning product available on the market. If it fails to live up to that claim then people are not going to buy another bottle – they will go back to their previous brand.

Having come up with a new product, there are three things that must be got right:

- achieving distribution (getting shops to stock the product, see 'Marketing mix', Unit 6)
- **product trial** (getting people to buy it for the first time)
- **repeat purchase** (moving customers on from trial to buying it again and again).

Achieving product trial

It can be hard to get people to try a new product. Not always, of course – for example, people who buy chocolate bars, canned drinks and magazines are quite willing to 'risk' their 50p or £1.50 on trying a new product. But

Talking Point

Can you think of any examples of products that dare us to try them? Why might a business do this?

most markets are not like this. Adults are very reluctant to 'risk' £12 on a new brand of whisky that they may not like and that may hang around on a shelf for months or years. When the first Xbox came out, people who had grown up with PlayStation were reluctant to buy the newcomer.

People who buy chocolate bars are willing to 'risk' their 50p on trying a new product

Getting people to buy a product for the first time can be hard when:

- buyers are locked into existing brand loyalties, such as always buying Heinz beans, Gold Blend coffee or Marmite

- buyers are locked in by earlier decisions (it's too expensive for them to switch), e.g. PlayStation games, Microsoft Office, or someone who is halfway through a mobile phone contract

- your new business has not yet established a reputation/brand image, so there is no reason for people to risk their money with you.

To overcome resistance to product trial is very difficult. Either it must be achieved by huge advertising spending, building up a clear brand image and persuading people that 'it must be good'. Or product trial must be started on a small scale, steadily building up sales by recommendation and word of mouth. Häagen-Dazs ice cream began in Britain with distribution in small shops, plus free samples given out at places like Wimbledon and Glastonbury. This built a network of customers who asked friends, 'Have you tried Häagen-Dazs yet?'

Repeat purchase

Repeat purchase by consumers is vital to a business's success. Launching a new product is far too expensive to make a profit if people buy once but never again. To achieve high repeat purchase (that is, **brand loyalty**), certain factors are crucial:

- The product/service must be at least as good as the customer expected – preferably much, much better. Adults may have been buying *The Sun* for 20 years; it would take a fantastic new newspaper to get them to switch permanently away from 'their paper'.

- The brand image must match the customer's image of himself or herself. Lots of people have tried Yakult, but not many

feel that its quirky image is what they feel about themselves; people identify far better with Actimel's fun, family image.

- The product must seem value for money, either because it is cheap for what you get (*The Sun*) or because it gives you exactly what you want/need (the *Financial Times* newspaper for business people).

Once a product has become established as a reliable brand, managers can look to expand their product range and know that they have loyal customers who would be willing to try something new. For example, most of us trust Cadbury's chocolate and are happy to try any of its new products. From the company's point of view, this is an extra type of repeat purchase.

> '*You can get everyone in the world to try your product once, but if the experience is less than satisfactory, the likelihood of a repeat purchase would be as thirst quenching as sand.*'
> **Joseph Jaffe, marketing speaker/author**

The Marmite advertising campaign 'You'll either love it or hate it' was born out of talking to people and discovering that most of them really either love or hate Marmite! This was a bold move for the brand; it brings to life the effect of the spread on different people. Marmite was telling its customers: try

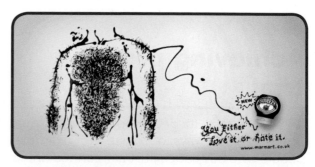

You'll either love it or hate it – Marmite's bold advertising campaign

it and if you don't like it, don't try it again. It effectively challenged consumers to try the brand with a hope that when they tried it, they would love it, and if they didn't that was OK because some people don't.

are likely to buy one of their products rather than an untried or unknown one when we go shopping. However, if any of these brands launched a product that we did not like or was of poor quality, it might cause damage to their whole business.

Customer loyalty

It is important for a business to encourage consumers to stay loyal to their brand. Large manufacturers Kellogg's, Adidas and Microsoft are all household names, which we associate with quality. As a result, we

> *'Your personal brand is a promise to your clients . . . a promise of quality, consistency, competency and reliability.'*
> **Jason Hartman, sales and marketing professional**

Revision Essentials

Product trial – consumer samples a product for the first time.

Repeat purchase – consumer regularly purchases brand.

Brand loyalty – a strongly motivated and long-standing decision to purchase a particular product or service.

Exercises

(30 marks; 30 minutes)

Read the unit, then ask yourself:

1   Explain what is meant by product trial and repeat purchase. (4)

2   Outline the importance of repeat purchase to a business. (2)

3   Describe why businesses try to encourage customer loyalty. (4)

4   Explain Unilever's decision to use the 'love it or hate it' advertising campaign for Marmite. (5)

5   Identify and explain three methods that businesses can use to encourage customers to repeat purchase. (6)

6   Decide whether these advertising slogans were designed to create product trial or repeat purchase. Briefly explain your answers.

    a   'I'm lovin' it.' (McDonalds)

    b   'The Lynx effect.'

    c   'Have a break. Have a Kit Kat.' (9)

Practice Questions

'Double Whopper, fries, Coke – oh, and a measuring tape, please.' The Advertising Standards Authority (ASA) has upheld a complaint against Burger King that a junk food portion was too small.

In comparison with the tall tower of meat, lettuce, tomato and bun featured in a recent television advertisement for the fast food franchise, investigators discovered that an actual store-bought Double Whopper burger came up short.

It is said that the camera puts on several pounds, but the ASA insisted the advert could not be re-broadcast until the size of the burger was reduced to correspond more closely to the product.

The investigation into the relative size of the Double Whopper was triggered by three complaints from consumers who believed the burger was smaller and less substantial than the product featured in a TV advert.

The Advertising Standards Authority upheld a complaint against Burger King

To check the chain's products, two ASA investigators purchased two Double Whoppers at separate London restaurants. After careful examination, they concluded that the burgers were smaller and thinner than those in the advert.

The conclusion drawn by these culinary detectives was that the advert did indeed give a 'misleading impression' of the size of the Double Whopper burger.

Questions

(25 marks; 30 minutes)

1　To what extent do you believe the Burger King brand will have been damaged after the complaint to the Advertising Standards Authority? (5)

2　Discuss what actions Burger King should now take to keep its existing customers following the complaint against it being upheld. (5)

3　Briefly explain how the news of this embarrassment for Burger King might affect:

a) product trial and b) repeat purchase of the Double Whopper. (8)

4　If you were invited to invest in a Burger King restaurant at this stage, what changes would you insist on beforehand? Explain your reasoning. (7)

Product life cycle

When deciding on its marketing strategy, a firm will have to examine the existing position of its products and services. Only by looking at how its products are doing will it be able to decide what to do next. One technique a firm can use to do this is the product life cycle.

All new products have an expected life cycle. A product's life cycle is the amount of time a business expects the product to sell. There are four stages in the product life cycle. These give an idea of where the product is in its lifetime – a bit like a human life.

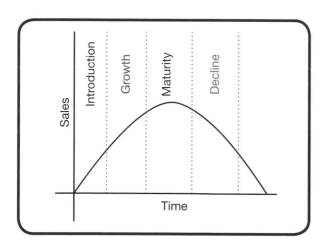

The product life cycle

Stage 1: Introduction

First the company spends a lot of time and money researching the product and the market for the product. The product will be tested and market research carried out before it is launched. There will be no sales at this time. The business will be preparing an advertising campaign. At this stage costs are high and there are no sales. The product

is then launched and placed on the market. There will be low product sales and small-scale distribution. Any advertising will be informative to make people aware that the product exists. The product might be the only one of its kind at this stage so the selling price will probably be high. At this stage sales are low and costs are high.

At a product's introduction a business may be preparing an advertising campaign

Stage 2: Growth

At this stage the product becomes known in the market and there will be a wider distribution network. The business will continue with advertising but it will be less frequent than at the product's launch. At this stage customer awareness increases, the price will still be high and sales and profits start to rise.

Stage 3: Maturity

The market may become saturated as 'me-too' or copycat products are launched onto the market. Sales growth flattens out and cash flow improves. Advertising is persuasive and is used to remind the market that the product exists. The business may try to increase promotion in an attempt to maintain market share – money spent on reinforcing the brand image or packaging. Profits are still good. The product is in a highly competitive market and weak brands often disappear at this stage, as they cannot compete.

Stage 4: Decline

The product's sales and profits start to fall. The product is no longer offering what customers want or new technology used by other products has made it out of date. Some businesses will stop their marketing to cut costs but will still make some profits between now and when the product is finally withdrawn. Eventually the product is taken out of production. The last products are often sold at a reduced price, meaning a further reduction in profits. The product is withdrawn from the market.

In reality very few products follow the cycle exactly. The length of each stage will vary a lot. Businesses can take actions to prolong a stage, such as heavy brand advertising to try to stop maturity turning into decline. Not all products go through each stage – some go straight from introduction to decline (think of Chico from *The X Factor*!).

It is important for businesses to know what stage of the life cycle their products are at so that they can plan the correct marketing strategy for the product.

Just because a product has reached the maturity stage or even started to decline does not necessarily mean it is the end. Some products will have **extension strategies** launched for them to start to increase sales again, for example by changing the product's design or use.

> 'Marketing is not an event, but a process . . . It has a beginning, a middle, but never an end, for it is a process. You improve it, perfect it, change it, even pause it. But you never stop it completely.'
> **Jay Conrad Levinson, author on marketing**

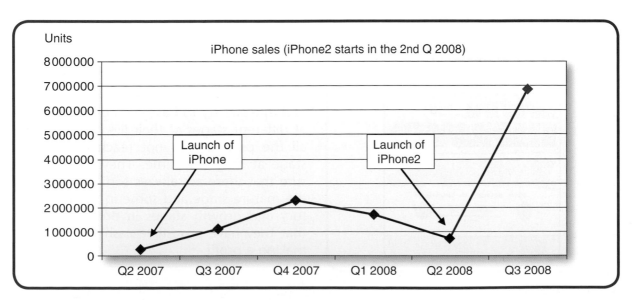

Product life cycle of the first iPhone – over one year

Extension strategies

Firms may try to prevent sales going into decline by using extension strategies. There are various techniques they can use:

- **Find new uses for the product**. Johnson's Baby Powder was originally marketed only for babies; realising its sales potential among women was a major breakthrough for the company.

- **Develop a wider product range.** Fairy washing-up liquid, Fairy Power Spray, Fairy dishwasher powder/tablets.

- **Change the appearance, format or packaging.** Coke cans, bottles, etc.

- **Encourage use of the product on more occasions** – e.g. shampoo, wash hair twice; cereals, not just for breakfast; ice cream in the winter.

- **Adapt the product**. 'New and improved.'

- **Reduce the price** – e.g. when the product moves from being newly introduced to an everyday item.

Adapting the product is one possible extension strategy

Cash flow and the life cycle

Cash flow is the term used for the money going into and out of the business. Cash flow is affected by the different stages of the product life cycle.

At the start of the cycle there is no cash flow inflow as money is paid out to design, develop and launch the product. Cash flow then improves until the product reaches the end of growth. By the time the product moves into maturity, cash flow is positive. This remains the case until the product starts to go into decline, when cash flow will become negative again unless the business introduces an extension strategy.

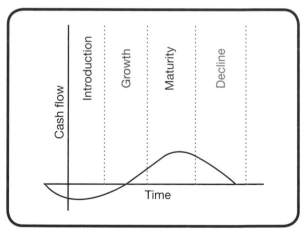

Cash flow over the product life cycle

Businesses try to have a range of products at different stages of their life cycles so that all the products do not reach the decline stage at the same time. They try to make sure that there are always some products at the mature stage and some in the introductory and growth stages in order to ensure that they have a positive cash flow and are making a profit.

Revision Essentials

Extension strategy – an attempt to prolong the sales of a product and prevent it from declining.

Exercises

(25 marks; 30 minutes)

Read the unit, then ask yourself:

1 Describe what happens during the introduction stage of a product's life. (2)

2 Outline what could happen to profits for a product that is at the maturity stage. (2)

3 Explain why some products have much longer life cycles than others. Use examples to illustrate your answer. (4)

4 Look at the examples below and match up the statement to the life cycle. (4)

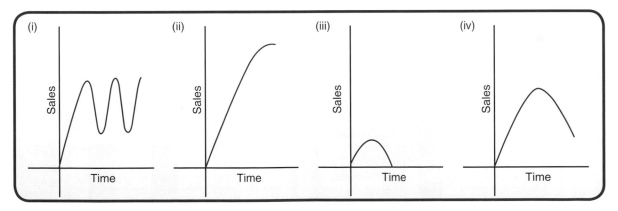

Sales/Time graphs

    a A product that is very popular but which after a time loses its popularity.

    b A new product that flops.

    c A product that becomes popular very quickly and continues to have good sales.

    d A product for which sales vary, season by season.

5 Think of examples of real products that would match up with the product life cycle descriptions in the previous question. (4)

6 Draw a product life cycle for the Volkswagen Golf and then describe the stages and explain what is happening to cash flow at each stage. (9)

Class Discussion – Sony v Nintendo

In business there are many head-on clashes: Coca-Cola v Pepsi, Cadbury v Mars and Boeing v Airbus. And then there's Sony v Nintendo. This is an interesting one because it appears to be straightforward: electronics giant Sony versus the relatively small Nintendo.

In 2005/6, most analysts would have been sure that Sony would always win this battle.

But as the bar charts show, Sony struggled in the following years, while Nintendo shot ahead. The bar charts also show the product life cycle, i.e. how some products hit a decline phase that means they must be replaced by something new.

A disappointment to Sony has been the relatively weak performance of the PS3. Fortunately for the business, the PS3 helped Sony win a different battle, in the market for High Definition DVDs. Sony included its own HD DVD (the Blu-Ray) in every PS3.

This helped force Toshiba to withdraw its HD DVD from the world market in early summer 2008.

Big businesses always to have to think between three and five years ahead. Sony's strategy meant that they won one battle, but seemed to have lost the other. Is there any way back for Sony in games consoles?

Talking Point

1 Use the bar charts to identify one product in its growth phase, one in its maturity phase, and one in its decline phase from within the Sony and Nintendo brands.

2 Discuss how Sony might set about recovering sales growth in the games console market, in order to halt the growth of Nintendo.

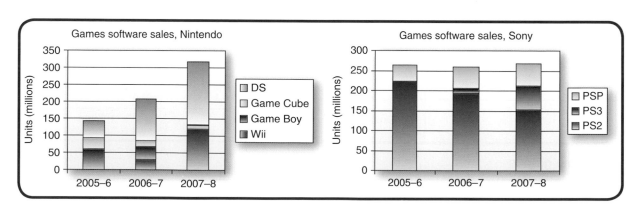

Games software sales, Nintendo and Sony

Practice Questions

When Cadbury Dairy Milk chocolate was introduced in the early 1900s it made an immediate impact, quickly becoming the market leader. The success story has continued. It is still the top-selling chocolate brand in the UK and the Cadbury mega brand's broad family of products today has an international retail value approaching US$1 billion.

As an international brand Cadbury Dairy Milk carries the same distinctive image all over the world. Wherever you buy a bar of Cadbury Dairy Milk the pack design will be exactly the same, only the language will be different.

The famous slogan 'glass and a half of full cream milk in every half pound' with the picture of milk pouring into the choc-

Wherever you buy a bar of Cadbury Dairy Milk the pack design will be exactly the same

olate bar is one of the all-time greats of British advertising.

The first two additions to the Cadbury mega brand family were Fruit & Nut in 1928 and WholeNut in 1933. The family has since been extended and there are now ten varieties of Cadbury Dairy Milk bars in the range.

Source: www.cadbury.co.uk

Questions

(25 marks; 25 minutes)

1 Outline what you think has made Cadbury Dairy Milk so successful. (3)

2 Draw a product life cycle for Cadbury Dairy Milk and describe what is happening at each stage. (6)

3 Explain why Cadbury might have decided to introduce new varieties of Dairy Milk. (4)

4 Identify other strategies that Cadbury might have used to boost sales. (4)

5 Describe how the product life cycle might help Cadbury in its marketing planning. (4)

6 Outline two possible extension strategies Cadbury could use if sales of Dairy Milk started to decline. (4)

The Boston Matrix

Product portfolio analysis

Most businesses do not rely on selling just one product; they have a range of products that they sell. This is called their product portfolio. All these products will vary in their popularity. Firms such as L'Oreal have many different products and brands. The managers need to decide which of these to concentrate most of their effort on. A tool that can be used by a business to compare their products and to work out how they are doing is the Boston Matrix.

The Boston Matrix

The Boston Matrix allows businesses to measure the extent to which an individual product is succeeding within its market. It looks at the success of a brand in terms of its market share and market growth.

Businesses need a variety of products to be available at any one time to ensure that they are not only making profits today but also have good profit prospects tomorrow.

The Boston Matrix helps decision-making using portfolio analysis. The analysis looks at the position of these products or services

in their relevant markets. The Boston Matrix looks at the market share and growth in the area in which a business operates. There are four categories within the Boston Matrix: Rising Star, Problem Child, Cash Cow and Dog. A business would look at each individual product in its range (or portfolio) and place it onto the matrix. It would do this for every product in the range.

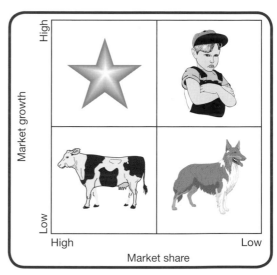

The Boston Matrix

Problem Children are products that have low market share in a high-growth market. They need lots of money spent on them if they are going to become stars. They are frustrating because they have so much potential yet aren't successful. Should the company try to turn them into stars? Or accept that they are flops? Nestlé's water brand Perrier is in that position.

Talking Point

Why is it important for a business to have a balanced portfolio of products?

Problem Child

Rising Stars are products with high market share in a high-growth market. They generate lots of sales but often need lots of money to be spent on them as the market is growing as well. Stars tend to generate high amounts of income. Businesses should keep and build their stars. Stars are destined to become the Cash Cows of the future.

Rising Star

Cash Cows are products with high market share in a low-growth market. They generate lots of sales and huge profits. Examples include Coca-Cola and Persil detergent. Profits from these products are used to help fund Problem Children or Stars. Cash Cows generate more than is invested in them. They are best kept in a portfolio of products for the time being.

Cash Cow

Dogs are products with low market share and low growth. They may have been Cash Cows or Problem Children before they moved into the Dog category. Businesses want as few Dogs as possible because they add little to the portfolio. Sometimes a business retains Dogs because they still make some low sales, which may attract customers to buy other products from the business. They have no real future, so as soon as they stop generating cash they are 'put to sleep'.

Dog

Working with the Boston Matrix

Sony BMG Music Entertainment is a global recording music joint venture with a roster of current artistes that includes a broad array of both local artistes and international superstars. The artistes signed to Sony BMG include

Leon Jackson, Leona Lewis, Rick Astley and Westlife, among many others (source: www. sonybmg.co.uk).

> 'The toughest thing about success is that you've got to keep on being a success.'
> **Irving Berlin**

We can use the Boston Matrix to analyse the 'products' of Sony BMG (see figure). Sony BMG can look at the artistes and where they are positioned on the matrix to make decisions about them.

Leona Lewis

The Boston Matrix

Leona Lewis won the 2006 series of *The X Factor*. Since then she has become a worldwide star, with Number 1 albums and singles in the USA. From Sony BMG's point of view, she is still a Rising Star with huge potential.

Leon was the surprise winner of *The X Factor* in 2007. Sony BMG achieved a Number 1 single in the UK, but it took a year to bring out his first album. Perhaps the company thought that this Problem Child might never become a Cash Cow.

Westlife generate a lot of sales. When they release a single, it goes to Number 1. There are plenty of Westlife fans who have supported the band for years. This Cash Cow does not need lots of marketing and promotion. Their fans love them!

Rick Astley was a big star in the 1980s. Then, he would have been positioned as a Star on the matrix, but the market changed and he is now more of a Dog. However, there has been an 80s revival in recent years, which is perhaps why Sony BMG still has him signed to its label.

Problems with the matrix

Businesses often assume that they will make more profit if the market share is high, but this might not always be the case. When Airbus launched the new A380 plane, it gained a high market share quickly but the extremely high costs of development still have to be covered.

Sometimes things can be over-simplified. A product may be a Dog, but sales might pick up. Heinz announced it was to stop making salad cream a few years ago, but sales recovered and it is now a Cash Cow once again.

Revision Essentials

Boston Matrix – a tool that can compare the products of a business and work out which ones have the best prospects for the future.

Stars – products that are in high-growth markets with a relatively high share of that market.

Problem Children – products with a low share of a high-growth market.

Cash Cows – products with a high share of a slow-growth market.

Dogs – products with a low share of a low-growth market.

Exercises

(25 marks; 30 minutes)

Read the unit, then ask yourself:

1   What is meant by the Boston Matrix? (3)

2   Describe the benefits to a business of using the Boston Matrix to help make business decisions. (6)

3   Identify two limitations to a business of using the Boston Matrix. (2)

4   a Complete a portfolio analysis for a manufacturer that you know well, such as Kellogg's, Cadbury or Nike. Consider how their brands fit into the Boston Matrix categories. (6)

    b Discuss whether the firm seems to be managing its product portfolio effectively. (8)

Practice Questions

Unilever has been trading for more than a century. Its website says that its aim is to meet people's everyday needs for nutrition, home hygiene and personal care. It does this with brands that help people 'feel good, look good and get more out of life'.

Sixteen out of forty brands are market leaders, including Persil, Dove, Magnum, Flora, Marmite and Lynx. You can find Unilever products in the kitchens, fridges, freezers and bathrooms of nine out of every ten UK homes. Unilever has annual UK sales of nearly €2.5 billion.

One important category of brands is 'home hygiene'. The brands are Cif, Comfort, Domestos, Persil, Persil Washing Up Liquid and Surf. Within these brands there are liquid, tablet and gel forms of the products.

Questions

(20 marks; 25 minutes)

1 Explain one possible reason why Unilever produces such a vast range of products. (3)

2 a Complete a product portfolio analysis of Unilever's home hygiene range. (5)

   b Justify the choices you have made. (4)

3 Discuss the importance to a company such as Unilever of having so many market leaders within its portfolio. (8)

Branding and differentiation

Have you heard of Apple? Do you know what it makes? What does the name mean to you? Does it mean quality? Does it mean expensive?

Apple manufactures a range of products, from iMacs to iPods to iPhones. We see the Apple logo (shown below) and we instantly recognise and know what it means. How do we know this? Apple has created a **brand**; it has bombarded consumers with advertising and promotion that have made us remember its logo. We are convinced about the quality of the company's products and image. Existing customers trust a strong brand such as Apple as they know what to expect. The **logo** on a product is an important part of the product.

The Apple logo allows customers to recognise the brand

Branding gives an identity to a product. Producers hope that consumers will become loyal to their brand and always buy their product rather than any other. Every business wants to be a customer's first choice. Building and managing a brand can play a significant part in making that happen. Brands give potential customers a firm idea of what they're buying before they buy it, making the purchasing decision easier.

A brand can be the name of a product, such as Dairy Milk, or it can be the name of a company that markets a number of products under its brand name, Virgin for example.

> 'Products are made in the factory, but brands are created in the mind.'
> **Walter Landor, German designer**

Branding is establishing an identity for your product that distinguishes it from the competition. Brands aren't just for big companies – they can make smaller businesses stand out from the crowd, particularly in competitive markets. Successful branding adds value to an item and can ensure brand loyalty. Brand loyalty exists when consumers buy your product on a regular basis.

Types of branding

- **Family branding**: products are distinguished under a company heading. Apple's product mix consists of iMac, MacPro, Apple TV, iPod, iTunes and iPhone. All the products are distinguished under the Apple banner.

- **Line branding**: products are distinguished from other producers' products, e.g. Wrigleys Extra, Extra Thin Ice, Juicy Fruit, Hubba Bubba, Airwaves, Orbit Spearmint and Doublemint.

Some retailers use **'own-label'** brands, where they use their name of the product rather than the manufacturers', like Sainsbury's 'Taste The Difference' range of food. These tend to be cheaper than the normal brands, but usually give the retailer more profit than selling a normal brand.

Some brands are so strong that they have become **global brands**. This means that the product is sold in lots of countries all over the world and the contents are very similar. Examples of global brands include Apple, Coca-Cola, Warner Bros., BMW and Lexmark.

The advantages of having a strong brand are:

- it encourages **customer loyalty,** leading to repeat purchases and word-of-mouth recommendation

- companies are able to charge **higher prices**, especially if the brand is the market leader

Retailers want to stock top-selling brands

- retailers want to stock top-selling brands. With limited shelf space it is more likely the top brands will be on the shelf ahead of less well-known brands.

> '*A product can be copied by a competitor; a brand is unique. A product can be quickly outdated; a successful brand is timeless.*'
> **Stephen King, WPP Group, London**

The disadvantages of branding are:

- there are high costs associated with promotion in order to gain brand recognition in the first place

- constant promotion is necessary to maintain the brand

- a single bad event may affect all the brand's products

- brand names have to be protected by being registered worldwide.

All companies try to make their products different to those of their rivals, even if only in some tiny or cosmetic way. They attempt to differentiate their products, in other words to make customers believe the product is really special. A strong brand name helps hugely in this process.

Product differentiation

Product **differentiation** makes customers feel there is a good range of products to choose from. But it can lead to higher prices for consumers. For example, in the market for sweets there are many different types of mint: Tic Tacs, Softmints, Extra Strong Mints, Polos and so on. All are made from sugar plus mint essence, i.e. they are the same. But the differentiation is clear, with different strengths of mint, types of packaging, hardness/chewiness and so on.

There are several other ways in which businesses can differentiate their product or service from the competition:

- logo
- name
- quality
- content
- packaging
- design.

A product has a **unique selling point (USP)** when it has an important feature that other products do not have. For example, Bounty's USP is that it is the only chocolate bar in the Mars range with a coconut filling. Having a USP is the ultimate form of product

Revision Essentials

Logo – a symbol or picture that represents the business.

Brand – a product with a unique character, for instance in design or image.

Differentiation – the process of making a product seem distinct from its competitors.

Unique selling point (USP) – a key feature of a product that is not shared by any of its rivals.

Exercises

(37 marks; 35 minutes)

Read the unit, then ask yourself:

1 Give two reasons why it is hard to develop a business rapidly. (2)

2 Explain in your own words what is meant by branding. (2)

3 Think of a brand you know. Identify what type of branding the manufacturers have used. (2)

4 Describe what a business must do to turn a product into a brand. (3)

5 Outline **two** benefits to a business of creating a brand. (4)

6 Identify the advantages and drawbacks to a small business of creating and maintaining a brand. (6)

7 Explain why a business would want to differentiate its products from those of its nearest rivals. (4)

8 There are many brands of cola, each of which is fairly well differentiated. Identify how the different brands on the market have been differentiated. (3)

9   Discuss whether there are real differences in the products or whether it is all just image and reputation. (5)

10 Which do you think is the number one brand in the UK today for the following products:

  a   MP3 players

  b   Trainers

  c   Breakfast cereals

  d   Dog food

  e   Jeans

  f   Toothpaste. (6)

Practice Questions

Pizza Hut has changed...its name to Pasta Hut

For the first time in its 50-year history, Pizza Hut has changed its name. It has invested a large amount of money and made significant nutritional changes, as

Pizza Hut temporarily rebranded as Pasta Hut

well as launching a range of 12 pasta dishes that are to be included on the menu of its 700 restaurants. To mark the dawn of a new era for the company Pizza Hut has decided to rebrand itself as Pasta Hut on a temporary basis.

CEO Alasdair Murdoch explains: 'We have made significant changes to every aspect of the business over the past few years and we wanted to create a moment in time for people to sit back and take notice. We are confident that people will like what they see when they come into the restaurants.'

Alasdair explained that the name change reflects the improvements in the nutritional content of their menu, although they will still sell the same number of pizzas. The name change will be supported by a multimillion-pound marketing campaign and Pizza Hut plans to invest £100 million in its restaurants over the next six years. This year, the company has spent £17 million updating more than 100 restaurants to give them a more contemporary look and state-of-the-art equipment.

(Source: adapted from www.pizzahut.co.uk/restaurants/news/posta–hut.aspx)

Questions

(25 marks; 30 minutes)

1 Explain what is meant by the term 'brand'. (2)

2 Outline why Pizza Hut might want to change its brand image. (4)

3 Describe the process Pizza Hut will have to go through in order to create the brand for Pasta Hut. (4)

4 Outline the impact of the decision on Pizza Hut's current customers. Do you believe they will be happy with the change? (5)

5 Explain whether or not there is enough flexibility in the name change? Would 'The Hut' been a better name for the rebrand? Explain. (5)

6 Evaluate the potential advantages and disadvantages to Pizza Hut of not changing the brand of Pizza Hut. (5)

Practice Questions

What's the first thing that springs to mind when the brand 'Club 18–30' is mentioned? Whatever it is, that is the purpose of a brand – to create an identity with a product or service that draws people to that product or service over those of a rival. The Club 18–30 brand is owned by Thomas Cook. It has decided to try to 'change the perception' of the brand but not, it claims, change the image. The perception of a brand is how people see it; the image is what the brand reflects, what it wants to be associated with.

Thomas Cook has introduced new activities on its Club 18–30 holidays, including scuba diving, paint-balling and golf. It believes that it has to respond to a changing market. It suggests that the youth market at which it is aiming is becoming more sophisticated in what it wants from a holiday. It employed an advertising agency to spearhead a £1.5 million marketing campaign and planned to boost sales by 10 per cent.

Club 18–30 has been at the centre of a number of unfavourable news items in recent years. Incidents have involved Club 18–30 staff who have caused offence in Greece, where Faliraki had become the centre of the 'yob culture', according to papers like The Sun.

Faliraki has now become yesterday's resort and new venues are being sought as the fun centres for holidays for the young. Club 18–30, it seems, is trying to reflect that changing market. This is not the first time Club 18–30 has tried to change its image. In 2004 it announced that it was not encouraging bar crawls and wet T-shirt competitions. It also dropped Benidorm from its list of resorts as it was becoming too much like 'Blackpool on the Med' and not the sort of thing its more sophisticated market segment wanted out of a holiday.

(Source: www.bized.ac.uk)

Questions

(20 marks; 25 minutes)

1 Explain what is meant by the term 'brand'. (2)

2 Describe how Thomas Cook has differentiated Club 18–30 from other packaged holiday firms. (4)

3 Explain why Thomas Cook might have chosen to differentiate Club 18–30 in the way that it did. (6)

4 Outline why Thomas Cook might want to change the brand image of Club 18–30. (4)

5 Describe the process Thomas Cook will have to go through in order to recreate the brand for Club 18–30. (4)

Building a successful marketing mix

In 2006 more than 1 million of bars of Cadbury's chocolate had to be recalled and destroyed. The company had found traces of salmonella (a nasty stomach bug) in one of its factories. Putting this right cost Cadbury more than £30 million. Despite this embarrassment, however, 2006 provided the company with one success – the launch of the Cadbury's Creme Egg bar.

Given that one in six new products fails, how did Cadbury succeed despite the salmonella scandal? It could be argued that this is down to successful marketing.

> 'Advertising doesn't create a product advantage. It can only convey it.'
> **William Bernbach, legendary American advertising agent, 1911–1984**

Years ago people believed that all you needed to do was to 'build a better mousetrap'

The **marketing mix** is made up of four elements – product, price, promotion and place. In order to be successful a firm must make sure it has:

- the right product/service (that customers like and want to buy)

- at the right price (communicating the right **image** – not so low as to seem 'cheap', nor too high to seem value for money)

- promoted using the right medium (TV, radio, magazines, newspapers, special offers)

- is available in the right place (Chanel at Selfridges; Lynx at Superdrug).

Product

The easiest route to sales success is to have a great product. Years ago, people believed that all you needed to do was to 'build a better mousetrap' and sales would flow. In other words, make the best product and you will get the highest sales. This is less true today, when no one is sure what is 'the best' product. One year people are eating low-calorie yoghurts, the next they are told that Omega-3 yoghurts are better.

Well-run firms try hard to keep in close touch with customers to find out what they want. Then they can provide the right product (or service) to match the customers' needs. Examples of great products include:

- the Lexus 430: the ultimate smooth saloon car – the Japanese car that conquered America
- Cadbury's Creme Egg: just hits that pre-Easter spot
- *The Sun*: the first newspaper to realise that most people prefer their news to be fun rather than serious
- Primark: realising the opportunity for up-to-date but affordable fashion.

Price

The key is to ensure that the price is 'right'. In some cases this may be very expensive. A Lexus 430 costs £55,000; it will never outsell the Ford Focus, but Lexus customers wouldn't want everyone to have one! At £55,000, though, Lexus customers are able to convince themselves that they are getting value for money.

Broadly, there are two different types of product/service: price-makers and price-takers. Price-makers have, like Lexus, such a strong brand name and such a good product that they can set their own price. Others may follow. In the case of a price-taker, the producer is a follower. The *Daily Express* follows the price lead set by the *Daily Mail*; British Airways' European flight prices follow the lead set by Ryanair.

Strong brands are price leaders; weaker ones are price-takers.

Talking Point

Which of these brands do you think are price-makers? And which are price-takers?

- Arsenal season ticket
- Vauxhall Vectra car
- Heinz baked beans
- easyJet flights.

Promotion

In this case, promotion means all the ways companies can use to persuade customers to buy. These include advertising, which may be used as a way of building a strong brand identity in the long term ('L'Oreal, because I'm worth it'). There are also many ways of trying to boost short-term sales, such as sales promotions: Buy One Get One Free (BOGOF), enter a competition, introductory prices and so on.

The key to successful promotion is that it should not only build sales but also build the brand image. Tactics such as BOGOFs can cheapen the image of a brand.

Talking Point

How would you feel if Apple started selling 'Buy one iPod, get one free'?

Place

This element of the marketing mix is about how to get the product from the producer to the customer. The easiest way, today, is to sell directly, via the internet. Many people love to go shopping, though, so retail sales remain very important. There are three main distribution channels: traditional, modern and direct (see overleaf).

In addition to choosing the most appropriate channel, firms must decide the type of store they wish to be distributed in. Posh crisp maker Tyrrells decided it would rather not have its products on sale in Tesco. The directors believed the image of the brand would be built more successfully by being seen in small shops, plus the more upmarket retailers such as Waitrose and Booths.

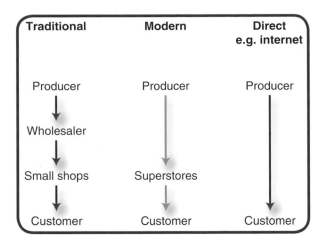

Distribution channels

There are 30 women's weekly magazines in the UK market

Why do some products fail?

Launching new products is difficult in all markets because customers get used to the papers they read, the soaps they watch and the chocolate they munch. Most markets are so crowded that it is very hard to find room for a new product success. This is clear when you read this insight into a 2007 new product launch.

There are 30 women's weekly magazines in the UK market. Yet February 2007 saw the launch of another weekly – *Look* magazine. The front cover of the preview issue featured pictures of Posh Beckham, Kate Moss, Lindsay Lohan and Angelina Jolie, plus there was an insert shouting 'Just In At Primark!' Nothing new here, then.

Fewer than one in eight new magazines becomes successful – could *Look* be lucky?

Owners IPC magazines invested £18 million in 18 months of planning for the launch and hired a massive editorial staff of 40. The sales target for *Look* was to sell 250,000 copies a week within 12 months. This seemed an ambitious target, as *Grazia* magazine was already filling a similar niche (for a glossy,

fashion-orientated weekly) but selling only 175,000 copies.

Editor Ali Hall targeted *Look* at 24-year-old women, keen on celebrities, even keener on shopping, and with a Saturday High Street ritual of Topshop, H&M, Primark and Dorothy Perkins. Hall thought this was distinctly different from *Grazia*, which, she said, was for 30-year-olds who were into brands such as Burberry and Chloe. *Look* would target youth, celebrities and style – not brands.

At the heart of the product is the promise that *Look* gives readers the quickest insights into what's hot and what's not. Sections include 'High Street's Hottest' and 'High Street Spy'. The latter tracks down what celebs are wearing and where to buy it (or the High Street imitation).

For £9 million of marketing spend, IPC launched a huge promotional programme, giving away 1.2 million copies at supermarkets plus shopping malls such as Bluewater and the Trafford Centre. There was also a big TV launch campaign.

A key decision has been over pricing. Unlike celeb magazines such as *Heat* and *OK!, Look* is produced on high-quality gloss paper. It will look as good as rival *Grazia* and monthlies such as *Marie Claire*. Despite the expensive gloss paper, *Look* was priced at £1.30, significantly below *Grazia*'s £1.80.

Eighteen months after launching, in autumn 2008, Look could proudly boast being the UK's top-selling fashion weekly. The one in eight chance paid off.

The *Look* marketing mix

PRODUCT	PRICE
Glossy, high production values, expensive-to-produce magazine. Targeting 24-year-old women with a sharp eye on fashion and celebrities	£1.30 launch price compared with Grazia at £1.80. Other top-selling weeklies include: OK!: £2.00 Hello: £1.85 Heat: £1.65 Now: £1.10
PROMOTION	PLACE
TV advertising plus a huge programme of giveaways for the launch issue (1.2 million copies given away). This is known as sampling and selling	Standard distribution through newsagents, supermarkets and sweet shops. *Look* achieved good distribution in WH Smith (though had to pay to get good display positions, e.g. by the cash desks)

What does a successful marketing mix look like?

According to statistics from ALVA (Association of Leading Visitor Attractions), Blackpool Pleasure Beach was the UK's leading visitor attraction for 2007. Yet In 2006 the nearby rival Southport Pleasureland had to close down. So what makes Blackpool Pleasure Beach so successful?

Blackpool Pleasure Beach

The Blackpool Pleasure Beach marketing mix

PRODUCT	PRICE
A theme park with rides for all ages, e.g. bumper cars, soft play areas and white-knuckle rides. Home of the biggest roller coaster in the world (The Big One). It also houses bingo halls and arcade games, plus a circus and shows including ice dance. The park offers a range of refreshments in restaurants and bars. It has themed areas, e.g. Wild West, and offers visitors souvenirs and the chance to buy photos of themselves on rides	Visitors are charged for the rides they use and can therefore budget; visitors are not penalised for waiting times. They do have pre-paid wristbands available. It is a cheaper day out than competitors such as Alton Towers and provides out-of-season special offers. More popular rides are more expensive and there are cheaper rides for younger visitors. Visitors can leave the park and come back later in the day

PROMOTION	PLACE
The park is well known and has a good reputation (word of mouth). It uses a variety of promotion methods, including TV advertisements, the internet, special offers, regional newspapers, free news coverage for charity events and the illuminations and when celebrities visit (e.g. Robbie Williams who rode The Big One). The park puts leaflets in other local attractions and gives special offers through local accommodation providers	Close to large populations of Manchester and Liverpool and to other attractions in Blackpool. It provides onsite parking. Blackpool is a year-round resort with visitors to the beach during the summer, the illuminations in the autumn and Christmas breaks. There is no competition within Blackpool and Southport Pleasureland closed in 2006. There are many hotels nearby (though Blackpool really wants a big casino)

Revision Essentials

Marketing mix – how a business persuades customers to buy its products/services. It is focused upon having the right product/service that customers want/need, available at a price they are willing to pay, in a place they are willing to travel to and promoted in a way to appeal to them.

Public image – how a business is perceived by the general public, e.g. most people believe the Co-op to be an ethical business due not only to its business practices but also to the way it markets itself.

Exercises

(25 marks; 30 minutes)

Read the unit, then ask yourself:

1   At its launch, explain whether *Look* appears to have been a price-maker or a price-taker. (4)

2   Do you think *Look*'s marketing mix was the key to its successful product launch? Explain your reasoning. (8)

3   Choose one of the following products and outline what you believe to be its marketing mix: Sony PS3, Specsavers, Pampers, Maltesers. (8)

4   Looking at the marketing mix for Blackpool Pleasure Beach and explain what you think makes it successful. (5)

Practice Questions

Sony launches Photo Go software

Sony has launched new software that allows users to edit and share photos and promises to be 'a fun, fast and easy way to organise, edit and share digital photos'. Photo Go software lets users import photos from a camera or computer, then, using built-in editing tools, rotate, straighten and crop photos. Users can also adjust colour, brightness and contrast, and remove red eye.

When they have finished editing, users can share their images in a slideshow, print them using their own digital photo printer, email photos to family and friends, or upload them directly to the Sony ImageStation processing site.

The new consumer photo-editing software enables quick searching for pictures using tags, titles and other keywords. Photo Go software supports all popular image formats including .jpeg, .tif, .bmp and .png.

The key features of Photo Go are interactive Show Me How tutorials and the ability to:

- import pictures from a USB-connected camera, memory card reader or CD/DVD ROM
- coarch for pictures using tags, titles and other keywords
- rate favourite pictures for reference organise photos using customisable data labels
- group photos by year, month, day and file size
- create and view slideshows on computer
- rotate, straighten, mirror and crop photos
- adjust colour, brightness and contrast to create the perfect look
- auto-adjust photos with one click
- correct photos with red eye reduction email photos to family and friends
- order prints online directly from www.imagestation.com.

Photo Go is available now priced £19.99 and includes a coupon for 100 free 4x6 prints from Sony ImageStation

(Source: What Digital Camera, January 2007 © What Digital Camera / IPC+ Syndication)

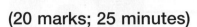

Questions

(20 marks; 25 minutes)

1 Part of Sony's promotion includes the coupon for free photos from Sony Image Station. How else should the company promote this software? (6)

2 Why has Sony charged £19.99 instead of £20? (2)

3 The article does not tell you where you can buy the product. What would you recommend for the 'place' element of the marketing mix? Explain your answer. (6)

4 Why might this new product fail? (6)

SECTION **6**

Exam-style Questions

DON'T RUSH; check answers carefully

1a. Look at this diagram of the Boston Matrix then decide which of the four statements is NOT a segment within the Boston Matrix.

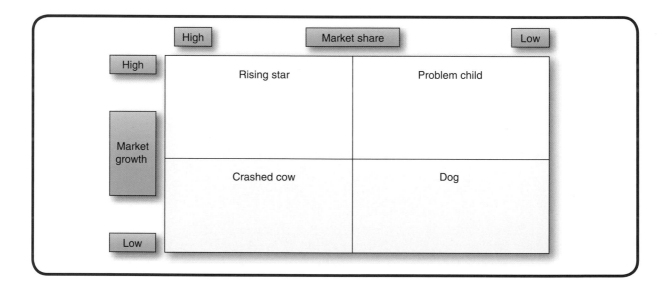

Select one answer.   (1)

a) Rising star

b) Dog

c) Crashed Cow

d) Problem Child

1b. Outline two possible benefits to a business of using the Boston Matrix.   (4)

1c. Explain why the Boston Matrix might not be helpful to a one-product business such as Liverpool F.C.   (3)

2a. Which one of the following is most likely to encourage repeat business at a restaurant.   (1)

a)   A 'buy one get one free' promotion

b)   Very good food and excellent service

c)   Heavy advertising on local radio

d)   An impressive new sign outside the restaurant

2b.   Identify two reasons why repeat purchase is very valuable to a company.   (2)

2c.   i.   What is meant by the term 'product trial'?   (1)

ii.   Explain why product trial may be hard to achieve for a car produced by a brand new company.   (3)

iii. Describe why brand names may help in achieving customer loyalty.   (3)

3.   In 2009 Mars launched the Malteaster Bunny as a rival to Cadbury's Creme Egg. It was priced higher than the Creme Egg but Mars felt confident that it would achieve a high level of distribution.

3a.   Within the marketing mix, distribution is known as which one of the following: (1)

a)   Position

b)   Place

c)   Packaging

d)   Prominence

3b.   i.   What is meant by the term 'marketing mix'?   (1)

ii.   Identify the two elements of the Malteaster Bunny's marketing mix that are not mentioned above.   (2)

iii. Explain why it is important for a new product to achieve a high level of distribution.   (3)

3c.   Explain why Mars may be wrong to price the Malteaster Bunny higher than Cadbury's Creme Egg.   (3)

4.   Before Pepsi launched 'Raw' cola into Britain, it carried out qualitative and quantitative research among those who did and those who did not buy cola drinks already.

4a.   Which of the following is an example of qualitative research?   (1)

a)   Depth interviewing

b)   Sampling and selling

c)   Questionnaires

d)   Population statistics

4b.   Identify two items of information that a business might discover through quantitative research.   (2)

4c. Explain why the findings of quantitative research might prove unreliable. (3)

4d. Explain how and why it might be useful to Pepsi to do research among people who don't usually drink colas. (6)

MEETING CUSTOMER NEEDS

Introduction to meeting customer needs

In January 2007 Apple announced the launch of its iPhone. Everyone had known that Apple had been working on a phone iPod, yet boss Steve Jobs managed to make the audience gasp with surprise and delight. His design team had produced such a distinctive, original product that everyone could see huge sales potential. That day, Apple shares rose by 7 per cent in the stock market, making the company worth an extra £500 million.

Apple had thought deeply about what customers would want from a single handset. The answer was a phone, a music player, a camera, text messaging and internet access – all in an attractive, convenient package. The design solution was to give it a touch screen and no buttons – and to make it look beautiful.

As he launched it, Steve Jobs said: 'The iPod changed everything in 2001. We're going to do it again in 2007 with the iPhone.'

Steve Jobs presenting the iPhone

On both occasions, Apple's skill was in anticipating customer needs and desires – then finding a way of beating **customer expectations**. Apple made the iPhone a 'must-have' item, then set a UK launch price of £300+.

Despite the success of the iPhone, little more than a year later Apple launched the iPhone 2. With fast (3G) internet access and a launch price of just £100, Apple was responding further to customer needs.

Key factors in meeting customer needs

1 Keeping close to the customer. Every Friday, Tesco boss Terry Leahy gets out of his office and visits a couple of stores. By talking directly to shop floor staff, he is confident that he will keep in touch with ordinary shoppers. For the same reason, he will join a checkout queue and chat to a few of his customers.

Hard though he is trying, Terry Leahy cannot always get it right. After all, he is boss of a business with more than 250,000 staff, so how can he see them all?

Every week, *The Grocer* trade magazine reports on customer service among the supermarkets. Each week a different town is visited and a secret visit is made to all the main stores. Then a winner is announced: the shop of the week. The judging is based on how well each store meets customer needs. The grocery trade believes these are:

- a full range of stock

- short queues at the checkout

- a clearly laid-out store

- friendly, helpful staff.

In other businesses, different factors will be the key to success in meeting customer needs. The table below sets out some of the possibilities.

Business Situation	Keys To Meeting Customers' Needs
Cafe in university student area	Cheap, with generous portions; open until late; internet access; some reference to organic or Fair Trade items.
Dentist	Minimum wait; minimum pain; minimum sense of guilt (at too many Mars Bars; too little flossing).
Buying a new Volvo car	Friendly, efficient service; reliable car that's easy – or fun – to drive; terrific sound system; petrol usage less punishing than expected.
Manufacturing scarves	Great designs – to meet different people's needs; different price levels: £6.99 scarves for teenagers, £14.99 scarves for middle-aged customers; making sure stock is available, especially in the autumn.
Professional football club	Three points this Saturday, no matter how poor the game, the pies and the programme.

2 Being efficient and reliable. Customers want their needs met consistently. The trains on the London–Manchester route are smart, new and fast. This meets many customer needs. They also have a highly varied pricing policy, which lets students travel for £30 return while businesspeople are paying £270 to be on the same train. No one will be happy, though, if the service is unreliable. Success relies on careful planning and an eye for detail. In the case of a railway or an airline, engineers should check regularly to prevent things going wrong, rather than waiting to fix things that have broken down.

> 'To all our nit-picky, over-demanding, ask-awkward-questions customers: Thank you, and keep up the good work.'
> **Dell computers advertisement**

3 Providing great design. Many customers value design and style above price. They want clothes that make them look great, cosmetics that make them look older – or younger – and cars that make them look successful, or exciting, or smooth. As mentioned above, it boils down to getting close to the customer. Some people will buy only the best; others want £2.99 T-shirts for some

Many customers value design and style above price

days but £24.99 tops for Friday and Saturday nights. Well-run businesses learn what customers want, then recruit people with the right skills to be able to supply them.

> *'You ponce in here expecting to be waited on hand and foot, well I'm trying to run a hotel here.'*
> **Basil Fawlty, hotelkeeper, aka John Cleese, actor,** *Fawlty Towers*

Revision Essentials

Customer expectations – what consumers expect they are going to receive for the service they have paid for. Clever companies aim to provide even more than was expected.

Exercises

(15 marks; 25 minutes)

Read the unit, then ask yourself:

1 Nokia, the world's biggest-selling producer of phones, would be worried about Apple's new iPhone. Outline two ways in which Nokia might respond to the launch of the iPhone. (4)

2 Re-read the table on page 261, then suggest the keys to meeting customers' needs for a supplier of:

  a baby car seats (3)

  b lipstick. (3)

3 Name two types of customer who might not 'value design and style above price'. (2)

4 Put in your own words what is meant by the phrase 'get close to your customer'. (3)

Practice Questions

On 2 January 2007 Little Chef went into liquidation (it closed down). It was quickly bought for £10 million, but that was little compensation for owners Lawrence Wosskow and Simon Heath. They had paid £52 million for the business just one year before. It was also a very worrying time for Little Chef's 3500 employees – the new owners made it clear from the start that they would close at least 60 of the 235 outlets.

Staff would be especially concerned because Little Chef eateries have always been on A roads, i.e. roads going between towns or cities, and therefore often in the middle of nowhere. There would be few alternative jobs nearby.

When reporting on the collapse of the Little Chef chain, many newspapers said it was 'stuck in a timewarp'. Started up in 1958, it expanded in the 1970s and many outlets still looked the same today.

Its 2007 menu of an 'Olympic Breakfast' (£6.99) and 'Gammon & Pineapple' (£7.50) was crazily far away from the modern concern for healthy eating. Even the firm's logo was a problem because outside every Little Chef was the 'Fat Charlie' symbol – looking just the way that no one wants to look today.

In the 1950s, 1960s and 1970s, Little Chef served up the big portions of greasy food people wanted. As tastes changed, the business stayed stuck with a Fat Charlie outlook and image. One reporter visited a Little Chef in Tabley, Cheshire and mentioned the cheery, quick service. Yet good service means nothing if the wrong products are being offered or the prices are too high.

Fat Charlie has had his day.

Fat Charlie – the Little Chef logo

Questions

(25 marks; 25 minutes)

1 Outline two reasons why staff at Little Chef would be worried about the news they heard about the business in early 2007. (4)

2 A section of the text mentions the importance of friendly, helpful staff. How does the story about Little Chef show that this factor is not enough to ensure business success? (4)

3 Discuss whether Little Chef managed to stay close to its customers during recent years. (8)

4 Discuss a suitable strategy the new owners might adopt to make the most of their £10 million investment. (9)

Design and R&D

Introduction

In July 2006 the *Dragons' Den* TV programme featured a new invention. James Seddon was trying to get £75,000 of investment for his 'Eggxactly' water-free egg cooker (a kind of boiled egg sandwich toaster). James invented the product to meet a specific 'customer need'. His three-year-old daughter loved soft-boiled eggs, but James kept overcooking them. Therefore he had to throw the egg away and start again.

As a scientist, James saw that soft-polymer plastics could grip an egg and provide the thermal contact for wires to heat and cook it. Electronic controls could then provide the timers and the heat controls to generate a perfect soft-boiled or hard-boiled egg (and ring a buzzer when the egg was cooked).

Scientific research such as this can provide a business with an edge over its competitors.

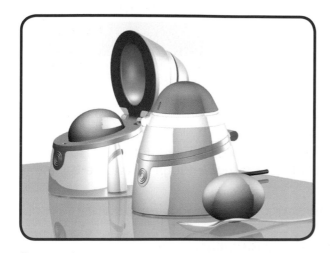

Eggxactly

When the research leads to the discovery of a new product, a **patent** can be registered. This provides the inventor with up to 20 years before anyone else is allowed to copy the idea. During this long period of time, the inventor has the opportunity to charge prices that are high enough to recover the costs of the original scientific work.

Although the *Dragon* investors offered James his £75,000, he later turned this down, deciding to finance it himself. It was to take him two more years to get Eggxactly ready for its UK launch.

> 'You can design and create and build the most wonderful place in the world. But it takes people to make the dream a reality.'
> **Walt Disney**

Design and the design mix

Having come up with the Eggxactly idea, James Seddon then needed to consider what the egg cooker would look like. Would it be shaped like a chicken? Or would it just be a square box, looking like a sandwich toaster?

James needed to consider the three aspects of the design mix:

1 **Economic manufacture**: making sure that the design allows the product to be made cost effectively; a complex design might add 50 per cent to the manufacturing cost, making the product too expensive for some customers.

2 Function: the design must make sure that the product works well and works every time. The Sony Bravia TV does not look any different from other flat-screen TVs, until you turn it on. Then the higher quality picture shines through. Sony invested heavily in making it function better than other TVs. In the case of the egg cooker, precise controls will be essential – to make the perfect soft-boiled egg, time after time.

3 Aesthetics: how well does the product appeal to the senses? It may work well and be inexpensive to make but look or feel cheap. No one buys a Mercedes sports car just because it's fast and reliable – they buy it because it looks beautiful outside and looks, feels and smells terrific inside. For James Seddon, the look of the product is not as important as whether it works well. Yet he cannot ignore the aesthetics altogether. If it looks cheap, people will expect it to be cheap to buy (and may doubt whether it will work). James intends the first Eggxactly product to be black and chrome, to look classy and to look like a serious piece of kitchen equipment.

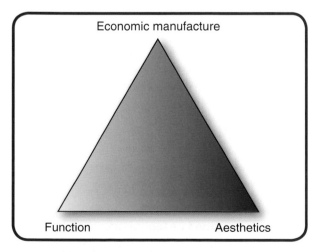

The design mix

Design and product differentiation

Product differentiation means making your product stand out from the competition. Making people see it as really different and distinctive. This may help the product become a market leader, as *The Sun* is within the British newspaper market. Or, like BMW, the distinctiveness may allow high prices to be charged, but without ever becoming a huge-selling product. The table below gives some more examples.

Product differentiation

Market	Differentiated Product
Cars	BMW
MP3 players	iPod
Newspapers	*The Sun*
Drinking yoghurt	Yakult

High differentiation is important because customers can become loyal to something that they see as different, even unique. Most *Sun* readers buy that paper and that paper alone; most iPod users would buy a new iPod if their original one was lost or stolen.

Design plays a crucial part in this process. It starts with a brand logo, such as the Nike 'Swoosh' (the tick). This makes products recognisable in a shop and when worn. In many cases there are other key characteristics. As a Merc sweeps past, it is usually recognisable without seeing the badge on the bonnet. Its designers try to keep all Mercs looking as if they are from the same family of cars.

A well-designed product will stand out from the crowd and will make the user take pride in using it/wearing it. That will help in achieving product differentiation.

> *'Profit in business comes from repeat customers, customers that boast about your product and service, and that bring friends with them.'*
>
> **W. Edwards Deming, quality guru**

Research and development

Every business needs to think about how to do things better and to make better things. This is where R&D becomes important. The R stands for Research. This does not mean market research. It is scientific research, such as James Seddon with his soft-polymer plastics. In effect, it is white-coat, laboratory science – experiments with new materials or chemicals. The D stands for Development. Engineers are needed to take a new idea and then see how it could be put into practice. This involves designing the machines to make the product and designing the factory to produce it.

Today there is increasingly tough competition from abroad, especially for producing low-cost goods. Clever firms try to keep one or two steps ahead by inventing new ways of working. Spending on R&D helps in this process.

Research and development

Conclusion

It is hard to run a business if competition is too direct or too fierce. A business has fixed overhead costs such as rent and salaries, so enthusiastic price-cutting by a competitor is very threatening. If you cannot make money at the prices being charged in the marketplace, you may be driven out of business.

This is why every firm wants to be differentiated from its rivals. Design is an important way to achieve this. It can give customers what they want – stylish, modern but practical products – yet at the same time give the producer what it wants – a degree of security.

Revision Essentials

Aesthetics – appeals to the senses, such as products that look, smell or feel good.

Patent – registering a new way of making something, so that no one can copy the idea for 20 years.

Exercises ✔

(20 marks; 20 minutes)

Read the unit, then ask yourself:

1 Briefly explain how James Seddon made use of these factors to help design the Eggxactly egg cooker: an understanding of science, an understanding of the market. (5)

2 What is the importance in product design of 'economic manufacture'? (3)

3 Discuss how McDonald's might use the design mix to help it develop a new 'Olympian Burger' for 2012. (6)

4 How can design be used to differentiate:

   a a pair of Diesel jeans from other brands on the market. (3)

   b a bottle of Tesco shampoo from one from Sainsbury's. (3)

Practice Questions

The portable high chair – Totseat

Edinburgh company Totseat has developed an innovative fabric highchair. Founding Director Rachel Jones came up with the original Totseat idea after her own experiences as a mother.

But to develop Totseat's design to perfection, she conducted extensive testing and research with several other families. 'The first Totseat prototype was made from the lining of my wedding dress and the second from a sheet,' says Jones. 'Nineteen versions later, and after more

Totseat

than 900 testing experiences, Totseat was born.'

The detailed research process, which majored on safety and adaptability, revealed that parents wanted to be able to take their babies to any cafe or restaurant, not just to 'child-friendly' places.

Fabric highseats have been around since the 1950s but were far from perfect – the Totseat meets the needs of parents who want something easy to use and adaptable for every shape and size of chair. Parents also asked for a product that was compact, comfortable, durable, washable, stylish and, above all, safe for their children to sit in.

Taking the time and effort to understand the needs of customers to evolve the product's design has paid off, with leading UK and European retailers, including John Lewis and Mothercare, now selling Totseats. The product also recently won the Grand Prix at the Scottish Design Awards.

(Source: Design Council website: www.design-council.org.uk)

Questions

(20 marks; 20 minutes)

1 Explain why a mother might have confidence that Totseat will work effectively. (4)

2 Is it possible for a business to take too much time and care over design? Explain your answer. (4)

3 Outline two key elements in Rachel Jones's approach to designing Totseat's product range. (4)

4 Totseat products are now distributed in more than 100 shops in Britain. Discuss the importance of design in this success story. (8)

Managing stock

Why stock management is difficult

In early December 2006 the Nintendo Wii was launched in Britain. The **stock** of 50,000 units was sold out within 12 hours, leaving thousands of gamers disappointed. Without stock, sales cannot happen. So manufacturers and **retailers** have to make sure they supply the right amount of goods to keep the shelves full.

Yet simply ordering lots of stock carries other risks. In September 2006 Honda hired 700 extra staff at its Swindon factory. It wanted to increase production of its new CV-R 4x4. Two years later, plunging car sales meant that Honda had far too many CV-Rs in stock. To cut stocks it cut production in December 2008. Full-time staff kept their

Stock of 50,000 Nintendo Wii units was sold out within 12 hours

jobs, but more than 200 temporary staff were put out of work.

As consumers, we are hugely demanding and quite intolerant. We expect to find every product we are looking for in stock, whenever we want it. Yet the retailers have to find a balance between too little stock and too much. If all they do is keep masses of stock of every item, their costs will be too high to stay in business. As shown in the figure below, even Britain's top supermarket chains struggle to achieve 100 per cent stock availability.

> *'Why should a customer wait weeks if he can buy from someone else's shelf?'*
> **Anon**

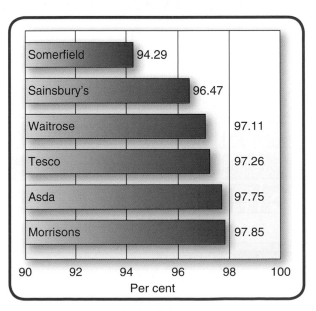

Stock problems at Britain's leading supermarket: shelf availability of stock, Jan-Dec 2006 (Reproduced by permission of *The Grocer*, © William Reed Publishing 2006)

Stock graphs

Successful stock management requires the right balance between reliability and cost. Too little stock and customers can be let down. Too much stock and high costs will force high prices (or losses and potential closure).

The traditional approach is shown in the graph below. It illustrates how stock levels should ideally be maintained. It is based on three things:

1 The level of demand for the product. If it's a popular item, plenty will need to be kept in stock and orders for fresh supplies may have to be sent regularly.

2 A decision on the right level of buffer stock. This is the minimum amount of stock the manager thinks should be held at all times. For example, a busy sweetshop might like to keep a minimum of one box of Cadbury Dairy Milk in stock (48 bars) as customers expect to always find it on the counter.

3 A decision on how often to order from the supplier, e.g. weekly or monthly. A monthly order would be four times the size of a weekly order and might therefore provide bulk-buying benefits.

Take, for example, the management of stocks of Heinz beans at Bob's Grocery. He has steady sales of 20 cans a week and likes to buy four boxes of beans at a time, each containing 20 cans. This is because when he buys four boxes his supplier gives him an extra 10 per cent discount. He chooses to keep a minimum of 10 cans in stock at all times (his buffer stock).

The bar gate stock graph below shows how the delivery of 80 cans pushes his stock up from 10 to 90. Then, as shoppers steadily buy the cans, stock slips down from 90 to 70, then down to 50, then 30, then 10. At this point he needs a new batch of 80 cans, which pushes the stock back up to 90. As long as customers keep buying 20 cans a week and the supplier delivers on time, this process will go on working smoothly.

Graphs such as this one are built into the scanning software used by many shops. When the barcode scanner shows that stocks

A busy sweetshop might like to keep a minimum of one box of Cadbury Dairy Milk in stock (48 bars)

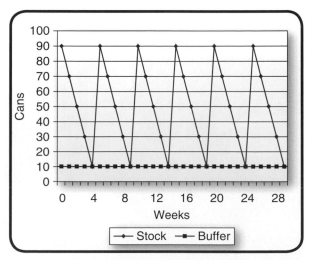

Bar gate stock graph for Heinz beans at Bob's Grocery

of baked beans have fallen to ten tins, it can either flash a warning to the shopkeeper or reorder automatically from the supplier.

Just In Time

Buffer stocks help ensure that customers always find what they want on the shelf. Yet they not only cost money, they also use up space. Ten years ago, a supermarket might have used up 20 per cent of its floor space in stockrooms. These rooms were closed off from the public, just holding stocks. Tesco was one of the first stores to recognise that this was a terrible waste. Why not turn the stock room into an extra sales floor, perhaps to stock non-food items such as clothes?

So Tesco started insisting that suppliers should deliver more frequently, but in smaller quantities. Therefore there was less need for a big storage room. Furthermore it started using 'Just In Time' (JIT). This means ordering extra supplies 'just in time' before the old supplies run out. In other words it does away with a buffer stock. Tesco believes it is so efficient that it does not need a buffer. It will order the right quantities at the right time. The table on page 269 shows that even Britain's most successful retailer runs out of stock from time to time (2.74 per cent of the time, to be precise). Yet clearly its managers find that the benefits of Just In Time outweigh the costs of lower customer satisfaction.

Conclusion

Managing stocks is difficult to get right. All it takes is for Jamie Oliver to mention 'pukka Thai noodles' one night on TV and the shelves of Britain will be empty by 10 a.m. the next day. If a business sets its sights on providing fantastic customer service, it may need to set high buffer stocks to ensure that no shelf is ever empty. If, however, the business (like Primark, Aldi or Lidl) is focused on low prices and low stocks, a JIT system may be needed to keep costs down. Different firms have different needs and therefore different policies.

Advantages and disadvantages of Just In Time

Advantages of JIT	Disadvantages of JIT
Eliminating buffer stocks cuts storage space, allowing more sales space.	A greater risk of running out of stock and therefore disappointing customers.
Low stocks and frequent supplier deliveries mean fresher produce.	Buying smaller quantities more often means losing out on bulk-buying discounts.
Less of the business's capital is tied up in stocks.	Any mistake or misjudgement could cause out-of-stocks and poorer customer service.

All it takes is for Jamie Oliver to mention pukka Thai noodles one night on TV and the shelves of Britain will be empty by 10 a.m. the next day

Revision Essentials

Buffer (stock) – the minimum stock level held at all times to avoid running out.

Retailers – businesses that sell goods to the public, i.e. shops.

Stock(s) – items held by a firm for use or sale, e.g. components for manufacturing, or sellable products for a retailer.

Exercises

(35 marks; 35 minutes)

Read the unit, then ask yourself:

1 Look at the the bar chart on page 269 and answer these questions:

   a Which supermarket ran out of stock 2.15 per cent of the time? (1)

   b Which supermarket ran out of stock 5.71 per cent of the time? (1)

   c What impact might this have on customers' loyalty to each of these stores? (4)

2 Outline one reason why a small grocer's shop might set:

   a a low buffer stock for fresh grapes (2)

   b a high buffer stock for Cadbury's Creme Eggs. (2)

3 Look at the the bar gate stock graph on page 270 and answer these questions:

   a In what way does the graph show that Bob wants to keep ten cans in stock at all times? (1)

   b What is the maximum number of cans of beans held in stock? (1)

   c Explain what the graph would show if Bob's supplier forgot to deliver the 80 tins of beans. (5)

4 Give two reasons why a factory owner might be worried about ordering raw materials on a JIT basis. (2)

5 Take one of the disadvantages of JIT shown in the table on page 271. Explain how it might affect sales at

   a a shoe shop in a busy shopping centre (3)

   b The Manchester United Club Shop, Old Trafford. (3)

6 Each week, the mobile phone shop at Meadowhall, Sheffield sells 90 Nokia phones. It receives its supplies from Nokia at the end of each four-week period. Nokia requires two weeks' notice for delivery, i.e. the order must be placed two weeks before the

delivery is required. The phone shop likes to have a minimum stock level of 40 Nokia phones.

a   Onto the graph below, draw the firm's buffer stock level. (1)

b   Draw a graph plotting the shop's stocks of Nokia phones. The shop starts with 400 units at the start of the month. Use the axes set out below. (6)

c   Label the graph carefully. (3)

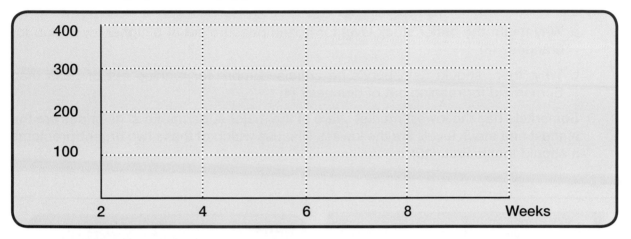

Practice Questions

Caught short

Supermarkets have been running out of basic items in the run-up to Christmas. Shoppers have found staples such as bread and milk missing from shelves, according to a survey released yesterday. It found that stock levels at the big six – Tesco, Sainsbury's, Asda, Morrisons, Somerfield and Waitrose – have deteriorated over the past six months. The survey, by *The Grocer* magazine, was based on weekly checks on the availability and price of 33 commonly purchased items.

The magazine's Gaele Walker said: 'Availability levels in the UK's top six supermarkets have plummeted over the past six months. Somerfield's performance was by far the weakest, with 48 "out-of-stocks" – 22 more than previously.' Items missing from Somerfield's shelves over the past 26 weeks included apple juice, oranges, Wall's sausages, Cathedral City cheddar and Andrex toilet tissue.

Sainsbury's was out of 30 staples over the same period including frozen peas, four-pint containers of semi-skimmed milk and baguettes. The top three chains, in order, were Morrison's, which was out of 18 products, Asda and Tesco.

The survey yielded some good news for Asda which was found to be the cheapest of the chains for the cost of buying the 33 basic items. Tesco ranked second, with Morrisons and Sainsbury's vying for third place. Most expensive were Somerfield and Waitrose.

(Source: Sean Poulter, *Daily Mail*, 18 December 2006)

Questions

(20 marks; 25 minutes)

1 Explain the meaning of the term 'stock levels'. (3)

2 Somerfield ran out of oranges while Sainsbury's ran short of frozen peas.

a Why might the buffer stock level for frozen peas be set at a higher level than for oranges? (3)

b Why, then, should Sainsbury's be criticised more for running out of peas than Somerfield for running out of oranges? (4)

3 Somerfield has the lowest market share of the major supermarkets. Its prices are the highest and stock levels are the lowest. Discuss which of these two urgent problems it should tackle first. (10)

Practice Questions

Sloppy stock management

On 8 January 2007 photographic retailer Jessops announced that Christmas sales were 6.9 per cent down on the year before. It blamed 'supply shortages' of popular Canon and Nikon SLR digital cameras.

A few months before, the company had trumpeted a 53 per cent increase in sales of these cameras. So how could it have run out in the crucial pre-Christmas period?

There are three possible reasons for running out of stock:

• an overly-cautious sales forecast, meaning ordering too little stock

Jessops

• setting the buffer stock too low

• being let down by suppliers, failing to deliver as promised.

In its announcement, Jessops tried to suggest that the problem was caused by the manufacturers. Inevitably, the managers did not say: 'It was our fault, we kept our stock levels too low.'

Whatever the cause, the results are clear:

- Jessops' profits would be hit (some reports said by as much as £2 million)
- Disappointed customers would remember that Jessops cannot be relied upon to provide the top-selling product lines.

Nothing smacks more of sloppy retail management than running out of stock.

Questions

(20 marks; 25 minutes)

1 Jessops' managers knew that sales of SLR digital cameras were 53 per cent up in the first half of the year. How should they have used this information when ordering stocks for the Christmas period? (2)

2 Outline two ways customers may react to being disappointed by Jessops. (4)

3 a What is meant by the term 'buffer stock'? (2)

   b Examine the possible effect on Jessops of 'setting the buffer stock too low'. (4)

4 Discuss whether Jessops should move to a 'just-in-time' method of stock management. (8)

Managing quality

Introduction

Quality is the ultimate test of a business organisation. Do customers who arrive or phone or email have a positive experience? For producers of goods, quality is about practical matters such as reliability. For service businesses, quality is often about personal things such as polite staff.

Hitachi recently increased the **warranty** period on its personal computers from one to three years. A new quality management system gave it the confidence to do this. Customers, of course, were delighted – boosting sales and market share.

With restaurants, quality is partly to do with the product (is it well cooked and served hot?) but also to do with the service: are staff friendly, well trained and on the customer's side? A customer who leaves feeling angry will never return; even a weakly positive response may not be enough. To return, we have to be thrilled. Customers should be delighted, not just satisfied.

Quality control

Many firms regard quality as a management issue, to be controlled by careful systems. Managers may put in place practices such as:

> ### Talking Point
>
> Over the past few weeks, what was your worst and what was your best consumer experience of quality?

- factory inspectors at the end of a production line, who check every fifth car or carpet before it's sent to the customer; if several cars fail to start, they might decide to check the whole day's output; any faults found are corrected

- a 100 per cent inspection system, just as Gordon Ramsay does in his restaurants: the head chef checks every plate before it's sent to the high-paying customers; if the steak is slightly burnt, Ramsay throws away the whole plate of food and demands that his chefs start again

- a feedback system, such as a customer feedback questionnaire, which you might find in a hotel room or be given at an airport. This is a check on the final experience enjoyed or suffered by the customer.

A customer feedback questionnaire is one system of quality control

The problem all these systems share is that they rarely feel part of the life of the worker. A car worker who is putting left front doors on Minis all day long cannot even see the end of the line where the inspectors are checking the quality. Similarly, the hotel cleaning staff do not see the feedback questionnaire responses – indeed they may rarely see a hotel guest. Only in the Ramsay kitchen does the chef see his cooking thrown away in disgust by an angry head chef.

Most systems of **quality control**, therefore, are flawed. They try to put a lid on a problem rather than solve it. They work on the basis of 'acceptable' quality. In effect, they accept that staff will not think much about quality, therefore the managers have to 'sort it out'.

> '*It is quality rather than quantity that matters.*'
> **Publilius Syrus, Roman writer 42 BC**

Quality culture

In the ideal business, quality is fundamental to everyone's attitude to work. If you're going to an ice cream parlour, what you want is someone behind the counter who delights in offering you free samples of 'two terrific new flavours' – and enjoys building up the ice cream on the cone to make it look great. When you go to Next, you want the staff to really help you find something that fits well, rather than look frustrated when you don't buy the first couple of things you try on. Ideally, everyone would be enjoying their job of serving you.

Business **culture** means the general attitudes and behaviours among staff within a workplace. Years ago, the Arsenal dressing room was famous for a hard-drinking, hard-gambling culture. Then came new boss Arsene Wenger, who steadily transformed the culture to a passion for sporting excellence, rather than excess. Successful businesses ensure that a quality culture develops among staff. This would come from pride in the business and what it does for its customers.

In Japan, Toyota recruits only graduates for its factory floor jobs. It wants engineers who gain experience of what car production is all about before they get promoted to supervisory or management jobs. Toyota wants its workers to spend their days thinking about how the process can be made more efficient and how quality can be improved. In this way, Toyota has risen to overtake Ford as the world's second biggest car producer – and from 2007 it became the world's Number One. The culture of quality that is famous at Toyota (and Honda) has helped these Japanese companies dominate quality surveys in America and Britain for years.

JD Power 2008 UK car customer satisfaction index

Top 5	Bottom 5
1 (Best) Lexus	1 (Worst) Fiat
2 Skoda (Volkswagen)	2 Mitsubishi
2 Honda	3 Chevrolet
4 Toyota	4 Kia
5 Jaguar	5 Citroen

How to develop a culture of quality

When Tim Waterstone started the Waterstone's bookshops, his aim was to create a bookstore run by people passionate about books, able to influence the range at the stores they ran. Today's Waterstone's offers staff similar opportunities to tailor their range to suit local demand and interests. Booksellers are encouraged to highlight their own favourite books in-store, to create their own themed promotions and their own busy, interesting and entertaining events programme.

The children's books section of a
Waterstone's bookstore

This approach was brilliant because quality
develops when staff get satisfaction from
their jobs. If they believe in what they are
doing, believe in the products they are selling
and care about their customers, quality has
arrived.

To develop a quality culture, new staff
must learn from the start about the high
standards expected from everyone. Those
standards must be set every day by every
manager, so that no one doubts that they
are real. If a customer returns an ice cream
that was melted and then refrozen, a good
manager will check the rest of the batch and
if she or he finds them all ruined, will take
them all off sale. This sets the standard for
all staff.

In a school, a quality culture will be seen
in a staffroom where teachers talk about the
successes of the students – on the hockey
pitch or in the classroom. In other schools,
staff moan about the students or talk about
anything other than work.

> 'They didn't want it good. They wanted it
> Thursday.'
> **Ronald Reagan, former movie actor
> and US President, talking about early
> movie producers he had worked for**

Quality assurance

Although the best businesses create a high
quality culture, this cannot be achieved overnight. If staff treat customers as an inconven-
ience, the short-term solution may be to use
quality assurance. Whereas quality control
is a system of checking at the end, quality
assurance attempts to build quality into the
system. In other words, every member of
staff has quality responsibilities. These are
set out on paper, often in detail. In this way,
everyone knows exactly what they must contribute towards quality.

Job Role	Quality Assurance Task
Car factory worker responsible for fitting windscreens	Must test every fitted windscreen for two minutes by spraying water to check that the screen is air- and water-tight
Hospital nurse going round each evening to give sleeping pills to patients who need them	Keeping careful records of who took what and when, e.g. recording 'I saw Mrs J take her two aspirins at 20.40'
GCSE teacher	Must test students once every three weeks to ensure that new subject knowledge is understood; records of test results must be kept

A hospital nurse's quality assurance task may be to record the medication that patients have been given

The hope is that, over time, making individuals responsible for quality will ensure better results. Once staff see quality as their personal responsibility, they may see ways to do things even better. Then a system of quality assurance can build into a quality culture.

Conclusion

High quality is achieved by providing an efficient service: the right product of the right quality at the right time – with a human face. This is hard to attain 100 per cent of the time because mistakes happen. The best way to achieve it is to establish a culture of quality based on motivated staff who care about the customers and about the company's reputation.

Once the culture is established, further quality controls may not be necessary. For example, if a fully qualified surgeon is carrying out an operation, no one else will peer over his or her shoulder to check on the quality. He or she is trusted. However, at Gordon Ramsay restaurants and at Toyota car factories, further inspections are carried out to make 100 per cent sure that the quality is spot on. So a combination of quality culture and quality control is probably the best of all worlds.

Revision Essentials

Culture – 'the way we do things round here', in other words the accepted attitudes and practices of staff at a workplace.

Quality control – putting measures in place to check that the customer receives an acceptable level of quality.

Warranty – the guarantee by the producer that it will repair any faults in a product for a specific period of time – usually one year.

Exercises

(20 marks; 20 minutes)

Read the unit, then ask yourself:

1 Explain how 'customer delight' might affect a firm's sales. (3)

2 Outline one possible weakness in a quality control system based on factory inspectors checking a sample of the finished product before it's sent to customers. (2)

3 MG Rover went out of business in early 2005, after years of a worsening reputation for quality. How may that reputation have affected the business? (3)

4 At school, you and your parents are 'customers'. Outline one example of good and one example of poor quality service that you or your parents experience from the school. (5)

5 Explain why highly motivated staff are more likely to deliver high-quality service. (3)

6 Would a system of quality control or quality assurance be better for:

a Boeing, which manufactures passenger aeroplanes (2)

b Mars, which produces chocolate bars. (2)

Practice Questions

Toyota production

The cornerstone of Toyota's quality control system is the role of the team members in the production process. The principles on which Toyota was founded are employed at the Georgetown plant, USA.

Toyota involves its team members by:

● encouraging an active role in quality control

● utilising employee ideas and opinions in production processes

● striving for constant improvement (called kaizen in Japan).

New-product planning emphasises a product that is as defect-free as possible. In other words, Toyota designs quality into the automobile. Then Toyota's quality control during production ensures that the correct materials and parts are used and fitted with precision and accuracy. This effort is combined with thousands of rigorous inspections performed by team members during the production process.

Team members on the line are responsible for the parts they use. They are inspectors for their own work and that of co-workers. When a problem on any vehicle is spotted, any team member can pull a rope – called an andon cord – strung along the assembly line to halt production. Only when the problem is resolved is the line restarted. This process involves every team member in monitoring and checking the quality of every car produced.

Questions

(20 marks; 25 minutes)

1 a Identify three ways in which Toyota is ensuring high-quality output. (3)

   b Briefly outline the benefits of these methods to Toyota customers. (3)

2 From this text explain how Toyota may be benefiting from the high-quality standards it achieves. (6)

3 Discuss whether Toyota's quality management at Georgetown is based upon quality control or a quality culture. (8)

Cost-effective operations

In early 2007 Ford of America announced that it planned to cut its US costs by £1000 per car. This would involve cutting 14,000 office jobs and closing 16 factories. The total cost saving aimed to be more than £2500 million per year. This became necessary because Ford's sales had been slipping for some years, pushing the company into huge losses. The rise of Toyota and the fall in sales of Ford's gas-guzzling trucks were largely to blame.

Even companies as massive as Ford have to make sure that they keep costs low enough to be competitive. If Toyota is offering a luxurious, fuel-efficient family car for $18,000 (about £9500), Ford has to make sure that its production costs are low enough to do the same. If it costs Ford $20,000 to make each car, everything it sells will be at a loss.

The same is true for a local builder. If he has to charge £1000 for building a wall but a rival can do it for £700, there is only one possible result: the more expensive builder must either give up or find a way to operate at a lower cost.

> 'The three most important things right now are costs, costs and costs. And costs can be summed up in one word: productivity.'
> **Financial analyst,** *New York Times*

Keeping costs down

What are the costs involved in building a brick wall?

1. **Materials**: bricks and cement. These must be ordered in the right quantity and at the lowest prices available from suppliers.

2. **Other costs directly involved**: hiring a cement mixer for a day or two; hiring a skip for the building waste.

3. **Labour**: this is a function of the amount of work involved, the hourly wage of the workers and the productivity of those workers.

4. **Fixed costs**: the fixed costs of the management time taken to win the order, supervise the work and deal with office administration.

The costs of building a wall may include: bricks and cement; the cost of hiring a cement mixer and of hiring a skip for the building waste

To keep costs to the minimum, careful ordering of materials and other supplies is very important. Every business, though, will be trying to buy at the lowest price and making sure not to buy more than is needed to complete a job. Therefore cost savings through purchasing are rarely crucial.

Far more important is good management of labour costs. Labour costs per hour vary dramatically in different parts of the world (see the table below). The figures show that, in 2006, a firm could employ 32 workers in India for every one in Britain. Even within the European Union the differences can be stark, with new entrant Romania having average earnings that are less than one tenth of the British level.

Weekly average earnings* (based on 40-hour weeks)

Germany	£505
Britain	£485
South Korea	£325
Czech Republic	£100
Romania	£45
China (in towns)	£23
India	£15
*Median average earnings Source: Federation of European Employers, April 2006	

> 'People are most productive in small teams . . . and the freedom to solve their own problems.'
> **John Rollwagen, CEO, Cray Research**

For companies to keep employing workers in Britain, they must find a way to get value out of the high wages being paid. This could come about if British workers have skills that cannot be found elsewhere – for example, the ability to write computer games or deal in foreign exchange. Or people can be worth the money they are paid if they are highly productive; in other words they produce a lot of work in the time they are employed. This means having high productivity.

Gavin is a bricklayer. He can lay 800 bricks in a day and is paid £120 per day. His friend John is a builder who is skilled at many different tasks (plastering, flooring, carpentry), but he can only lay 400 bricks a day. So, if both are paid £120 for a day's work:

	Pay	Output	Labour cost per brick
Gavin	£120	800	15p (£120/800 = £0.15)
John	£120	400	30p

Labour costs per unit depend upon productivity

Productivity is efficiency, usually measured as output per person. In this case, Gavin is twice as productive as John, therefore John is twice as expensive to hire, from the point of view of a company. High productivity enables the labour cost to be spread across lots of output. Low productivity (John) means higher labour costs per unit.

Productivity differences can be much bigger than this. In 1999, Renault bought the Romanian car business Dacia. It employed

27,000 people and made 110,000 cars a year. In the same year the Nissan factory in Sunderland, UK, was producing 270,000 cars with just 2750 people. Therefore the productivity difference was:

	Staff	Output (cars)	Productivity (cars per worker per year)
Dacia	27,000	110,000	4 cars per year
Nissan	2750	270,000	98 cars per year

Even at the much lower wage rates in Romania, it was far better value to manufacture cars in Britain. Since 1999, of course, Renault has set out to change this.

In general, higher productivity is one of the keys to success when up against competition. Ways of increasing productivity include:

● investing in up-to-date machinery to help workers work faster, or to replace them with **automated** equipment or robots

● encouraging workers to work more enthusiastically and therefore harder and faster; this can be achieved through improved morale and motivation

● encouraging staff to work smarter – to come up with new ways to do things more effectively. Toyota says it receives more than 100,000 employee suggestions per year.

> 'The best way to have a good idea is to have a lot of ideas.'
> **Linus Pauling, Nobel prize winner**

Keeping the business competitive

If high **productivity** keeps costs per unit down, a firm can compete. As shown in the following figure, if Ryanair cuts its prices, easyJet can compete, but British Airways will struggle. Ryanair and British Airways carry a similar number of passengers – but BA has staff costs that are nearly 20 times higher!

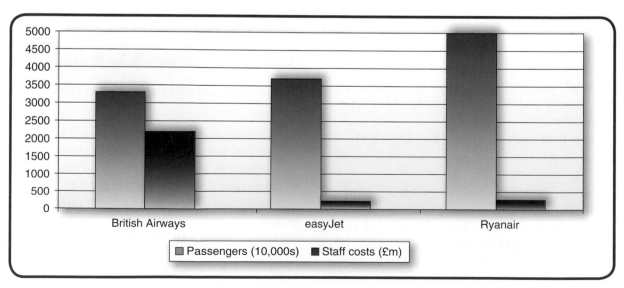

Passenger numbers compared with staffing costs. Source: Annual Report and Accounts 2007/2008 for these three companies

Conclusion

A well-managed business keeps a careful eye on efficiency. This is especially important for firms competing with overseas suppliers. While France and Germany may have higher wage costs than Britain, many other countries have remarkably low-cost workforces. In the long run, every country, every company and every employee in Britain will need to be a bit special to keep successful.

Revision Essentials

Automated – processes that are fully carried out by machinery rather than people.

Productivity – efficiency, measured by output per worker per hour.

Exercises

(20 marks; 20 minutes)

Read the unit, then ask yourself:

1   Toyota can sell a car for $18,000 that costs Ford $20,000 to make. In this situation, how might productivity improvements help Ford? (3)

2   a Bartex Ltd, a small lighting factory, employs 150 staff and has a monthly output of 180,000 lamps. What is the factory's monthly productivity? (3)

   b A rival based in Hull pays similar wages and has monthly productivity of 1500 lamps. Outline two ways this might affect Bartex. (4)

3   Gavin is twice as productive as John. Give three possible reasons why this may be the case. (3)

4   Explain how improved staff motivation might affect productivity. (3)

5   Outline two ways in which Renault may have tried to improve productivity at Dacia since 1999. (4)

Practice Questions

The plastic microchip

Plastic Logic's factory in Dresden, Germany

In January 2007 Plastic Logic, a company originally founded in Cambridge, announced that it was setting up a US$ 100 million factory in Dresden. The factory would be the world's first producer of e-paper (electronic paper) displays made from plastic rather than silicon on glass. The factory was expected to employ 140 people by the time it went into full production In 2009.

But why would a company that started with an invention that came from Cambridge University set up its factory in Germany? Plastic Logic considered a number of other locations, including Singapore and New York State, but chose Dresden, in part, because of its large skilled workforce.

Wage rates are higher in Germany than in Singapore or Britain, but the city has a network of over 200 semi-conductor companies, creating a large pool of highly skilled and very committed workers.

When Plastic Logic's factory opened in September 2008, the company's managing director praised 'the ingenuity, dedication and tireless efforts' of its employees.

Questions

(20 marks; 20 minutes)

1. What is meant by the term 'productivity'? (2)

2. Explain how productivity will be affected by staff being highly skilled and very committed. (6)

3. Explain why high productivity can make high wages more affordable for an employer. (6)

4. Discuss whether the owners of Plastic Logic should be paid by the British government to keep the factory and jobs in Britain. (6)

Effective customer service

It had already been an unlucky day for four teenage Wigan supporters on 13 January 2007. Chelsea had just beaten their team 4–0, with the Wigan defence handing out presents like a bunch of Santas. Then they missed the Supporters' Club coach home from Stamford Bridge and were left with hardly a penny between them. They sat down and wept. Fortunately the Wigan players saw them, had a whip round which collected over £200, and sent them home to Lancashire. That's customer service.

This marked a big turn-round for the club. Just two months before, manager Paul Jewell had criticised the fans for staying away. Home attendances had slumped. Then the club started to talk to its supporters (the customers). For the pre-Christmas home game against Chelsea the ticket price was halved to £15 – and the ground was packed. With loud support behind them, Wigan were unlucky to lose 3–2. The Boxing Day derby against Blackburn saw ticket prices move back up and attendance slump by 7000.

By early January, though, the club realised that some ticket prices had to be cut down to £15 (Portsmouth, West Ham and Middlesbrough) and others to £20 (Newcastle and Spurs). The club was finally providing an effective customer service.

To be effective, customer service must be:

- rooted in a clear understanding of what customers really care about
- practical and cost-effective enough to ensure that it can be kept going regularly
- based on a genuine wish to help, rather than the attempt to seem helpful
- offered at the right time in the right way at the right place.

> 'People perform best, and give the best customer service, when they like what they do.'
> **Source: unknown**

Wigan Athletic football club

Making it efficient

Good customer service is designed for the customer, not the company. It is efficient because it works well, works quickly and gives the customer the sense of being cared for. A call to the school is answered by the school secretary who knows that the head is out today. With bad service, a call puts you into a voicemail loop and you wait several minutes listening to tinny 1970s' music. Only then do you get through to someone at a call centre 25 – or 10,000 – miles away. That person knows nothing about the school, or the head teacher.

Efficient service:

- gets products to you exactly when you want them

- in good condition. . .

- . . . but if there is something wrong, it will be sorted as soon as possible and in the right spirit (if you leave a jacket in a shop, it would be great for them to contact you, instead of you having to figure out which shop you left it in).

Good service may cost the customer extra, but that is fine as long as it represents value for money.

Good customer service must relate to what customers want and what they are willing to pay for. A discounted 'Upper Class' flight on Virgin Atlantic to New York costs £2,800 return. This is about ten times the cost of a standard class ticket. For that you get a seat that doubles as a bed, an on-board massage and better food. It is hard to see that this *can* be value for money – yet some people (or their companies) are happy to pay it.

Ryanair, meanwhile, offers no 'customer service'. Boss Michael O'Leary boasts his contempt for the way most airlines offer service frills rather than the real thing. If you put 'Ryanair customer service' into Google you get over 400,000 items. Most are hostile about the 'scrum to get a seat', 'not even a cup of tea', or 'charging you to put a bag on the plane!' O'Leary, though, would point to some important facts. Ryanair is Europe's

most punctual airline. If all you want is to get cheaply, quickly and efficiently to Spain and back, Ryanair is for you, as you can see in the table below.

Airline punctuality January–September 2008

Percentage of planes arriving more than one hour late	
Ryanair	2.7%
British Airways	8.6%
easyJet	5.7%
Virgin Atlantic	12.9%

Bad customer service

In the past, bad customer service was sloppy because it risked losing a customer. These days, YouTube and many other websites have made bad service potentially suicidal. If the family is going out for a birthday restaurant meal, mum or dad will probably check out www.toptable.co.uk. A glance at the 'latest reviews' posted by customers shows up a September 2008 review of a London restaurant called *La Spiga*: 'Service was a little brusque and food below average. My plate was also dirty. Not a great experience.'

Word of mouth is always an important factor, as people love to talk about their holiday or eating-out disasters and successes. Today, though, the internet has made it so

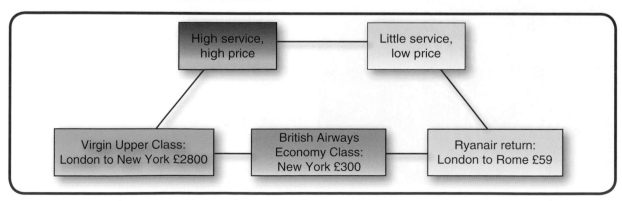

Flight companies flow chart

The internet has made it quicker and easier for bad news to spread

much quicker and easier for bad news to spread.

Staff need to be trained not only to provide good service but also how to cope when things go wrong – what to do when the steak ordered well-done has been left, bloody, on the plate (quietly apologise, say it won't be charged for and offer a free alternative). Intelligent, generous service can turn a disaster into a bit of a triumph, with the customer going away really impressed.

'There is only one boss: the customer. And he can fire everyone in the company, from the chairman on down, simply by spending his money somewhere else.'
Sam Walton, founder of the multi-billion retailer, Wal-Mart

Customer service and repeat purchase

For the business, the reason to provide great customer service is because it keeps customers coming back. In business, nothing beats repeat purchase. It can cost a lot of money to persuade someone to try something new. Advertisers believe that people need to see a TV commercial at least five times before it has an effect on attitudes. Five national TV commercials on ITV can easily cost £400,000. So it is madness to risk losing these people through poor service.

Some families return year after year to the same hotel, in Brighton or Biarritz. They like to feel confident that they will always be welcomed and always served well. Some go to the same pub because the staff are always friendly. Repeat custom adds to revenue, cuts marketing costs and therefore can multiply profits.

Exercises

(20 marks; 25 minutes)

Read the unit, then ask yourself:

1 Explain the importance of:

  a rooting customer service 'in a clear understanding of what customers really care about'. (4)

  b designing customer service 'for the customer, not the company'. (4)

2 Explain how Ryanair might be said to provide good customer service. (4)

3   You and your family are spending a night at a hotel in Scotland, as there is a family wedding the following day. You get there, tired and hungry, to be told by the receptionist: 'No, we have no record of a booking in your name. And all we have is one single room. You'll have to squeeze in there ... and the restaurant closes in ten minutes, so you'd better be quick.'

  a Outline two faults in the quality of the receptionist's service (4)

  b Outline two possible impacts on the hotel that may be a result of this incident. (4)

Practice Questions

A newly arrived visitor found an infestation of flies, mosquitoes and frogs

In June 2006 *HolidayTravelWatch* had to deal with a mass of complaints about the Miramar holiday resort in Obzor, Bulgaria. It is used extensively by Britain's biggest tour operator, Thomson Holidays.

The problems began at the end of June, when serious flooding caused the sewage system to fail. Holidaymakers were evacuated so the mess could be cleared up, but the same people were returned to the hotel a few days later. One report from a holidaymaker said that 'the swimming pool was full of sludge and it was difficult to find the exact position of the pool because of the extent of the flooding'. A newly arrived visitor 'could not understand why everything seemed damp and he has reported finding an infestation of flies, mosquitoes and frogs on the balcony of his room'.

Over the following months, there were repeated complaints about stomach bugs requiring medical treatment. Despite many protests, travellers were advised by the tour operator that their health problems stemmed from an 'airborne virus' and that the hotel had passed its health and safety check.

The Managing Director of the *HolidayTravelWatch* website later said: 'This major tour operator appears to have ignored the common sense approach to this problem. Instead of abandoning the hotel and taking care of their customers, they have compounded the problem by adding fresh holiday victims to this appalling situation.'

In January 2007, the hotel was still being promoted by Thomson Holidays, describing it as 'opulent'.

(Source: adapted from www.holidaytravelwatch.com)

Questions

(20 marks; 25 minutes)

1 Examine one reason why this tour operator might have acted in the way it did. (4)

2 Discuss how the tour operator should have handled the situation following the flooding. (8)

3 Examine the possible longer-term effects of these events upon the tour operator. (8)

Consumer protection

Starting a business is easy. You just let the Inland Revenue know, then get on with it. Turning it into a meaningful, long-term investment, though, is harder. You have to build a base of loyal customers who want to spend their money with you.

When Manchester City were relegated twice, ending up playing Carlisle instead of Chelsea, 30,000 supporters turned up every week. And kept buying the shirts, the scarves and the pies. A hairdresser needs the same, so even if you're a bit disappointed with one haircut, you return a month later. Fundamentally, you see it as *your* hairdresser.

If all businesses worked this way, we would not need laws to protect the consumer. Unfortunately, it is not quite like that. Although many small firms do their best to build customer loyalty, others are not so careful.

This might be for the following reasons:

- The business is in a **monopoly** position, i.e. it has no competition and therefore becomes sloppy. Hygiene standards at a college canteen might slacken, with customers moaning but still buying – until an outbreak of food poisoning.

- A large business in a competitive market allows its ethical standards to slip, i.e. managers make decisions that could not be defended morally.

- Individual business owners get greedy and are unable to resist an opportunity to make big profits in the short term.

On 18 December 2006, Julie's Restaurant in posh Holland Park, London, was fined £7500 for swindling famous customers such as Kate Moss, Kylie Minogue and U2. The menu had boasted of 'organic, marinated roast chicken', 'organic sausages' and 'organic lamb'. But it was a lie. Environmental health officers found that none of the meat sold in the restaurant over a two-month period was organic. During October and November 2005 the restaurant had saved itself £4186 just on the chicken. As *The Independent* newspaper put it: they 'bought cheap meat and pocketed the change'. A local councillor said: 'Customers have a right to receive what is advertised on the menu. For many visitors to the restaurant, this has led to a betrayal of lifestyle.'

Julie's Restaurant was fined £7500 for falsely claiming to use organic meat

'If there were no bad people there would be no good lawyers.'
Charles Dickens

Key consumer protection laws

Sale of Goods Act

Originally passed in 1893, this Act is one of the world's earliest examples of a law passed by Parliament to protect the consumer. It has been updated many times, the latest being 1994. This is the Act that gives you the right to take back a faulty item and get your money back, e.g. the dress in which the zip gets stuck the second time it's worn, or the vacuum cleaner that breaks down after six months.

The key features of the Sale of Goods Act are:

- goods must be fit for the purpose for which they are sold

- relevant aspects of 'fit for purpose' include freedom from defects, the appearance, finish, **durability** and safety

- the buyer has a right to get his/her money back, or could choose to have it repaired at the seller's expense

Talking Point

An angry householder wrote on the website 'Cowboy Builders': 'Our attic conversion was completed using the wrong materials, the insulation was incomplete and our new deck has been built without sufficient supports.' How might the householder benefit from the Sale of Goods Act?

The Act is not stupid, as it accepts that low-cost items may wear out quickly. If you buy a £1.99 umbrella, do not expect the Act to get your money back four months later. In other instances, however, the Act will accept compensation claims up to six years from the purchase date. So faults in a brand new house might give rise to a claim for a refund five years after the purchase date.

- the person responsible for correcting any problem is the seller (the shop), not the manufacturer.

Trade Descriptions Act

The owners of Julie's Restaurant were breaking the Trade Descriptions Act when they called chicken 'organic' when it was not. This Act (passed in 1968) put an end to 100 years of misleading advertisements. Before the Act, Guinness said 'Guinness is Good For You', dogfood PAL claimed to 'Prolong Active Life' and – much earlier – brands of cigarettes claimed to be healthy, such as 'Heartsease' – good for your heart.

An old Guiness advertisement

The Trade Descriptions Act insists that all advertising, pack labels and public statements made by firms about their products must be 'demonstrably true'. In other words, there must be evidence for them. Key features include:

- it is an offence for a trader to use false or misleading statements

- it is an offence to misleadingly label goods and services

- the Act carries criminal penalties and can therefore lead to a jail sentence.

Although specific statements must be provable, e.g. that Yakult helps the digestion, advertisers can still get away with clever ways round the Act. Many of the claims about Omega-3 have little scientific support. Manufacturers of foods containing Omega-3 keep mentioning 'the brain' in their advertising, even though they cannot claim that Omega-3 makes children cleverer.

Despite the tricks some companies use, there is no doubt that the Trade Descriptions Act has reduced substantially the number of customers being conned by suppliers.

Other key Acts

Among many other Acts passed to protect consumers are:

- the Consumer Credit Act (1974): every item sold on credit must have a clear indication of the APR – the annualised percentage interest rate – being charged
- the Weights and Measures Act 1985 (updated in 2006): if the bag says 500 grammes, that is what it must contain
- the Food Safety Act (1990): to prevent illness from eating food sold to the public, by insisting that sales staff have hygiene training and that premises are inspected regularly.

It is not important to remember these other Acts. However, it is important to know that there are more than just the two main Acts. This is because firms often complain that they are overwhelmed by the amount of legislation they must learn to cope with.

Are firms held back by legislation?

The Federation of Small Businesses has carried out research among the owners of small firms. The results showed that 50 per cent thought that excessive regulation would hinder their growth in the next few years. But are firms right to feel this way? After all, just as football managers have always got

'reasons' (excuses?) for their latest defeat, so it is possible that business owners like to blame government for their own failings.

Many businesses say:

- too many rules mean too much paperwork which costs time and money
- rules can restrict our creativity and initiative
- we don't mind rules that apply directly to us, but we object to '**red tape**' that we have to complete but isn't designed for 'firms like mine'.

Others argue that:

- it helps firms to know what is acceptable and what is not – that lets them concentrate on doing things better
- rules do take time and money, but not enough to damage firms' drive for success
- consumer protection law is too valuable to dismiss just because firms find it time-consuming; people can die from faulty drugs, unsafe cars or a dodgy kebab.

In the 'credit crunch' of 2007–9 many banks collapsed

During the 'credit crunch' of 2007–9 many banks collapsed. They were guilty of reckless lending at a time when the government had relaxed the rules on banking. The managers, customers and shareholders of the banks would have benefited from more, not less, 'red tape'.

> *'Ignorance is no excuse.'*
> **Legal maxim**

Revision Essentials

Durability – how strong the product is and therefore how well and long it lasts.

Monopoly – when there is only one supplier, i.e. no competition, so one company has the market to itself, e.g. BAA with London airports (it owns Gatwick and Heathrow).

Red tape – implies tangling firms up in too many rules and regulations; stifling them.

Exercises

(15 marks; 15 minutes)

Read the unit, then ask yourself:

1 Explain why there would be no need for consumer laws if every business was aiming to build long-term customer loyalty. (4)

2 Julie's Restaurant has had terrible publicity following its prosecution.

   a Outline two possible reasons why it pretended its meat was organic. (4)

   b Explain one reason why Julie's may be able to keep going, despite this setback. (3)

3 State whether the following incidents are covered by the Sale of Goods Act, the Trade Descriptions Act or neither:

   a A shop puts up a 'Sale' sign but doubles the prices before 'slashing them by 50%!'. (1)

   b A pair of running shoes splits open when the wearer is running fast, eight weeks after buying them. (1)

   c An advertisement promises that 'L'Oréal For Men will cure baldness in a week'. (1)

   d A 'Kate Moss' dress, bought last month, is condemned by *The Sun* as being 'more like last year's cast-offs than this year's fashion'. (1)

Practice Questions

Prosecutions to protect consumers in South Ayrshire, Scotland

A Greenock man was found guilty of offences under the Trade Descriptions Act 1968 and the Trade Marks Act 1994. The man had been selling counterfeit clothing and football tops at Ayr Sunday market.

A Chinese woman was found guilty of selling counterfeit DVDs contrary to the Trade Descriptions Act 1968, the Trade Marks Act 1994 and the Video Recordings Act 1984. The woman was admonished by the court.

On 19 May 2004 a local jeweller was fined £400 after being found guilty of offences under the Trade Descriptions Act 1968. The jeweller had misled a local consumer into believing that a bangle she had supplied to her had been made by her from the consumer's own gold (as requested by the consumer). The bangle was in

A local jeweller was fined £400 under the Trade Descriptions Act for misleading a customer

fact made of hollow gold and had been bought from a jewellery catalogue.

A farmer pleaded guilty to offences under the Cattle Database Regulations 1998, Trade Descriptions Act 1968 and the Cattle Identification Regulations 1998. The farmer had applied a false date of birth to a bullock, therefore making it over 30 months of age when presented for slaughter. He was fined £350 at Ayr Sheriff Court.

Source: Adapted from South Ayrshire Council, www.south-ayrshire.gov.uk

Questions

(15 marks; 20 minutes)

1 Outline two possible reasons why the jeweller may have chosen to mislead the customer. (4)

2 All four prosecutions were for breaking the Trade Descriptions Act. Which of the four do you think was the worst and therefore deserved the harshest treatment? Explain your answer. (5)

3 To what extent do these examples prove the need for legislation to protect consumers? (6)

Exam-style Questions

DON'T RUSH; check answers carefully

1. Between them, the 20 staff at BMax Ltd produce 600 chairs a week. The productivity level of the staff is twice as high as that at Balex, a major competitor.

1a. What is the productivity of the BMax workforce? (1)

a) 30 chairs per week

b) 600 chairs per week

c) 300 chairs per week

d) 12,000 chairs per week

1b. i. What is the formula for calculating productivity? (1)

ii. Outline one possible reason why BMax has higher productivity than Balex. (3)

1c. Explain one problem Balex will have in competing with BMax. (3)

2. Look at this graph of stock levels then answer the questions below.

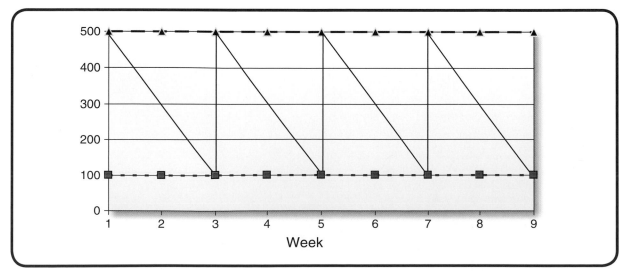

Stock of baked beans at JB Grocers

2a. What seems to be JB Grocers' maximum stock level for baked beans? (1)

a) 100 tins

b) 500 tins

c) 300 tins

d) 9 tins

2b. i. How many tins are delivered to the shop every two weeks? (1)

ii. Outline one possible reason why BMax has higher productivity than Balex. (2)

2c. Explain why JB Grocers might want a delivery every 2 weeks instead of once a week. (3)

2d. Explain one possible disadvantage to JB Grocers of setting its minimum stock level at a higher level than 100 tins. (3)

3. Look at this diagram and answer the questions below.

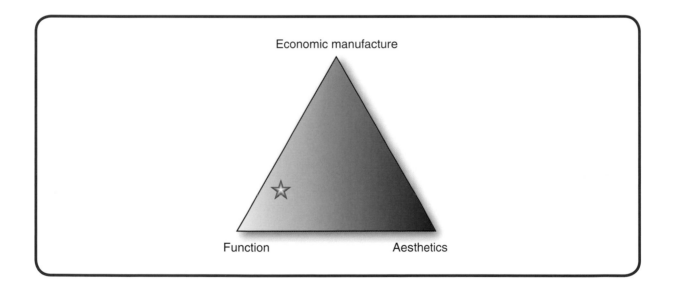

3a. What is the name given to this diagram? (1)

a) The boston matrix

b) The design mix

c) The product life cycle

d) The marketing model

3b. i. What is meant by the term 'economic manufacture'? (1)

ii. Outline why economic manufacture may be important to a firm. (2)

3c. FP Ltd's new product is shown on the diagram as a star. Explain what FP Ltd should focus on in producing its new product. (3)

3d. Explain how good design helps achieve product differentiation. (3)

4a. Which of these is a benefit of using a system of quality control? (1)

a) It guarantees that every customer enjoys products of the highest quality.

b) It ensures that everyone in the business cares about quality.

c) It keeps the costs of quality management down to the minimum.

d) It ensures that products are inspected at the end of the production line.

4b. Explain one weakness of quality control as a way of managing quality. (3)

4b. i. Explain what is meant by the term 'a culture of quality'. (2)

ii. Explain how a culture of quality might help a manufacturer of mobile phones achieve a high level of repeat purchase. (6)

EFFECTIVE FINANCIAL MANAGEMENT

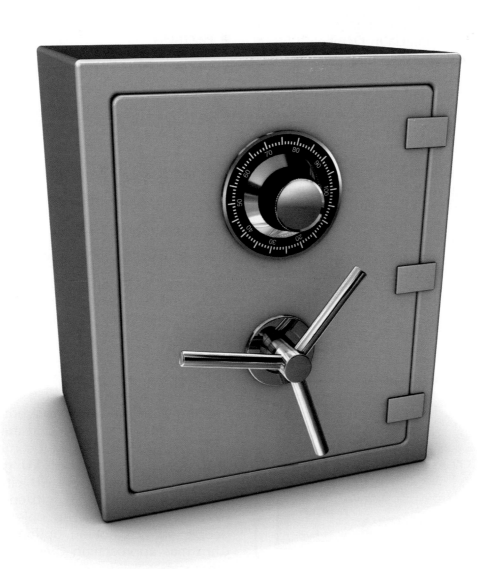

How to improve cash flow

'Happiness is a positive cash flow.'
Fred Adler, New York venture capitalist

Helen and David Madueno-Jones opened their hotel in Andalucia in October 2006. At the time it felt like they had finally reached the end of a very long journey – they bought a plot of land in 2004 and then spent months negotiating planning permission, architects' plans and builders before finally arriving at opening day.

However, the real endurance test was just about to begin. Within a month of opening they were in trouble – they basically had more money going out of the business bank account than was coming in. They had to take swift action, otherwise they risked losing everything they had worked for and more – David's parents had allowed the couple to use their house as security for Helen and David's loans.

Hotel

Outflows and inflows

The couple first drew up a list of their outgoings (outflows). These included:

● mortgage repayments

● electricity

● car running costs

● wages for two staff

● laundry costs (bed linen from the hotel and table cloths and napkins from the restaurant)

● food supplies

● wine for restaurant

● beer and spirits

● advertising (specialist magazines).

Their income (cash inflows) came from hotel guests and customers in the restaurant. Their problem was how to improve their cash flow.

They first looked at how they could reduce their outgoings. When a business is struggling, laying off staff is the usual option. Helen and David were both working full time in the hotel and restaurant and employed two other full-time members of staff. A condition of their **EU grant** was that they employed four EU citizens – as they themselves were EU citizens they had to employ two other people, so laying people off was not an option. Also, with Christmas approaching they really needed more staff.

They considered cancelling their contract with the laundry but soon realised they could not manage the task themselves – they were rushed off their feet and had an eight-month-old baby.

They tried to find cheaper suppliers for their restaurant to cut costs that way but their unique selling point was that they used only fresh organic ingredients, so switching suppliers would mean their **USP** would be lost.

> '*In God we trust; all others pay cash.*'
> **Anon**

Overdraft

Helen and David took swift action with the bank at the end of their first trading month and negotiated a larger overdraft – in the short term this meant they could pay all their bills. Luckily the bank manager was a fan of the restaurant and agreed.

Credit terms

With Christmas and New Year fast approaching, the cash flow crisis could not have come at a worse time. Both the hotel and the restaurant were very busy and would not be able to function unless suppliers were paid. Helen and David chanced upon the solution when placing their order for wine and spirits for the festive period. The wine dealer offered them two months' credit (this meant they could have the supplies and pay for them two months later, allowing them to sell the items before paying for them). At last the couple had a chance to manage their cash flow better.

Christmas 2006 was their first festive season operating the hotel and restaurant, but despite the lifeline being given to them by one of their suppliers they still could not afford the extra staff they needed for the busy Christmas and New year period. Their solution was to call on family and friends who travelled down from Madrid and came from North Wales to help the couple out.

Payment from guests

Initially hotel guests were asked to pay a 50 per cent deposit on booking their room and paid the balance when checking out. Helen and David started asking for payment at the time of booking as another short-term solution to their cash flow problems.

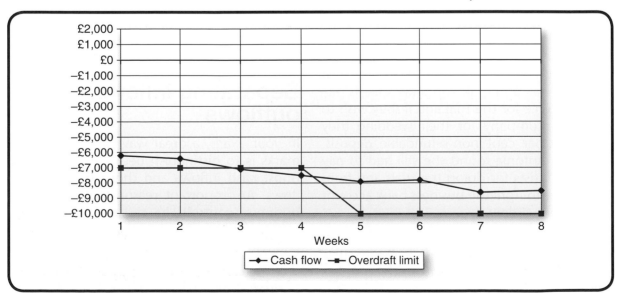

The need to negotiate a bigger overdraft

Other ways to improve cash flow

Favourable customer credit

Elle Au Naturel is a wedding hair and make-up business

Antonia Krieger is a sole trader running a wedding hair and make-up business called Elle Au Naturel. From May to September she has at least one wedding every weekend and her cash flow is very healthy. During the winter months she has fewer weddings but has more hair and make-up trials. Clients pay a booking fee for the trial and if they wish to book the company for their wedding they pay a 10 per cent non-refundable deposit. However, Antonia found she still had to pay make-up artists for doing the trials and from November to April the business bank account was often overdrawn.

Her solution was to increase the client deposit to 50 per cent. This meant that she could afford to pay the make-up artists without going overdrawn and the brides-to-be much preferred this arrangement as they

had fewer bills to pay on their big day, so the solution was a great success for all involved.

> 'It is not the employer who pays the wages. Employers only handle the money. It is the customer who pays the wages.'
> **Henry Ford**

Destocking

Having cash tied up in stock is a problem for many companies.

A company having cash flow difficulties can try to sell off stock to release cash to put into the business bank account and to make the bank balance healthier. In the difficult autumn of 2008, Debenhams ran a short '70 per cent off' sale to cut stocks. That's not unusual in January or July, but it is unheard of in October. Customers weren't buying, so Debenhams needed to destock.

With the use of bar codes, major retailers are able to operate a **Just-In-Time (JIT)** approach to their stock levels (this means they order only products they need, when they need them). The advantage is that they are not left with lots of unsold stock that they either have to sell at a loss (e.g. the reduced counter in Tesco for items about to reach their sell-by date) or throw away.

Separating inflows from outflows

In your exam, a great way to improve your marks is to distinguish between factors that boost cash inflows and those that cut outflows. An important reason why is that no business 'controls' its cash inflows. It may assume that a customer will pay £2000 on Friday, but will the cheque arrive?

In October 2008 celebrity chef Tom Aiken's business went into liquidation when his bank failed to provide the extra capital that he thought had been promised. When Land of Leather was suffering a 29 per cent fall in sales in the 2008 'credit crunch', it did everything it could to try to cut cash outflows: it stopped opening new stores, it stopped spending money on redecoration and expansion of existing stores and it cut back on its £22 million advertising budget. Although, ultimately, it was not able to do enough and the company went into administration in January 2009.

As shown in the table below, there are many options for improving a firm's cash flow. The key is whether or not they are within the management's control. A good starting point is to analyse whether the cash flow boost will come from bringing more cash in, or cutting the amount flowing out.

Boosting cash in	Largely within firm's control	Cutting cash out	Largely within firm's control
Getting customers to pay more quickly	X	Cutting orders on new stock	✓
Getting shareholders to invest more	X	Stopping investments in expansion, e.g. new shops	✓
Running a 'Blue X' sale – 25 per cent off everything for one weekend	✓	Stopping hiring temporary or seasonal staff	✓
Getting a bank to provide a medium-term loan	X	Delaying paying your suppliers (within reason)	✓

Revision Essentials

EU grant – a subsidy available to new businesses which set up in areas of regeneration but there are conditions attached. In Helen and David's case they have to employ four EU citizens and are not allowed to sell the hotel for five years. They are also not allowed to use the property as their own residential dwelling.

USP – unique selling point.

Just In Time (JIT) – a system designed to reduce cash tied up in stock – firms buy raw materials only when they need them and only produce goods to order, reducing storage costs.

Exercises

(20 marks; 25 minutes)

Read the unit, then ask yourself:

1   When facing a cash flow crisis a firm will often try to reduce cash outflows. How can it identify which cash outflows to reduce? (2)

2   It will also try to increase inflows. Name two ways it could achieve this. (2)

3   Will increasing inflows increase profit? Explain your answer. (4)

4   Will reducing outflows increase profit? Explain your answer. (4)

5   Why do you think Helen and David found it so hard to reduce their costs? (4)

6   If you were the bank manager, what would you advise the couple to do? (4)

Practice Questions

Merthyr Tydfil FC football club

In season 2007–8 footballers at Merthyr Tydfil FC agreed to take pay cuts. This was to help the club survive its awful financial position. This sacrifice seemed wasted in August 2008 when the club was taken to court for non-payment of debts. Inland Revenue was demanding £20,000, though this was just one part of a debt mountain: £200,000 of mortgage payments, £96,000 to the brewery supplier to the clubhouse and many others.

Later in August 2008, Merthyr owner Wyn Holloway offered to sell 25 per cent of the shares in the club to raise money from supporters. But supporters were always likely to be reluctant to invest in a club with a poor recent financial history. There seemed to be only two ways to help the cash flow: to keep on pressing the players on wages, or to have the good luck to get a good cup draw. In the past Merthyr had won the Welsh Cup and made it into Europe. Its 1987 defeat of Serie A club Atalanta has gone down in club history. Unfortunately, success requires good players, and if the manager wants to buy new players he will have to sell existing ones first.

Questions

(20 marks; 25 minutes)

1 What are the drawbacks of having to sell existing players before buying new ones? (4)

2 The club is selling more shares to generate more inflows. Discuss whether this is a good idea in the long term. (8)

3 You are the finance director for the club. Explain how you will improve its financial situation. (8)

How to improve profit

Multi-Michelin-starred Gordon Ramsay sharpened his knives and his tongue when, as part of the TV series *Ramsay's Kitchen Nightmares*, he visited a restaurant owner in crisis. The owners of Momma Cherri's Soul Food Shack had started talking about their options in the event of closure. If they didn't have a good December, then that was that. Enter Gordon Ramsay, the most feared and revered chef in Britain today, with his potent recipe of passion, perfectionism and inspirational leadership. Gordon had just one week to turn the business around.

Momma Cherri

> 'The measure of success is not whether you have a tough problem to deal with, but whether it's the same problem you had last year.'
> **John Foster Dulles, US politician**

Momma Cherri's Soul Food Shack

Momma Cherri's Soul Food Shack was an intimate 40-seater in Brighton. Owner Charita Jones was producing a menu of classic food from the Deep South, but at the same time facing financial disaster. £65,000 in debt and with the punters missing, Charita was spending more and more time in the kitchen.

Ramsay loved the food and said her home cooking should be the restaurant's unique selling point. But Charita was killing herself trying to do everything and paying herself only £200 a week. She was paying two chefs, but there were hardly any customers: a surefire way to ruin a business. Ramsay's solution was for Charita to get out of the kitchen and start running the business properly.

Ramsay was confused about the menu prices: the restaurant was offering specials at £8 but on the menu dishes were a hefty £14. Why the leap? Charita said her bank manager suggested boosting prices to make money. Ramsay said it was killing the business. Charita needed to cut prices and offer smaller portions.

They let locals sample Momma Cherri food – and they loved it. Gordon overhauled the menu by offering a weekday £10 three-course menu of 'Soul in a Bowl'. The idea was to let customers sample small portions of different foods during the week, so that hopefully they would return on a weekend for more. But at £10 a head, Charita had to fill the restaurant twice over each night to make it pay. It was a gamble that paid off: the customers loved the food, the front-of-house team pulled together and the vibe in the kitchen was professional.

Two years on, Gordon returned to find Momma Cherri now one of Brighton's biggest success stories. Charita had moved out of the shack to bigger premises round the corner. Momma Cherri's Big House was over triple the Shack's size. People were booking up to four months in advance. There was an average of 900–1200 customers a week and it seemed to be one of Ramsay's biggest success stories. Although the 'Big House' proved too expensive to run (going into administration in January 2008) the business is up and running again.

Adapted from: www.channel4.com

> 'To open a shop is easy, to keep it going is an art.'
> **Chinese proverb**

Improving profits

There are three main ways in which a business can attempt to improve its **profits**:

● by reducing costs

● by increasing **revenue**

● by expanding.

Reducing costs

Costs and profit have a direct effect upon one another. If costs are reduced then profits should increase. There is almost always some way in which a business can reduce costs. Momma Cherri found a way of cutting costs, which allowed her to lower her prices, therefore tempting more customers into the restaurant.

1 Reduce workforce

A business could look to cutting the size of the workforce as a way of reducing costs. There are various ways in which it could do this:

● lose some workers and divide the extra work out among the remaining staff (do you think the remaining staff would be happy with this?)

● reduce the number of managers and cut a management layer out of the organisation (would the business be as efficient?)

● automate some jobs and replace people with machines (what would be the impact on the remaining workers?).

> ### Talking Point
> If a pizza takeaway business needed to cut its costs, what would be its main options?

2 Contract-out the work

Many businesses today employ other firms to carry out certain jobs for them rather than employing someone full time. The most common example is with computer services – it is often cheaper to have a contract with a computer service company rather than employing your own.

> 'The definition of a consultant: someone who borrows your watch, tells you the time and then charges you for the privilege.'
> **Letter in *The Times* newspaper**

3 Cut wages

Students often suggest that a business should cut wages. But this would have a devastating effect on staff – and all the high-quality ones would look for new jobs. One of the implications is that this could damage levels of customer service.

Reducing the workforce can be expensive. To automate jobs involves huge capital outlay to purchase the machinery in the first place; redundancies are hugely expensive. To keep redundancy costs low, many businesses rely on what is called 'natural wastage'. This means that organisations wait for workers to retire, or offer early retirement and then not replace them. The same would happen when a member of staff leaves; they are not replaced.

Cutting wages would have a devastating effect on staff

Increasing revenue

This means increasing income from sales.

1 Raise prices

Momma Cherri's bank manager suggested that she put up prices to increase her revenue. Raising prices is an option, but the success of this action will depend on the market in which the business operates and its competitors. Gordon Ramsay discovered that all Momma Cherri's competitors offered food at a much cheaper rate than Momma Cherri, so the action of raising prices actually meant that customers were lost. In theory a rise in price could lead to higher revenues, but the level of demand must not be affected for this to be an effective strategy.

2 Increase sales

Gordon's approach was to attempt to increase the number of customers visiting the restaurant. Increasing sales volume is the more common way of attempting to increase revenues. This means, quite simply, setting out to sell more. By selling more at the same price, or even at a reduced price, means that a business can earn more. A business can use a variety of methods to attempt to increase the level of sales.

> 'There are three things you should spend your time doing: marketing, marketing, marketing . . . if you are not prepared to do that then everything else is irrelevant.'
> **Emma Harrison, entrepreneur**

- **Advertising**: Momma Cherri went out and about in Brighton, offering sample food and advertising what she offered. She attempted to increase awareness of the product she was offering.

- **Sales promotions**: Momma Cherri offered a £10 lunchtime menu – it didn't matter how many people were at the table, the lunch would be £10. The idea was that while the customers were eating they would be buying drinks to wash down the food and this was where the money was being made. Other special offers are competitions or tokens. The important thing to remember is that the increased revenue must be more than the cost of the marketing.

Talking Point

How costly are these options? What might be the impact on profit?

- **Attracting new markets**: Momma Cherri's was only known locally; now it is a nationally known restaurant with people travelling from around the country to visit.

- **Reduced prices**: Momma Cherri reduced her prices to tempt customers into her restaurant. As a business becomes more popular and new customers are attracted, prices could eventually be raised with a hope that the new customers stay. A business needs to be wary of this action as it does not want to price itself out of the market.

3 Introduce new products

Based on Ramsay's advice, Momma Cherri launched a new product, 'Soul in a Bowl'. This strategy normally increases sales and in this case it did. Businesses often launch a brand new or updated version of an existing product as a way of increasing sales – often they want to be seen as modern and up to date. There are many customers who look forward to having the latest version of a product – do you know anybody who raced out to buy the latest HD digital TV or know someone who is always in the latest new fashions? Some industries regularly introduce new products: fashion, technology and car makers.

In all these cases the reason for bringing out the new products is to increase sales and gain a competitive edge. Businesses that do not regularly update their products or services risk losing out to their competitors.

Expanding

Momma Cherri decided to expand her business so that she could make more profit.

> *'No one was ever ruined by taking a profit.'*
> **Stock exchange maxim**

There are two ways in which a business can grow: internally, by increasing levels of production and sales like Momma Cherri, and externally, by taking over or merging with other firms.

Internal expansion

After starting up in 2007, within a year London ice-cream parlour Scoop was ready to expand. Its Covent Garden shop was doing well, but there was a limit to the sales that could come from one small outlet. Every day owner Matteo Pantani produced fresh batches of (fantastic) ice-cream in the basement under the shop. In the time taken he could easily produce batches three times the size.

The answer was to open other ice-cream outlets nearby and deliver daily from the Covent Garden 'factory'. Opening the Covent Garden shop had required an investment of £200,000 to cover the shop and the state-of-the-art factory underneath. It would obviously be much cheaper to open branches that simply sold ice-cream. So he could aim to achieve three times the revenue but with far less than three times the total costs. This would boost profit hugely.

External expansion

Taking over another business is very risky. Research shows that most 'takeovers' prove unsuccessful. Yet they can be a success if they are managed with great care. In 2008 chocolate-maker Mars bought chewing-gum maker Wrigley. This boosted the total revenue of Mars but provided scope for costs to kept from rising as fast. Before the take-over, a Mars van and a Wrigley van would have delivered to wholesalers; now only one would be needed – bad news for delivery staff, some of whom would lose their jobs, but good for Mars profits. Usually, external expansion achieves higher profits in ways that benefit shareholders but not the staff.

Mars benefited from its takeover of Wrigley

Revision Essentials

Profit – the amount of money a business is left with after paying all of its costs. It is the difference between revenue and costs.

Revenue – the amount of money earned by a firm from selling its products/services. It is calculated by multiplying the price by the quantity of products sold.

Exercises

(20 marks; 20 minutes)

Read the unit, then ask yourself:

1 Suggest two reasons why it is important for a business to make a profit. (4)

2 Smith's Confectioners Ltd had the following costs and revenue:

   Costs   Revenue

   £2,318,000   £2,770,000

   How much profit did the business earn? (2)

3 A new competitor has started operating and Smith's revenue has fallen by 10 per cent. Yet costs have remained the same. What is the new revenue? (2)

4 What is Smith's new level of profit? (2)

5 Describe two ways in which Smiths could increase its revenue. (4)

6 The Managing Director of Smiths has suggested using cheaper ingredients in an attempt to increase profits. Explain the implications of this decision. (6)

Practice Questions

Pilgrims Frozen Food was in trouble. Pilgrims was a big distributor of everything from frozen pizzas to prawns. The company owed the bank £600,000 and could not pay. The business had gone bankrupt and the directors had left. The bank had appointed Buchler-Phillips as liquidator. It is the liquidator's job to raise as much money as possible from the sale of Pilgrims to pay the firm's creditors. The liquidator was going to try to sell the firm as a going concern and keep hold of the workforce.

The receivers eventually found a buyer for Pilgrims, Roy and Bruce Hodges. Roy and Bruce already owned Metrow Foods, a small local competitor of Pilgrims. They had outgrown the site they had been operating out of for 12 years, but buying Pilgrim's was a huge investment for them. Their main interest in buying the business was the premises, but they were also keen to see whether the business could support itself.

Metrow Food

The Hodges managed to get Pilgrims back on its feet, but they were wary of the business's profits level and wanted to keep a check on its performance. Profits are still not what they should be.

(Source: adapted from BBC, *Trouble at the Top*)

Questions

(20 marks; 25 minutes)

1   Give two reasons why the profit levels may not be as high for Pilgrims as for Metrow Foods. (2)

2   Roy and Bruce have noticed that the costs for Pilgrims have been rising. Suggest two courses of action that they can take. (4)

3   Roy and Bruce wish to increase the sales revenue for Pilgrims and they do not have a lot of money to spend on advertising. Advise them of two strategies they could use, outlining the implications of each. (6)

4   Roy and Bruce are considering two options: merge Pilgrims Frozen Food with Metrow Foods and open more outlets in different parts of the country, or move into another area of the food market – fresh fruit and vegetables. Give two points in favour and two points against each of the two options. (8)

Break-even

Tushingham Sails Ltd manufactures windsurf sails in Blackawton, Devon. The company identified a potential market for a new design of windsurfing sail. Everyone who has tried the sail reckons it will be a success. A few magazines have reviewed it and have told the company to mass produce it. Tushingham will sell the sail direct to customers through a website.

Tushingham Sails Ltd windsurfer

Before going ahead, Tushingham will have to make sure there is an opportunity to make some money out of the sail. One way of doing this is to calculate the **break-even point**. The break-even point is the number of sails the company must sell to cover all the costs of making them. It is the point at which it is making neither a profit nor a loss. Tushingham will begin to make a profit once it sells more than this number. If it sells less, it will make a loss. Knowing the break-even level is important for any business.

If you are failing to plan, you are planning to fail.'
Tariq Siddique

Fixed and variable costs

As you studied in Unit 1, costs in a business can be divided into two types: fixed costs and variable costs. Before a business can calculate its break-even point it must first collect information about production costs. A business will need to know its fixed and variable costs and its sales revenue if it wants to be able to calculate its break-even point.

The fixed costs for the new board are £18,000. Rental for the premises, managers' salaries and loan repayments are all examples of fixed costs.

The variable costs are £200 per board. The raw materials, packaging costs, etc. all go up and down in line with the number made and sold.

Tushingham Sails has carried out some market research which shows that people are prepared to pay between £400 and £500 for a board. This helps the business decide on a selling price of £450. Knowing the selling price will allow Tushingham to calculate its sales revenue at different levels of production.

Tom, the Finance Director at Tushingham Sails, has summarised these costs:

Fixed costs = £18,000

Variable costs per windsurf sail = £200

Selling price per windsurf sail = £450

Drawing a break-even chart

It can be helpful to draw a diagram that shows the profit or loss at every possible level of output. This diagram is called a **break-even chart**.

To draw a break-even chart you need information about:

● the variable costs

● fixed costs

● the revenue of the business

● the maximum output of the business.

Tom will also need to know the following:

Total costs = Fixed costs + variable costs

Variable costs = Variable costs per unit × number of wind surfboards

Sales revenue = Selling price per unit × number of windsurf sails.

Maximum monthly production output of the factory is 200 units.

Stage One

Tom now starts to record the information on a graph. First he has to decide on the scales to use. For the horizontal scale (across), he needs to know the maximum number of windsurf sails Tushingham is able to produce (200).

The highest figure on the vertical (up) scale is the maximum amount of money likely to be received. In this case, it is the maximum number of boards that can be sold multiplied by the selling price

200 × £450 = £90,000.

Below you can see the first stage of Tom's chart.

Talking Point

Why is it important to draw each line with care?

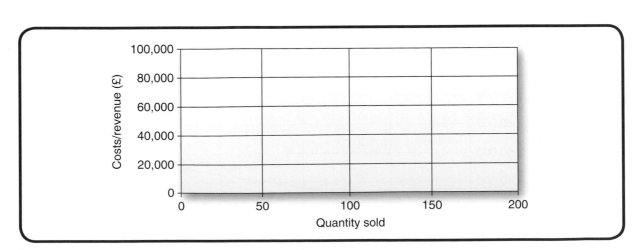

Stage One break-even chart

Stage Two

Tom needs to draw his £18,000 fixed costs line on his chart.

Talking Point

Decide whether these costs of Tushingham's are fixed or variable costs: shop heating and lighting; managers' salaries; material for sails; workers paid per board; advertising; delivery (using Parcelforce); factory rent.

The line is horizontal because the fixed cost figure is the same no matter how many windsurf sails are sold.

Stage Three

Tom next needs to show the total costs. This means adding the variable costs to the fixed costs. If Tushingham sells nothing, its variable costs will be £0 (£200 × 0). If it sells 200 windsurfs, its variable costs will be £40,000 (£200 × 200). These costs however are on top of fixed costs. Tom must start the total costs line from where the fixed costs line meets the vertical axis. The gap between the total costs and the fixed costs shows the variable costs.

Talking Point

Why is it important to think of future revenue as an estimate, not a fact?

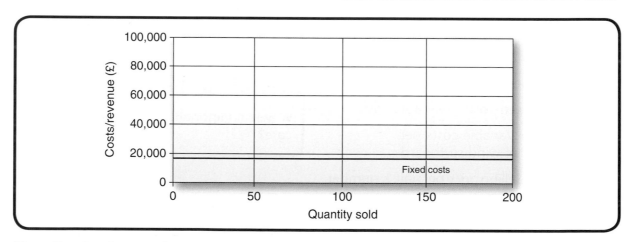

Stage Two break-even chart

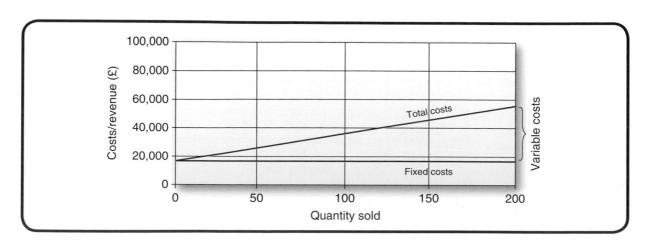

Stage Three break-even chart

Stage Four

The third line drawn shows Tushingham's income from sales, the revenue. If no sails are sold, then no revenue is made (£450 × 0). So the line starts at zero. If all the windsurf sails that the company produces are sold, then £90,000 sales revenue would be received (£450 × 200). This is where the line should end.

Stage Five

The point on the chart where the sales revenue line crosses the total costs line is the break-even point. Tom can now draw a vertical line down to the quantity sold and identify the number of sails the firm has to sell in order to ensure that all costs are covered.

Talking Point

Is it possible to calculate the break-even point without a graph?

Tom reads the graph and can see that the line meets the horizontal axis at the number 72. This means that Tushingham needs to sell 72 windsurf sails before it starts to make a profit.

The distance between the total cost line and the revenue line shows the loss which would be made at that level of sales. After the break-even point, the difference between the two lines represents profit. From the graph Tom can calculate that Tushingham will lose £18,000 if it sells no windsurf sails yet could make a maximum profit of £32,000.

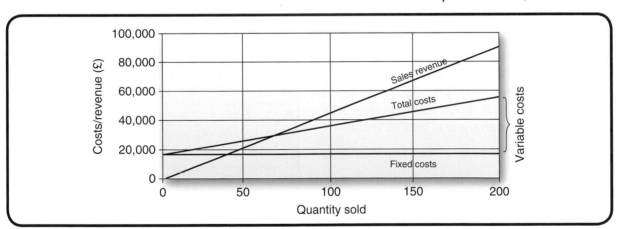

Stage Four break-even chart

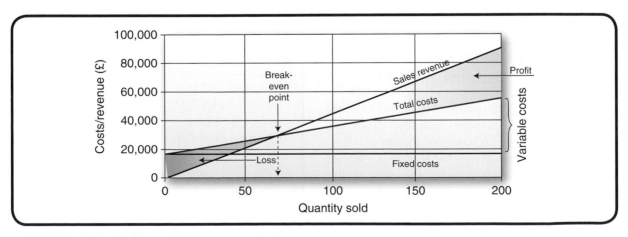

Stage Five break-even chart

Using break-even charts

Tushingham would be able to get other information from the break-even chart. Tom would be able to read off the graph the expected profit or loss to be made at any level of output.

Tom would be able to examine the effect on profit or loss of certain business decisions. For example, if a competitor brought out a similar windsurf sail and Tushingham needed to alter its prices, it could show the new situation on another break-even chart.

The value of break-even charts

Business is all about the future, i.e. making decisions today for the sake of things happening tomorrow. The history of a business might be interesting, but building a business is all about tomorrow. Therefore managers need methods that help them make decisions. Break-even analysis is one of those.

Break-even can help a manager answer questions such as:

● What if we put our prices up by 10 per cent? What would this do to our break-even sales level?

● The price of wheat has risen 25 per cent. What will this do to our profit if we leave our prices unchanged?

The following table shows this in more detail, but the key thing is that these are critical questions for a business. They can all be answered on a calculator, but a break-even chart shows the answer visually. That will often make it easier to use, for example when explaining to staff why the business cannot afford to pay a 5 per cent pay rise at the moment, or why three staff have to be made redundant.

Crucial business questions can all be answered with a calculator but a break-even chart shows the answer visually

Questions break-even can help answer	Impact on the break-even chart
● Our landlord has increased our rent by 40 per cent; what will it do to our profitability?	● Fixed costs line will rise, pushing the total cost line closer to the revenue line, i.e. cutting profits
● The recession has cut demand for our organic eggs by 20 per cent; what will be the impact?	● No lines on the chart will change, but the 20 per cent sales fall will reduce the **margin of safety**, or perhaps wipe it out
● Is it right to cut our prices by 10 per cent? Will it increase or cut our profits?	● The revenue line will rise less steeply, pushing it down towards total costs; profits can only rise if the sales volume leaps ahead. Is that likely?

Revision Essentials

Break-even point – the level of sales at which total costs = total revenue. At this point the firm is making neither a profit nor a loss. All output below this point is at a loss. All output above this point is at a profit.

Break-even chart – a graph which shows total costs and total revenues and the break-even point where total revenue equals total cost.

Margin of safety – the amount sales can fall before the firm's profit is wiped out.

Exercises

(A: 15 marks; 20 minutes. B: 20 marks; 30 minutes)

A. Read the unit, then ask yourself:

1 John sells hot dogs for a living. He calculates his fixed costs at £20 per day and his variable costs at 10p per hot dog. John sells each hot dog for 75p and is able to cook 50 hot dogs to sell every day. What are John's fixed costs if he makes and sells 25 hot dogs? (1)

2 What would John's variable costs be if he sold no hot dogs at all? (1)

3 What are John's total costs if he sells 20 hot dogs in an afternoon? (2)

4 What would be the maximum sales revenue that John could take in one day? (2)

5 Explain what is meant by the term break-even. (3)

6 Outline two reasons why a business might want to be able to calculate the break-even point. (4)

7 Explain how to find the break-even point on a break-even chart. (2)

B. 1 Toys 4 Fun is a manufacturer of children's wooden toys. The company has calculated the monthly costs of producing the average toy as follows:

Rent/Rates:	£2000
Electricity:	£100
Salary bill for managers:	£2700
Other fixed costs:	£200

Average variable costs for producing each toy come to £5.00. The average price for each toy amounts to £25.00. The factory's capacity is 300 units. Calculate the total costs and total revenue of the business over the following outputs: 0, 50, 100, 150, 200, 250, 300. (8)

2 Plot these figures onto a graph and estimate the break-even output. What is the profit/loss at the following levels of output: 100, 200, 300? (6)

3 If the company could not sell more than 150 in a month, what might the management do? (6)

Practice Questions

Pride Hair Design

Pride Hair Design is a Preston-based hairdressing salon, set up and run by Sue. It was partly funded by a bank loan on which there is an interest charge of £400 a year.

Sue is the only hairstylist. She allows herself £18,000 as a yearly salary. Roy keeps the accounts. Sue has an assistant who works in the shop full time, doing jobs such as washing hair, sweeping up and answering the phone. Sue pays her £8000 per year. The average price she charges for all types of work, including OAP reductions, is £20.

Sue pays £5000 a year in rent and £600 a year in heating and lighting. It costs Sue 50p per person to shampoo and condition each customer's hair. Other variable costs such as hair gel, hair spray, etc. cost on average £2 per customer. The maximum number of hair cuts Sue can do each week is 100. On average Sue gets 90 customers per week.

Questions

(30 marks; 45 minutes)

1 Identify Sue's fixed costs and variable costs. (4)

2 Using the information given, construct a break-even chart by carrying out the following tasks: (10)

On graph paper, draw and label the two break-even chart axes.

Draw the fixed and total cost lines and label them.

Draw in the revenue line.

Identify the break-even point.

Give your chart a suitable title and ensure the axes are labelled correctly.

3 From the chart, estimate the profit or loss if Sue had:

10 customers

70 customers

100 customers. (6)

4 Evaluate the potential success of Sue's business using the information you have. (5)

5 Sue thinks she could perhaps charge £40 per hair cut. Discuss the probable effect of increasing her prices to £40 per cut. (5)

Practice Questions

Dealing in the downturn

What do you do if demand for your products has slumped by 20 per cent? Or what about 60 per cent? Clearly, you could be dragged from profit to loss, and cash flow could quickly become a serious problem.

This is the position of car dealerships up and down the country. A 17 per cent fall in car sales in August has been followed by a 21 per cent fall in September. Among the hardest hit have been Jeep showrooms. UK sales fell from 1,695 in September 2007 to just 660 in September 2008.

Explanations for the slump in Jeep sales are not hard to find. Higher petrol prices encouraged people to switch to smaller cars, as did consumer concern for the environment. Then came the economic downturn reinforced by increasing uncertainty about banks and the 'credit crunch'.

For a company owning four or five Jeep dealerships the position could quickly become a major concern. The business in the graph on the next page has fixed costs of £300,000. Its Finance Director wants to act to cut these costs but the Managing Director has said: 'That's foolish, we can't cut the fixed costs, we must focus on the variable ones.'

Economic downturns can catch out the businesses that are slow to react. Those running Jeep dealerships had better move fast.

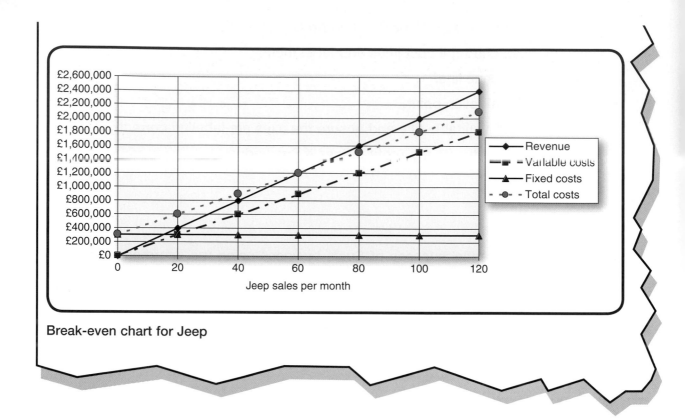

Break-even chart for Jeep

Questions

(25 marks; 30 minutes)

1 Briefly explain how a sales slump could 'drag' a business from profit to loss. (4)

2 a Calculate the percentage decline in Jeep sales between September 2007 and September 2008. (3)

  b The Jeep dealer featured in the break-even chart sold 100 Jeeps in September 2007 but only 40 in the same month this year.

    What profit did the business make last September? (3)

    And what profit/loss did it make this September? (2)

3 a Help the Finance Director to explain why fixed costs can be cut. (4)

  b Explain two ways in which this Jeep dealer could return itself to break-even. Discuss which is the better option in the difficult 2008 car market. (9)

Financing growth

All businesses start off small. Subway has 26,868 restaurants in 86 countries. It has 865 stores in the UK and Ireland and hopes to have 2010 by 2020. The company was started in 1965 by 17-year-old Fred DeLuca, who borrowed $1000 to open a sandwich shop. All he wanted was to raise enough money to pay his college tuition fees. He later became a billionaire thanks to Subway.

Fred DeLuca, owner of Subway restaurants

How does a company finance expansion?

Internal sources	External sources
Profit	Share capital/ increasing the number of partners
Sale of assets	Debt
Personal funds	Flotation on the stock exchange

Profit

Richard Branson began his Virgin empire at the age of 17 when he launched the magazine *Student*. His early venture was so successful that he used his profits to set up Virgin, a mail-order record company. Using profit means no interest will have to be paid but shareholders will get a smaller dividend and may be opposed to the expansion plans.

Sale of assets

In 1992 Richard Branson sold Virgin Music to Thorn EMI for £560 million to raise capital to support other business ventures, mainly Virgin Airlines.

Smaller firms might sell off their buildings and then rent premises or may sell off computer equipment and choose to lease equipment instead. The main drawback is that while this can be an effective way of raising large sums of capital, it could cost the firm more in the long term. When Richard Branson sold off Virgin Music he sold the most successful and profitable part of his company.

Personal funds

In 1987 Richard Branson personally raised £200 million to buy out external shareholders and take back control of his business. This meant he could change the direction of the company as he saw fit.

Smaller businesses will not need to raise this type of capital. In 2005 Antonia Krieger expanded her wedding hair and make-up company Elle Au Naturel by creating a sister company and developing a new website. The investment needed was £10,000, a sum she raised herself by using the deposit she had saved to buy a flat. Using her savings meant that she did not have to pay interest, although for a time she had to continue living in rented accommodation. However by 2007 she was able to buy a property having paid herself back over £7000 of the original loan, from product sales over a two year period.

The Elle Au Naturel website

Share capital

A limited company can sell more shares to raise finance for growth. The drawback is that the original owner may lose control. If it wasn't for the willingness to sell shares – especially on the stock market – the Sainsbury family would just be grocers instead of members of the super-rich.

When Richard Branson started Virgin Records he sold his friend Nik Powell a 40 per cent share in the company. This helped raise the funds needed to open the first retail store in 1971.

Even in the difficult trading conditions of 2008, more than 80 new companies raised money by listing their shares on the London Stock Exchange.

Debt

A bank loan is probably the most common way a firm will finance expansion plans, but this comes at a cost – interest.

Helen and David Jones have financed their hotel in Andalucia by taking out a 25-year mortgage – they hope they will be able to pay the loan back sooner.

Flotation on the stock exchange

When Sumas, a Bristol-based financial advice company, wanted to expand by buying other businesses, it raised £3 million by going public and selling shares. It raised the funds needed for expansion, but the **flotation** cost £1 million and the business is now vulnerable to being bought up by a rival.

Minimising risk

One of the riskiest times for businesses is when they are growing fast. It is easy for the cash outflows to rise faster than the cash inflows. So it is important to get enough finance and to make sure it's the right type.

The worst type of cash inflow is an overdraft. This is because, if something goes wrong, the bank can demand to be repaid within 24 hours. The best type of finance for growth is share capital, because this never has to be repaid. The business has the shareholders' investment forever. If a shareholder wants to get their money back, all they can do is to sell their shares to another buyer (which is what the stock market is all about).

A good way to look at financing risks is to look at the difference between debt and shares. There are two main reasons why shares are less risky than debt:

1. Borrowing money forces a company to pay interest even in a tough year; whereas share capital involves dividend payments that can be cancelled if necessary. Debt (such as a bank loan) has interest that must be paid. If it isn't paid, the company can be closed down. With shares, the directors can decide that the

business cannot afford to pay dividends that year. British Airways, for example, paid not a penny in dividends to shareholders between 2001 and 2009.

2 Borrowed money has to be repaid, therefore a 3-year bank loan of £200,000 not only involves a lot of interest, but also the £200,000 has to be paid back. Money raised by selling shares *never* has to be repaid. So £200,000 raised by selling shares is much safer than £200,000 borrowed.

Revision Essentials

External sources – sources of finance from outside the business, e.g. bank loan, venture capital.

Internal sources – sources of finance the company already has, e.g. selling assets.

Flotation – when a firm offers its shares for sale to the public for the first time on the stock exchange.

Exercises

(20 marks; 25 minutes)

Read the unit, then ask yourself:

1 A 20-year-old wants to start an aerobics gym. It will cost £60,000 to set up, but she has only £6500. Outline two suitable ways of raising the rest of the capital. (6)

2 A local double-glazing company is considering expanding its product range to include conservatories – it needs £300,000 to do this. Discuss the external options available to the company to raise this amount of cash and make a recommendation about what it should do. (9)

3 A local hairdresser has the opportunity to buy a second shop. Her family has offered to buy a 60 per cent share in her business – this will give her the money she needs for expansion. Or she could take out a loan. What should she do? (5)

Practice Questions

Mermaid Pod

In 2006 James Seddon appeared on BBC's *Dragons' Den* looking for finance for his water-free egg cooker. He had developed his design and had built a prototype. He believed there was massive potential in his product but did not have the finance to take the product from the prototype to the global marketplace.

His TV appearance did not go to plan and he failed to demonstrate that his invention worked, even forgetting to add the egg during his first demo! Despite this, two of the Dragons – Richard Farleigh and Peter Jones – offered to invest £75,000 for a 40 per cent share in the company.

Matt Hazel also appeared on the programme, hoping to raise £100,000 for a 5 per cent share in his technology company so he could market his invention, the Mermaid Pod. The Pod was designed for sailors. All the crew wear the device and when one falls overboard an alarm sounds and the device gives the skipper a grid reference to show where the crew member fell into the water. Richard Farleigh came up with the £100,000 but insisted on a 30 per cent share.

Questions

(25 marks; 30 minutes)

1   Appearing on a programme like Dragons' Den means an entrepreneur gets media exposure for his or her business while having the opportunity to raise money from a venture capitalist. What are the drawbacks of this? (6)

2   Why do you think James Seddon chose to appear on Dragons' Den rather than take a loan from the bank? (4)

3   Matt Hazel did not want to give 30 per cent of his business to the Dragons and tried to negotiate Richard into settling for 20 per cent. Why would Matt be reluctant to sell such a large stake in his business? (6)

4   Matt has come to see you before his TV appearance. Would you advise him to go on the show? Explain your answer. (9)

Exam-style Questions

DON'T RUSH; check answers carefully

1a. Which of the following lines is not shown on a break-even chart?   (1)

a)   Total costs

b)   Variable costs

c)   Selling price

d)   Total revenue

1b. i. Calculate the break-even point for a firm with fixed costs of £600, variable costs of £2 per unit, a selling price of £6 and a sales level of 250 units.   (2)

ii. Calculate this firm's safety margin based on the data available.   (2)

1c. Explain one way in which a chain of shoe shops could use a break-even chart to help decide whether to close down a loss-making branch.   (3)

2a. Which one of the following factors would help a firm improve its cash flow?   (1)

a)   Cutting the time customers are allowed before paying

b)   Increasing the number of sales on credit

c)   Building up the firm's stock levels

d)   Repaying a bank loan

2b. Outline the effect on a firm's cash flow of hiring more staff.   (2)

2c. Explain why a firm might have negative cash flow during the winter months.   (3)

2d. In 2009 a leading manufacturer increased its credit terms with suppliers from 30 to 90 days. Explain the effect on those suppliers.   (4)

3a. Last month, DAQ Ltd sold 200 items at £15 each. Its fixed costs were £400 and variable costs were £4 per unit. What profit did it make?   (1)

a)   £2,556

b)   £3,000

c)   £1,800

d)   £4,200

3b.   i. Calculate DAQ's profit this month, if sales slump to just 100 units.   (2)

ii. Outline two ways in which DAQ might boost its profit.   (4)

3c.   Explain why actions to cut costs might cause revenues to fall as well.   (3)

4.   After the recession, the boss of a chain of mobile phone shops saw the opportunity for 6 new branches. This expansion would require £600,000 of new capital.

4a.   Which of the following sources of capital would be the best for financing this investment?   (1)

a)   An overdraft

b)   A five-year bank loan

c)   Longer credit from suppliers

d)   Cutting back on stock levels

4b.   i. Give two examples of external sources of capital.   (2)

ii. Examine one external source that is suitable for financing long-term investments.   (3)

4c.   Explain the main factors a farm should consider when deciding how to finance the purchase of a huge new field.   (6)

EFFECTIVE PEOPLE MANAGEMENT

Organisational structure

Among your group of friends, is there a 'pecking order'? Is there someone who makes the decisions for your group or who tells the others what to do? You might have someone who is in charge, who makes the final decisions. You might have a newer member of the group who is always the person told to go and make the drinks! If there is, you probably have what is called an informal hierarchy within your group. Without this structure and defined roles you might never get anything organised and get to go for any nights out!

In businesses it is no different: they have structures too. For a small firm there may just be the owner/boss and a few staff working for him/her. In a large company, the structure will be more complex. It will help identify who does what job and who is in charge of whom.

An **organisation chart** is a diagram showing the structure of a business. Let's take the example of a small business employing five workers. The structure will be straightforward, as in the figure below.

There may be a pecking order among your group of friends

The chart shows that there is one person at the top of the organisation who makes all the decisions and there are five workers below who follow the instructions given.

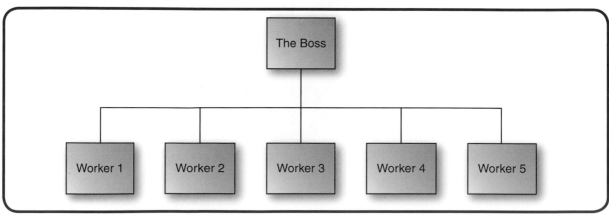

Simple organisational chart

Talking Point

Why do businesses need a clear organisational structure?

Let's look now at the structure for a large organisation like the Metropolitan Police. The Metropolitan Police Service has a complex command structure that reflects its wide range of activities.

The purpose of the organisation chart is to show the hierarchy, chain of command and span of control within an organisation.

Hierarchy refers to the levels of responsibility in an organisation. It is the formal structure of responsibility and authority and is usually shown in vertical layers. The further up the hierarchy somebody is, the more important they tend to be and the more power they have.

Talking Point

If you decided to start a business, would you prefer to be independent or buy into a franchise?

Chain of command refers to the route by which decisions are passed between the different levels in an organisation. It is the pathway of instructions and authority from the most senior people in an organisation down to the workers at the bottom of the hierarchy. A chain of command may be long or short depending on the organisation and the type of structure. Normally decisions are passed down the chain of command and issues/problems are passed up.

Span of control refers to how many other people someone is responsible for. A subordinate is a person who is directly responsible to a person of higher authority.

Almost everyone in an organisation is subordinate to someone else. In other words, the span of control is the number of subordinates that a person has direct authority over.

The example of the small firm with five employees we looked at earlier showed two layers in the hierarchy; the chain of command is vertical and the boss has a span of control of five.

Tall structures

Large organisations like public limited companies or multinationals have more complex management structures. The organisation is likely to have many layers in it and would perhaps look like the first diagram on page 335.

The chart is like a pyramid, with the people with the most responsibility at the top. The layers form a pyramid structure as there are fewer people at the top than at the bottom. The management structure has several clear levels of responsibility. The people they are responsible for are on the next line down on the chart. This structure is called a tall structure because the company has a narrow span of control: each person is responsible for only one or two others. The army is a really good example of a tall structure with many layers in the hierarchy.

Advantages include the following:

- communication should be better because the chain of command shows a clear line for messages

- lots of opportunities for promotion

- it is easy to maintain standards across an organisation, since authority is strictly passed down the line

- it is easier to check everybody's work because there are managers and supervisors at each level.

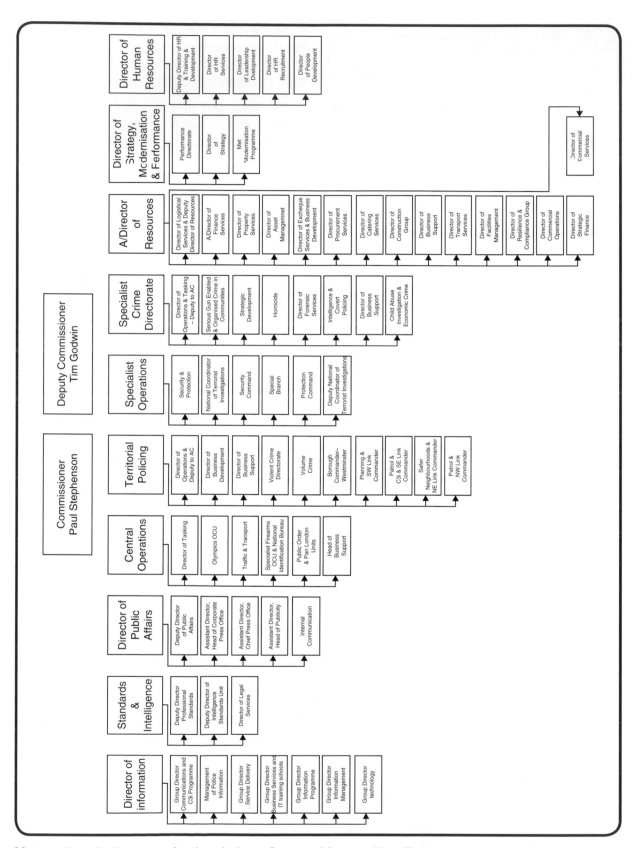

Metropolitan Police organisational chart. Source: Metropolitan Police, www.met.police.uk

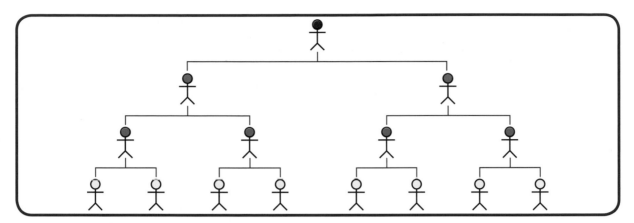

Simple organisational pyramid – tall structure

Disadvantages include:

- the system is rigid and inflexible

- people's position in the management structure shows their level of responsibility and authority and it is often seen as a status symbol with clear divisions between managers and the workers

- there can be too many layers of management and this will create a long chain of command

- a long chain of command will mean it takes decisions a long time to reach the workers at the bottom of the hierarchy.

To overcome the problem of long chains of command, some businesses prefer a flatter structure, with fewer layers of management.

Flat structures

In a flat organisation each manager has a wider span of control. This means that each manager is responsible for more people. People on the lower levels have more responsibility than those on the lower levels in a tall organisation. Managers therefore need to have confidence in their staff. They also need to be happy delegating work to their subordinates.

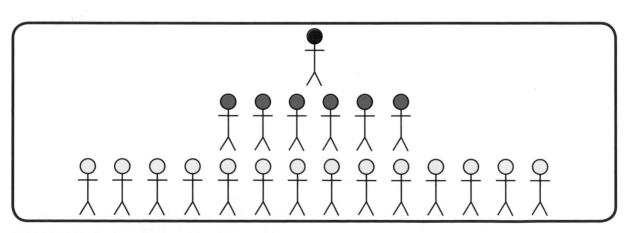

Simple organisational pyramid – flat structure

> *'The best executive has the sense enough to pick good men, and the self-restraint enough to keep from meddling.'*
> **Theodore Roosevelt**

Advantages include:

- fewer managers are needed, which saves money

- managers give more responsibility to the workers

- more responsibility leads to more job satisfaction for the workers

- there is faster, more efficient communication between staff and management

- it can lead to greater job satisfaction.

Talking Point

What might be the impact of a manager losing control of junior staff?

A disadvantage of a flat hierarchy is that every manager is responsible for more people

Disadvantages can be:

- each manager is responsible for more people

- managers have to rely on their subordinate staff much more to work efficiently and safely

- managers may lose control of subordinates as there is too wide a span of control for each manager

- it can lead to over-work and stress

- there are fewer opportunities for promotion.

Centralised organisations

Banks like Lloyds TSB and supermarket chains such as Sainsbury's are examples of businesses that are normally **centralised**. Local branch managers have little decision-making power: they are strictly controlled by head office and they have to follow the instructions they are given so that the branches operate in the same way. Managers are expected to send regular reports to head office. Head office will also arrange orders of supplies for all the branches; the branches have no control over finance.

Advantages of centralisation are:

- decisions can be taken with an overview of the whole company

- central managers are able to make sure that policies and decisions are followed consistently across the whole organisation

- decision-making and communication can be quick.

Drawbacks of centralisation are:

- it reduces delegation, which may lessen a company's ability to respond rapidly to changes in the market, since local managers have to refer to head office for decisions

- business opportunities may be lost because people are not allowed to make any decisions

- job satisfaction may be lost as staff are not able to feel involved.

Decentralised organisations

A **decentralised** organisation is one that shares out the power of decision-making to more people. Important decisions are made locally at either the branch or division. Head office will make the policy and still have overall control but important decisions about the running of the branch will be made by the branch manager, for example. Flat organisations emphasise a decentralised approach to management as the structure encourages high employee involvement in decisions.

> *'Management means helping people to get the best out of themselves, not organising things.'*
> **Lauren Appley,**
> **www.businessballs.com**

Revision Essentials

Organisation chart – a diagram that shows the internal structure of an organisation.

Centralised organisation – an organisation in which most decisions are made at head office.

Decentralised organisation – an organisation which allows staff to make decisions at a local level.

Exercises

(35 marks; 35 minutes)

Read the unit, then ask yourself:

1 Outline the differences between a tall and a flat organisational structure. (4)

2 Identify the benefits to a business of having managers with a small span of control. (2)

3 Explain the implications to a large firm of having too many layers in its hierarchy. (4)

4 Name two examples of businesses, one that is centralised and one that is decentralised, and comment upon why they might have chosen to run the organisation in that particular way. (5)

5 a Draw an organisation chart to show the structure of your school. (3)

   b Give reasons as to why the structure is designed as it is and evaluate its effectiveness. (5)

c Make suggestions for how the structure might be improved. (4)

d On your organisation chart highlight the areas where departments must communicate with one another. (4)

e Explain how each department in the school contributes towards the school achieving its objectives. (4)

Practice Questions

EduPlay is a medium-sized business located in a small town in Manchester. Sean and Rebecca Couzins set it up in 1986 after Sean lost his job with a multi-national group. The experience of redundancy made Sean wary and this affected the way he chose to run the business. He wanted to keep total control over the management and finance of the company, yet establish an atmosphere of trust and cooperation between all members of the company.

The company sells educational toys for the pre-school child (1–5 years) and classroom toys for primary schools (5–9 years). The firm's policy had been to keep costs down and sell through both the internet and mail order, so there has been no need for sales people. The annual catalogue is sent to schools and playgroup leaders and small advertisements appear in the national weekend press.

In the organisation's structure there are only two levels: the Couzins and everyone else. The 48 employees are spread out as follows:

Production	24
Packing	15
Warehouse	5
Office	4

In the early days, workers were expected to cover each other's jobs when needed. This is still true, with all employees earning the same hourly rate. This situation has led to a number of complaints in recent months, since some jobs are seen to be 'easier' than others. The main grumble is that the equal wage for all isn't good enough. Another issue has arisen from the fact that the Couzins are in charge of decisions made in production, marketing, finance, personnel and design.

Several of the older employees have complained that as the firm gets bigger, the Couzins just don't seem to be in control of day-to-day events. Others have claimed that the Couzins leave jobs half finished and it takes for ever to get a decision made because there are so many demands on the pair. The secretary in the office commented that 'the left hand does not know what the right hand is doing'.

It seems clear that the organisation structure that was suitable for the company of the early days has now been outgrown and a change is needed if the company is to survive.

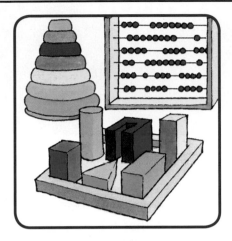

Wooden educational toys

Questions

(40 marks; 45 minutes)

1 The Couzins are the only ones who can make any decisions, everyone is on the same pay and there are only two levels in the hierarchy. Outline why this might lead to problems in the running of the business. (5)

2 a Describe exactly how the current structure of the organisation might affect the following:

the profitability of the company (4)

the morale of the staff (4)

communication in general. (4)

b Take each of the above in turn and suggest things the Couzins might do to solve these problems. (9)

3 Explain how EduPlay should be structured. Use an organisation chart to illustrate your answer. (8)

4 Explain how these changes might improve the operation and success of EduPlay. (6)

Motivation

Why do people go to work? Is it *only* so they can earn money? Then why do some people volunteer to work on Christmas Day providing food for homeless people? They don't get paid, so what is it that makes them do it? A sense of achievement? There are many things that motivate us to do something. Why is that some people have a strong will to work and some don't?

Why do businesses need to know why workers work?

> *'Motivation is the art of getting people to do what you want them to do because they want to do it.'*
> **Dwight D. Eisenhower**

Motivation theory

There are several theories as to what it is that makes people work harder. The best known is Maslow's Hierarchy of Needs.

Maslow's Hierarchy of Needs

Maslow believed that **motivation** lies within individual employees. He divided human needs into categories and said that to motivate workers you must meet these needs. This was formed into a hierarchy of needs.

Once a lower-level need is satisfied, individuals strive to satisfy needs further up the hierarchy.

Application of the Hierarchy of Needs

When looking to motivate the workforce, managers need to think how to provide the opportunities to satisfy workers' needs. This is vital because a dissatisfied workforce will have high absenteeism and low productivity, whereas a motivated workforce can provide ideas for improving working methods, can put a smile on the face of customers and can provide the managers of tomorrow.

1 Physiological needs

The first needs that Maslow identified were physiological. Also known as basic needs, these include food, shelter and clothing. These needs can be met by financial means, giving the person the ability to feed, clothe and house their family.

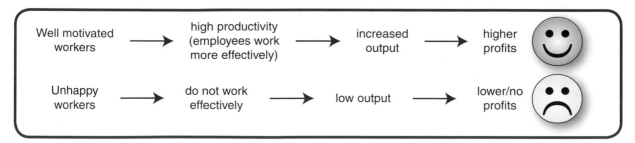

Motivation is vital to business success

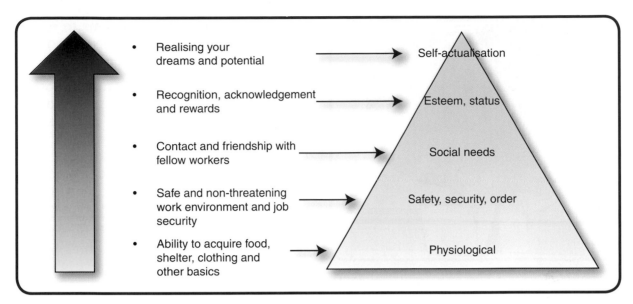

Maslow's Hierarchy of Needs

Financial methods of motivation: pay

- Time rate: this means that workers are paid for the amount of time taken to complete the job.

- Piece rate: workers are paid for how many items they finish. It is used to encourage workers to work faster in order to earn more money.

- Commission: commonly used in sales, the sales person is offered a basic wage plus commission – a percentage of the value of every item sold after the basic wage has been calculated.

- Performance-related pay: this is linked to the achieving of targets. If a worker exceeds the target, an extra bonus is earned.

- Perks or fringe benefits: one of the most common ways of motivating salaried staff is through fringe benefits or perks. These are extras, other than money, that the person may have in addition to his or her actual pay. Examples of perks are health insurance schemes, subsidised travel or accommodation, company cars and store discounts. It is often cheaper for the employer to provide goods rather than the money to buy them with. A good perk will make an employee reluctant to leave the business.

Talking Point

In 2008 staff at Carluccio's cafes were being paid £3.50 an hour, though tips pushed the figure up to the minimum wage. Would you work for that?

Maslow's hierarchy suggests that money is not enough on its own to motivate workers. Maslow felt that non-financial rewards acted as a better incentive for employees to work harder. Once an employee is earning enough money, they are seeking more than a financial incentive. Maslow's theory states that a worker could be earning a good basic wage but when this need is fulfilled they will then strive for more.

2 Safety, security, order

According to Maslow, people need to feel safe. They need to be sure that they are secure in their job. If their jobs are guaranteed, they can carry on meeting their basic needs and plan for the future. A business can fulfil this need by organising pension schemes, for

A business can satisfy their employees' need for security by organising a pension scheme

example. The threat of redundancy is a big demotivator in this category.

3 Social needs

Maslow suggests that people strive for a sense of belonging – they want to feel part of a group or team. Businesses can attempt to satisfy this need by organising social events or clubs. Some firms organise social outings or family days for their employees. Businesses can also give their workers the opportunity to work in teams or take part in team-building exercises.

4 Esteem, status

Businesses should allow their employees to feel respected and have a sense of status.

A company car can reinforce the status of a manager

It is therefore important for firms to recognise their employees' achievements and give them the chance of promotion.

Some jobs attract high status in society (nurse, vet, actor), while others are thought to be of low status (insurance sales person, window cleaner, street sweeper). Within a business, though, a good manager can make everyone feel important. The telephonist really is a crucial part of the team – so it is vital that the job is treated with respect. The status of managers in some sectors is reinforced with a company car.

5 Self-actualisation

This is the highest need that Maslow identifies. It is the satisfaction to be gained from challenging yourself to achieve more than you thought possible. It comes when you learn more about yourself and therefore can see yourself growing up into a new you.

Workers might get this from trying something scary and new – and then triumphing. The actor who has just done a love scene with a famous actress and did brilliantly. The sales person who has just made a huge sale to a difficult customer. This need can be fulfilled by someone doing an important job and taking responsibility.

Self-actualisation can come from both within and outside of work. Maslow believed that people always have the potential to set themselves ever greater challenges. A good manager keeps that in mind.

Advantages of a motivated workforce are:

- better productivity (amount produced per employee)
- better quality
- lower levels of absenteeism
- lower levels of staff turnover (number of employees leaving business)
- lower training and recruitment costs.

Real motivation is from within

A lot of research has been done into what motivates people. It all shows that real motivation is (as the business writer Stephen Covey says) 'a fire from within'. If your parents offer to buy you a car if you get seven C GCSEs, you'll work really hard to achieve this. Yet you may find that a friend – no brighter than you – does still better. You achieved your seven C grades (and your car) while your friend got 8 As and Bs. You had an incentive to work hard, but your friend was really motivated. You did all you could to get seven Cs, but no more. Your friend really 'got into' the work, even (secretly) enjoyed it, and did much better.

> 'Motivation is a fire from within. If someone else tries to light that fire under you, chances are it will burn very briefly.'
> **Stephen Covey, business writer**

Think of the extraordinary efforts of Olympic swimmers, who may swim for four hours a day, for four years! No amount of gold would make most of us capable of that level of dedication. Their drive and motivation comes from inside them, from within. This is why it is risky and often wrong to tempt people too much to achieve financial incentives. The bankers whose foolishness led, in part, to the 2008 'credit crunch' were trying to get their bonuses. They weren't working for the good of their employer, just jumping for bonuses as a sea lion might jump for a fish.

Conclusion

However large or small a business, the enthusiasm of employees, at all levels, can mean the difference between success and failure. People all have their own needs, drives, characteristics, personalities and contributions to make the business successful.

Revision Essentials

Motivation – **the will to work.**

Exercises

(25 marks; 30 minutes)

Read the unit, then ask yourself:

1   Identify three reasons why people work. (3)
2   Describe what is meant by the term motivation. (2)
3   What is it called when workers are given perks in addition to their pay? (2)
4   Describe how Maslow's Hierarchy of Needs would motivate someone to work. (4)

5   Explain what needs you think would be met if you took on a paper round. (4)

6   How could an employer increase the amount of job satisfaction gained by its workers? (4)

7   Identify and explain three benefits that a highly motivated employee brings to a business. (6)

Practice Questions

Salvatore gives his staff presents on their birthday

Salvatore's is a restaurant chain in the north-west of England. Staff put in long hours and the work is hard. Salvatore, the restaurant owner, started out washing dishes and he's done every job in the business, so he feels that he can empathise with staff.

To attract the best staff and more importantly to keep them working there, Salvatore pays above the minimum wage. 'We're nothing without our staff,' he says. 'We wouldn't get customers leaving happy and coming back for more without them! We try to make all our staff feel that they are individuals.'

Salvatore even gives his staff cards and presents on their birthdays and at Christmas. He employs 80 staff.

Staff at Salvatore's are paid above average wages, work regular hours and there is a company pension scheme. And it's not just the practical benefits that Salvatore likes to give: 'There's a real family atmosphere in the company and that's down to the staff,' says Salvatore.

(Source: adopted from www.ristorantesalvatore.co.uk)

Questions

(25 marks; 30 minutes)

1   Identify three reasons why staff are important to a business like Salvatore's. (3)

2   Outline the benefits to Salvatore of a motivated workforce. (4)

3   Use Salvatore's as an example to discuss why money is not enough to motivate staff in the restaurant industry. (6)

4 Explain how Salvatore encourages people to work hard. Make reference to relevant theory where appropriate. (5)

5 Salvatore wishes to introduce some more non-financial methods of motivation. Discuss three methods that he could use, explaining the advantages and disadvantages of each. (7)

Practice Questions

Getting the best out of staff

2008 was a very difficult year for the major supermarkets. It was boom time for discounters Aldi and Lidl, but tough for Sainsbury's and a nightmare for Marks & Spencer. In response, Sainsbury's decided to launch a massive customer loyalty drive in a bid to increase its sales by £1 billion. Unusually, the company decided that the staff – rather than the management – would be the key to success.

The retailer asked its staff to brainstorm ways to increase customer loyalty. Of the 16.5 million customers per week, just 2.5 million shopped only at Sainsbury's. If the rate of repeat purchase could be increased among 14 million customers, extra sales would inevitably follow. Although £1 billion is a vast amount, it would not require that big a percentage increase on the company's 2007 sales of £20 billion.

Sainsbury's told its staff, 'You meet customers every day and really know what they want, so we want you to tell us what we can do to keep our shoppers coming back, encourage them to shop with us every time, and see whether we can get them to put an extra £1.17 of goods into their baskets.'

Obtaining the bright new ideas was to be achieved in two ways. First, staff were encouraged to talk together about how to make improvements. This might lead to more creative ideas and would improve the sense of teamwork in-store. The second way was to offer a financial reward. A bright idea could receive an instant £100 and also be put forward for Suggestion of the Year.

The focus on staff was backed up by a new TV advertising campaign which focused more on shopfloor workers and less on celeb Jamie Oliver. The idea was to give staff more pride in their work, improving their self-esteem. Four months into the new programme, Sainsbury's trading was slightly better than arch-rival Tesco. And at Christmas 2008 its sales growth was nearly twice as high as Tesco.

Questions

(25 marks; 25 minutes)

1 Explain why 'extra sales would inevitably follow' an increase in the rate of repeat purchase. (4)

2 a Calculate the percentage increase in sales expected from the new staff initiative. (3)

  b Explain how the sales increase might affect the company's profit. (3)

3 a Identify three elements of Maslow's hierarchy that form part of Sainsbury's new plan for its staff. Briefly explain how each element relates to Sainsbury's initiative. (6)

  b Discuss whether Sainsbury's plan is likely to provide a major boost to staff motivation. (9)

Communication

The importance of communication

Imagine it is a Saturday afternoon and a group of you have gone into town shopping. You go into Frockshop and decide to try on some clothes. A couple of you try on the same dress; they are all different sizes. The dresses are too small (no one admits this to the others, of course), but as you leave the fitting room you do mention it to the fitting room assistant.

Later on the same day more customers try on the dress; they also mention that the dress is too small. By the end of the week several customers have felt unhappy with the size of the dress and have made the same comments to various shop floor staff, yet none of the assistants does anything with the information – they decide it's not worth mentioning. Eventually the store decides to drop the dress from its product line due to poor sales figures. You start to shop at Lara where the dresses fit properly!

At Frockshop, the fitting room assistants were not involved in checking the quality or monitoring sales of clothes. Their job was to ensure the fitting room was run and managed well. The story would have ended differently if the store manager at Frockshop had taken the time to meet and talk with the fitting room assistants. She or he could have asked: which item of clothing has been tried on most today? How many items that were tried on were then purchased? The store manager could then have assessed the problem: lots of dresses had been tried on, but none had been bought. The manager then would have been able to discover that in fact the batch of dresses was wrongly sized.

There are lots of different ways in which people can communicate. Even so, some businesses do not make the effort and take the time to communicate with all the staff within the business. Many employees in a business know and have an interest only in what their job is within their department. A really successful business will be one that communicates with its employees on a regular basis.

"Doesn't yours fit either?"

> 'The greatest compliment that was ever paid me was when someone asked me what I thought, and attended to my answer.'
> **Henry David Thoreau, US author**

What is communication?

Communication means passing information between people. Good communication is the one ingredient which is essential for a business to become a success. Those firms that do not communicate with their employees will never run as well as those firms which communicate in full. The most successful companies are those that discourage one-way communication and encourage two-way communication – that is, from the people at the very top of the organisation right down to the people at the bottom.

One-way and two-way communication

One-way communication is when the receiver of a message has no chance to reply or respond to the message. An example would be 'I want you to write me an essay on motivation by Friday'. In one-way communication, the receiver, the pupil, does not get the opportunity to contribute to the conversation or communication, to ask questions or to provide feedback.

Two-way communication is where there is an opportunity for the receiver to give a reply or a response. This could be a discussion or confirmation that the message has been received and understood. This should lead to better and clearer information. An example would be a teacher saying 'I want you to write me an essay on motivation by Friday', then a pupil responding 'Can you explain what key points you want me to include', resulting in the teacher explaining the essay question further.

The advantages of two-way communication are that:

● tasks get done effectively and efficiently, with fewer mistakes

● it creates good employee relations – workers should feel valued and listened to by the firm.

A business that aims to run efficiently needs to be communicating at all levels.

Barriers to communication

Sometimes in businesses not all communication is effective. This is due to a variety of reasons:

● the person sending the communication might not explain themselves properly

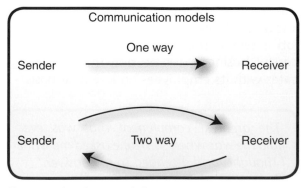

Communication models

A message may be distorted in its transmission

- the receiver of information may not understand the message due to the technical language or jargon used

- the receiver may not hear or receive the message in the first place, e.g. a problem with the medium

- the message got distorted in its transmission (e.g. like a game of Chinese Whispers).

All these **barriers** would be overcome if there was an opportunity for feedback to clarify the message.

> *'The greatest problem in communication is the illusion that it has been accomplished.'*
> **George Bernard Shaw**

Effective communication

To be effective, communications need to be:

- clear and easily understood
- accurate
- complete
- appropriate
- via the right medium
- with a chance for feedback.

Talking Point

How can managers make sure that they are communicating effectively?

The process of effective communication

A business needs to make sure that it has effective communication channels to allow the flow of information around it. The communication process involves a sender, e.g. a 14-year-old boy; a message, 'Mum, can you come and pick me up?'; an appropriate medium, a text message; a receiver, Mum; and most importantly an opportunity for feedback, 'What time and where do you want me to pick you up from?'

It is not safe for anyone to assume that just because a message has been given it has been received and understood. Some big mistakes have been made as a result of poor communication. The infamous 'Charge of the Light Brigade' happened because the instructions of an army commander were misunderstood by his commanding officer. The result was nearly 200 men killed.

Information overload

Developments in telecommunications have had a real impact on the world of work.

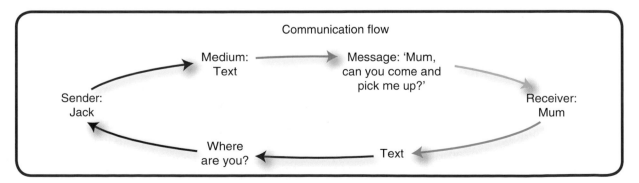

Communication model

Information and communication technology (ICT) can cut down the time it takes to send a message or information. Email and mobile phones mean that people can be contacted quickly. This should ensure more time to check that information has been received and understood properly, thus reducing the number of communication errors.

ICT can allow the same message to be sent to large numbers of people at once, for example using email. This could allow all the employees in a business to be kept informed of developments in the organisation, which could help to increase their motivation levels.

With so many methods of communicating, sometimes people suffer from information overload

> 'The more elaborate our means of communication, the less we communicate.'
> **Joseph Priestley, philosopher**

Advances in technology have meant that a person is confronted with lots of information every day – in emails, phone calls, newspapers, on radio and TV. With so many methods of communicating, sometimes

people suffer from 'information overload'. This term was introduced by Alvin Toffler in his 1970 book *Future Shock*. A study ('Dying for Information') found that more than half of all managers were unable to deal effectively with the information they had to process. It can also mean though that some people in business are working 24/7, constantly being bombarded with information, and sometimes it is just too much for some people to cope with.

The purpose of communication

So why is communication so important to the success of a business? Managers need to communicate in a business in order to do the following:

● **Provide and collect information about the business**. The store manager in Frockshop did not communicate properly with the shop floor workers and therefore a potentially profitable product line was dropped due to poor communication. Staff were not motivated to say anything. Managers will have no idea how the business is performing or what staff are doing without communicating.

Talking Point

Have you been on work experience? If so, how well did your manager communicate instructions and provide information about the business?

● **Give instructions**. It is important that staff understand what jobs they have to do. Once a manager has planned how the business's aims and objectives will be achieved, the next job is to put the plans into action. All managers in all organisations need to give workers instructions as to what task they are required to do, who is to do the task and when it should be done by.

- **Ensure all workers are working towards the same goal**. It is very important that all workers have knowledge of what the company is aiming towards. A business might have a goal of achieving more profit. It might intend to achieve this by launching a new product. But if the research and development department and the marketing department do not know about this planned course of action, the aim probably will not be achieved.

Without managers having this knowledge, the business cannot run smoothly.

Poor communication

There are some key consequences of poor communication.

- **Misunderstandings**. Employees and managers may be given the wrong information and bad decisions could then be made.

- **Time wasted**. If the wrong message is sent or it is given to the wrong person, this can lead to time and money being wasted. Having to correct mistakes also wastes time and means jobs might have to be done twice.

- **Costs increasing**. Some mistakes could be costly. If, for example, the marketing department spends time planning a television advertising campaign but in fact only a radio advert is required, this would be very costly to the business.

- **Inefficiency**. Sometimes workers in a particular area of a business may have an idea which could improve efficiency – they may be doing a job every day and have a suggestion as to how the job could be done better. If there is no opportunity to communicate their ideas, this could cost the business money.

- **Low levels of motivation**. If staff feel that their ideas are not listened to, they might feel that they are unimportant and have low self-esteem, which could lead to decreasing productivity levels. If workers are constantly getting things wrong because instructions are not clear and they have no opportunity to clarify their understanding, this will lead to low motivation and perhaps high levels of staff absences.

- **Profits lost**. If communication within the organisation is poor, this is ultimately going to affect levels of customer service or sales – think of the Frockshop example, where the customers turned to Lara. This will affect profits.

- **Disputes**. Poor communications between a business and its workers can lead to misunderstandings. In the worst cases this may lead to disputes and industrial action.

Revision Essentials

Communication – the passing of information from one person or organisation to another.

Barrier to communication – something that prevents the flow of communication.

Internal communication – communication that takes place between people within the organisation.

External communication – communication that takes place between the business and people or organisations outside of the business.

Exercises

(25 marks; 30 minutes)

Read the unit, then ask yourself:

1 Use the chapter to identify four reasons why good communication is essential to any organisation. (4)

2 Give two reasons why a business might experience barriers to effective communication. (2)

3 Outline why it might be useful to a manager to give his workforce an opportunity to have a regular meeting about working practices. (3)

4 Explain two problems that could arise as a result of poor communication between the sales department and the production department. (6)

5 Each year *The Financial Times* carries out a survey of staff attitudes to find out Europe's 'Best Workplaces'. In 2008 the winner was Microsoft. An article on why Microsoft did so well identified its communications as an exceptional strength. Below are some quotes about communications at Microsoft. Read them, then discuss the tasks listed underneath.

    1 'At Microsoft employees spoke about the open communication with their leaders.'

    2 'They (managers) share the goals and results without withholding any information.'

    3 'Ask management any reasonable question and get a straight answer.'

    4 'Microsoft is very transparent about its pay model and bonus plans.'

    5 'The entire company holds a "Happy Hour" on the second Friday of the month . . . a chance to eat and drink together.'

    6 'Higher management is open for a talk when you need advice or feedback'.

Tasks:

A Agree on the two questions you most need answered by your teacher about these six statements (for example, 'What is meant by a Happy Hour'?). (6)

B Decide which of these six statements is the single most important for successful communications in a workplace. Explain why you have chosen that one. (4)

Practice Questions

'The key thing I learned was the importance of good communication within any company. Without good communication on a day-to-day basis it can be very difficult to provide a good service.' A few years ago Pickfords' Removals

Pickford's Removals van

Director Grant Whitaker spent a week on the vans in Birmingham to find out how he could make the business better. Pickfords is a nationwide moving and storage company.

All removals depend on the salespeople, who visit the customers first to price the job and see how long it will take before letting the removal people know what they think. More often than not the drivers arrive late to jobs and find irate customers waiting for them. However, it is not their fault as often they have difficulties getting furniture up and down stairs and out of the houses.

One of the drivers showed Grant a set of aluminium ladders he had found that would make lifting the furniture much easier and quicker, but head office would not listen to his idea. The drivers often feel they are kept in the dark about the business. Grant took his findings back to the board of directors for discussion.

Questions

(20 marks; 30 minutes)

1 a What evidence is there to suggest that there were poor communications at Pickfords? (4)

   b Describe the benefits to the business of solving these problems. (4)

2 Explain the ways in which communications could be improved at Pickfords. (7)

3 Outline two methods of communication that Pickfords should use to improve their customer service. (5)

Remuneration

Do you have a part-time job? How are you paid for the work you do? Most likely you will be paid for the hours that you work and you will receive this money weekly.

For most people one of the most important things about going to work is the amount they are paid. People can be paid in different ways, depending on the type of job and company policy.

> 'I don't pay good wages because I have a lot of money; I have a lot of money because I pay good wages.'
> **Robert Bosch, German industrialist**

There are two main methods of paying people for their work: **wages** and **salaries.**

Wages are usually paid to shop-floor and manual workers. They are normally paid weekly, sometimes in cash and sometimes into a bank account.

One of the most important things about work is what you are paid

Salaries are usually paid to managers and office workers. They are usually stated at so much a year, although they are normally paid monthly. Salaries are paid straight into employees' bank accounts rather than in cash. People paid a salary are not usually paid overtime. They are expected to put in any extra time necessary to do the job.

Wages

Wages are based either on **time rates** or on **piece rates.**

Time rates

Workers are paid according to the time worked. Workers are usually paid a fixed hourly or weekly rate which can easily be calculated. The rate they are paid for a week's or an hour's work is their **basic rate**. This method does not depend on how much work the worker produces in the time worked. Time rate pay is often used for jobs where it is difficult to measure the level of output (the amount of work produced) by an employee. Workers will often have to 'clock in' or 'sign in' on arrival at work. In some organisations, if workers are one minute later than their starting time when they clock in, they lose 15 minutes' pay. So it is important to get to work on time! This method of payment makes it very easy to calculate workers' wages and the worker knows exactly how much will be in their wage packet.

> *'A fair day's wages for a fair day's work.'*
> **Thomas Carlyle, author**

Time rate is criticised because it means everyone is paid the same whether they work hard and fast or not. Businesses need to employ supervisors or systems to ensure that workers are at work on time and work the hours they are supposed to. Workers also need to be monitored to make sure that they keep working and that a high level of work is maintained.

Talking Point

Would you prefer to be paid the same every week or work on a bonus basis of good weeks and poor ones?

If the employee works longer than their normal hours, they will usually be paid **overtime**. This is the regular amount per hour plus an extra amount, perhaps time and a half. This system benefits employees as they are paid extra for any additional hours that they work. The offer of money is often a great incentive to encourage workers to put in longer hours during busy periods.

Example

The Co-operative Bank offers people £10 per hour to work as telephone customer advisors; these workers will be paid £10 for every hour that they work. The job requires the advisor to work 10 a.m. until 4 p.m. Monday to Friday.

The Co-operative Bank also offers premium pay (overtime payments) for hours worked between 6 p.m. and 8 p.m. Monday to Friday and weekends.

Jan works five hours' overtime during the week for which the premium pay rate is time and a half. She also works four hours on Sunday for which she is paid double time. What would her wages be for that week?

Basic pay = £10 × 30 hours = £300

Overtime, weekdays = £10 × 1.5 × 5 hours = £75

Overtime, Sunday = £10 × 2 × 4 hours = £80

Total pay for week = £455

Take the example of the Co-operative Bank. Ask yourself, what are the implications of staff working so much overtime? Will they be tired? Will they still complete their job efficiently and effectively? Will they start to make mistakes? The impact of this could be great on a business like the Co-operative Bank. Will the same level of service be offered if Jan has worked a 12-hour shift or might she get grumpy with customers?

Piece rates

This means getting paid a certain amount for every unit of output or 'piece' made, i.e. the more you make, the more you get paid. Piece rate pay can be used only where the work of one worker can be counted or measured. This type of payment is normally used in factories, as it can be used only where it is possible to measure the performance produced by an individual or a team. It is also popular for work based at home, for example sewing and knitting garments, or packing and filling envelopes.

> *'You have to learn to treat people as a resource . . . you have to ask not what do they cost, but what is the yield, what can they produce?'*
> **Peter F. Drucker, management guru**

Benefits of piece rate pay are:

- workers work harder because the more they produce, the more they are paid

- it is a fairer system than flat or time rate pay because hard workers are paid more than lazy ones

Piece rate work is popular for work based at home, such as packing and filling envelopes

- people can work at their own pace if they want to. Some may prefer to work at a speed that suits them rather than be worn out going for higher wages.

But there are drawbacks of piece rate pay:

- So that they can earn high wages, workers produce as many items as they can. This may result in poor quality work.

- Firms have to spend more money on quality control.

- Workers may also lose money, since they are not paid for work that is rejected or has to be corrected.

Payment by results

The more workers on a piecework produce, the more they get paid. It is a form of payment by results. There are also other forms of payment by results that are often paid in addition to workers who receive wages or salaries.

Commission. Sales people may be paid a basic salary, plus a commission (a percentage of the value of sales).

A & M Carpet and Bed Centre is a shop based in Wigan. Peter is the director of the business and is in charge of the day-to-day running of the shop. Tony is employed by the business as a salesman; he is paid a basic salary of £10,000 per year. Tony is also paid commission on every carpet or bed he sells; he receives 2 per cent of the value of anything he sells. What this means is that if Tony sells nothing he will still get paid the equivalent of £10,000 a year (roughly £833 per month).

If in one month Tony sells carpets to the value of £8000 and beds to the value of £2000, he will receive £1033 for that month.

How is this calculated? £8000 added to £2000 is £10,000; 2 per cent of £10,000 is £200; add this to the basic salary of £833 equals £1033. This means the more Tony sells, the more money he earns.

Bonuses. These are extra payments over and above the basic wage or salary. They are often paid as a reward for reaching a target. Bonuses are often linked in with piece rate pay; for example, if a worker produces more than their target they will be rewarded with a bonus.

The Co-operative Bank offers its staff a 10 per cent bonus if they reach their targets.

Talking Point

What are the advantages and disadvantages of: a) paying a striker huge bonuses for each goal he scores? b) paying a teacher a huge bonus per A* GCSE result?

Performance-related pay. This is a payment for reaching an agreed target. It may be a personal target agreed with an individual.

Share option schemes. Some firms also allow their workers to have shares in the business. This can make employees feel part of the business and can give them an incentive to work hard because if the business performs better, this means more profits and, therefore, more money for the worker.

Fringe benefits

Fringe benefits are non-monetary rewards given to staff. Often known as 'perks', these are benefits other than money, paid in addition to wages or salaries. Examples include a company car, health insurance, payments into a pension fund, free life assurance, discounts when buying the firm's goods, shares in the company, use of a company mobile phone, subsidised canteen and leisure facilities.

Pizza Hut gives its workers a discount card to get money off their meals at the restaurant.

Freelance and temporary workers

Tony is the only member of staff employed by A & M Carpet and Bed Centre. Peter decided not to employ carpet fitters full time and instead makes use of freelance carpet fitters. They are not employed by the business, they work for A & M only when there is work for them to do. The carpet fitters charge £2.50 for every square metre of carpet that they fit and £3.50 for every square metre of cushion floor that they fit. This cost is added to the price that customers pay when they order a carpet.

Peter decided to use freelance carpet fitters because carpet sales are highly **seasonal**. Sales boom in the spring, but February is dead. If Peter employed the fitters full time he would have to pay them a set wage or salary and would effectively be paying them for doing nothing. By using freelance carpet

A & M Carpet and Bed Centre uses only freelance carpet fitters

fitters Peter has flexibility; he can use several fitters when the company is busy and use and pay for none when it is not.

Talking Point

What might happen to temporary and freelance workers in a recession?

It is a similar situation with temporary workers. Often businesses will employ people on a temporary or a fixed-term contract to help out when they might be busy or when permanent staff are on holiday. This type of work benefits both the business and the individual – the business is able to operate efficiently at busy times or when there could be potential staff shortages. The individual is able to perhaps earn extra money at expensive times of the year such as Christmas and does not have to make a long-term commitment to a business.

Revision Essentials

Remuneration – payment to employees.

Wage – a method of paying employees for their work, usually on a weekly basis.

Salary – a method of paying employees for their work, usually calculated on an annual basis and paid monthly.

Commission – a method of payment where workers' pay is based on the value of products they have sold.

Piece rate pay – a method of payment where workers are paid per item or unit they produce.

Time rate pay – a method of payment where workers are paid per hour that they have worked.

Exercises

(35 marks; 35 minutes)

Read the unit, then ask yourself:

1 Outline the main difference between a time-based payment system and a salary payment system. (4)

2 Identify the difference between piece rate and a bonus. (2)

3 List five common fringe benefits given by companies. (5)

4 Identify which payment system might be suitable for each of the following jobs and briefly explain why: waitress, policeman, postman, manager, car assembly worker. (10)

5 Describe why businesses might offer workers fringe benefits. (4)

   a Explain how a results-based payment system works. (4)

7 a How much would Tony, the salesman at A & M Carpet and Bed Centre, be paid in a month if he did not sell anything? (1)

   b In January Tony sold £14,000 worth of carpets and £400 worth of beds. In February he sold £22,000 worth of carpets and £1000 worth of beds. How much would he be paid for each of these months? (3)

8 A firm agrees a performance-related pay scheme with its employees. If a firm's profits exceed £1.5 million, 3 per cent of the total profit will be shared between the 40 employees. If the business made £3 million that year, how much profit-related pay would each employee receive? (2)

Practice Questions

Clean Windows was established over 30 years ago and is a company that makes and fits double-glazing windows as well as other home improvement services. Clean Windows employs just fewer than 500 staff in total.

Clean Windows has a range of people working in various roles across the company. Senior management are paid between £50,000 and £60,000 per year. Senior management oversee the management of the whole operation. There are various levels of management, from junior managers whose salary starts at £20,000 per annum and middle managers who are paid from £30,000 per annum. All employees on the management team have use of a company mobile phone, use of the company gym and are part of a performance-related pay scheme where they receive a 5 per cent share of the total company profits that exceed £5 million. These staff are members of a share options scheme.

There is a sales team who are based around the whole country. They are paid a salary of £15,000 per annum and receive 3 per cent of any sales above £5000 that they make each month as commission. They also have use of a company mobile phone and a company vehicle. These staff are also members of a share options scheme.

Of the 500 staff employed by Clean Windows, 100 are production staff whose wages are calculated on a piece rate basis. Assemblers are paid 80 pence for each frame they make. These employees can also be members of the share options scheme.

Clean Windows uses freelance window fitters to fit all its windows. The fitters are paid £2 for every window that they fit.

A team of cleaners is contracted to work various shifts. They are paid £5.20 per hour. The staff are paid time and a half if they work in excess of their basic hours during the week (four hours a day, Monday to Friday) and double time if they work at the weekends.

Questions

(30 marks; 30 minutes)

1   Jodie is one of the sales team. She sold £8000 worth of windows during February. What money will she receive in her pay packet at the end of March? (3)

2   Nick, one of the assemblers, makes 500 frames in one week. Calculate his gross pay for the end of the week. (3)

3 The table below outlines the hours of the cleaners who work at Clean Windows. Using the information, calculate the three cleaners' pay for the week. (6)

Number of hours cleaners worked at Clean Windows

	Karen	Catherine	Gary
Monday	8	9	9
Tuesday	8	8	9
Wednesday	8	8	0
Thursday	10	9	9
Friday	8	8	8
Saturday	3	0	4
Sunday	4	4	0

4 Discuss the advantages and disadvantages of Clean Windows using freelance window fitters. (6)

5 Outline the reasons why a business like Clean Windows would offer its workers non-financial rewards. (4)

6 Explain the benefits and drawbacks of Clean Windows paying the assembly workers piece rate and the cleaners time rate pay. (8)

Exam-style Questions

DON'T RUSH; check answers carefully

1. Look at this organisational hierarchy for a small travel agency

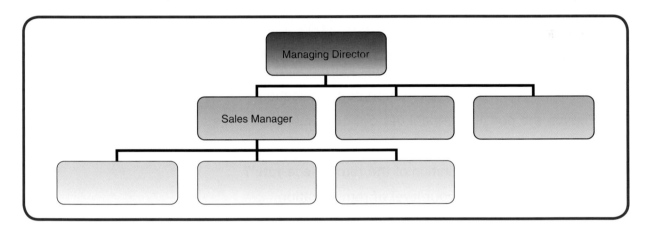

1a. What is the Managing Director's span of control?   (1)

a) 2

b) 3

c) 6

d) 1

1b. i. What is meant by the term 'chain of command'?   (1)

    ii. Explain one possible effect on a business of a long chain of command.   (3)

1c. Explain how a firm may benefit from being decentralised.   (3)

2a. Which type of human needs are at the top of Maslow's hierarchy?   (1)

a) Social needs

b) Physical needs

c) Esteem needs

d) Self-actualisation

2b. i. State what Maslow means by social needs.   (1)

ii. Outline the possible effect on staff if their social needs are not fulfilled at work.   (2)

2c. Explain how security needs of staff might be affected by the arrival of a major recession.   (3)

2d. Explain why senior managers care about whether their staff are motivated.   (3)

3a. Identify who a manager might be talking to if she/he was using horizontal communication.   (1)

a)   Another manager

b)   A junior member of staff

c)   Their boss

d)   A customer

3b. i. What is meant by the term 'barriers to communication'?   (1)

ii. Outline two possible barriers to communication.   (4)

3c. Explain the possible impact of poor communication on staff motivation.   (4)

4a. Which is the best definition of the term 'piece-rate'?   (1)

a)   Keeping calm about your level of remuneration

b)   The amount paid per piece produced

c)   The amount paid per week or month

d)   The pieces of money paid per week or month

4b. i. Outline one reason why a worker may prefer permanent to temporary work.   (2)

ii. Explain how staff might respond to feeling unfairly paid compared with their managers.   (3)

4c. Explain one advantage and one disadvantage to students, if teachers were paid a commission based on their number of GCSE A grades.   (6)

THE WIDER WORLD

Ethics in business

Close your eyes and think of a petroleum company. Think of the profits it makes, the impact of oil upon the environment, disasters such as the Exxon Valdez oil spill back in 1990 that reportedly killed 250,000 sea birds, 2800 otters and billions of salmon and herring eggs (www.wikipedia.com).

Are your eyes still closed? Are you imagining an **ethical** company with a social conscience? I thought not!

What does it mean to be ethical?

All businesses have to follow **legislation** and failure to do so will result in their being pros-ecuted, but this is not the same as unethical behaviour. Being legal means operating within the law; being ethical means doing what is right.

If your school holds a non-uniform day for Children in Need and your friend turns up to school in non-uniform but does not pay their £1 for doing so, they haven't broken a law but most people would believe they had behaved badly.

> 'Ethics is a code of values which guide our choices and actions and determine the purpose and course of our lives.'
> **Ayn Rand, Russian-American novelist and philosopher (1905–1982)**

Ethical behaviour covers every aspect of business, including who a business buys supplies from, how it treats its employees, how it acts towards its competitors, the impact it has on the environment and the impact it has on its local community.

The Exxon Valdez oil spill killed 250,000 sea birds

Ethical heroes

> 'There's a hole in the moral ozone and it's getting bigger.'
> **Michael Josephson, American ethicist**

Who	What	Why
Total is a leading multinational energy company with 95,000 employees and operations in more than 130 countries. Total is the fourth largest oil and gas company in the world	In 2005 Total became the first company to sell One water. One water is a **social enterprise** which sells bottled water and donates all the profits to building roundabout-powered playpumps across Africa. As children play on the roundabout they pump fresh water from deep underground to a storage tank. The sales of One water in Total garages have already funded one playpump in the village of Ndondeni in Kwazulu Natal, South Africa	While a business may lose out on profit by behaving ethically, it gains considerably in positive PR. The side of the water tank paid for by Total has a board displaying the company's logo. The tank is in a remote village miles from anywhere; the people who live in the village don't own a car so the publicity is wasted on them. But Total can use that image in its marketing material. Being associated with a life-changing project provides a better image than the ones you had at the start of this unit

But what about profit?

When behaving in a socially responsible way a business often has to put its money where its mouth is! Being ethical may mean being less profitable. One water donates all its profits to the charity and the founder Duncan Goose lives off a salary of just £12,000 (when he worked in advertising his salary was over £85,000). Other companies are making rather more money. At up to £1.30 a litre (£5.40 per gallon), bottled water is more expensive than petrol.

> 'Sharing money is what gives it its value.'
> **Elvis Presley**

At the start of this unit we were critical of oil companies and their behaviour. Yet with high petrol prices, do customers really care about the oil producers' behaviour, or do we just want petrol to be as cheap as possible?

The trade-off between ethics and profit

Businesses suggest that they are naturally ethical because high standards mean high consumer reputation. This generates the profits to keep standards high, as the diagram shows.

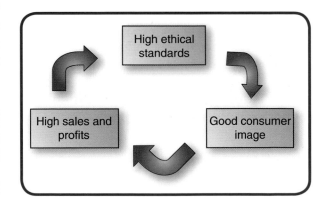

The trade off between ethics and profit

Unfortunately, that often proves not to be the case. A trade-off occurs when a business chooses one course of action instead of another. It's an either . . . or moment. A business might happily follow green policies when they save the company money. An example is when Marks & Spencer said they would no longer give away free plastic shopping bags at checkouts. But what if an ethical approach would hurt profit? What would a business do at that point? Go ethical or go profitable?

M&S carrier bag

Go ethical

Not that many years ago, cigarette companies were among the country's biggest advertisers. Many advertising agencies made a good living working on these multi-million pound campaigns. One advertising agency refused to deal with tobacco companies. One of the founders of Allen, Brady and Marsh had seen a loved-one die of cancer, so the decision was taken to never deal with cigarettes. At the time the ethical stance impressed no one in industry, so the decision was entirely for ethics at the expense of profit.

Profit, not ethics

The Total oil company deserves the praise given earlier for its work with One water. Yet this same company behaved shockingly towards the victims of the 2005 Buncefield Oil Depot fire. The fire followed a spillage of 300 tonnes of petrol that ignited to cause Britain's biggest ever peacetime explosion. People living nearby were blasted from their beds and it was a miracle that no one died. More than 40 people were injured and hundreds lost their homes.

Yet even though Total admitted negligence in operating the site, as late as October 2008 many of the local residents had still received no compensation. The lawyer representing the local families said that 1300 claims were outstanding, representing £370 million. As a result some people were still unable to return home three years later. For Total, £370 million is a minor sum of money, yet its behaviour caused unacceptable stress to completely innocent families. When it came to this trade-off between profit and ethical standards, profit won.

Pressure groups

A **pressure group** can be described as an organised group that seeks to influence government policy, legislation and business behaviour. Pressure groups include Greenpeace and Friends of the Earth (environmental), London Cycling online (a group which aims to make the city of London a world-class cycling city), Amnesty International (which campaigns for human rights) and Searchlight, which aims to combat racism and prejudice.

If a business behaves in a way that a pressure group disagrees with, the media may turn against the company. Nike suffered serious sales declines when its expensive trainers were revealed to be produced by low-wage Far Eastern factories. Pressure groups can embarrass companies and damage the company's image. This could lead consumers to boycott the business, damaging the profits and therefore upsetting the shareholders.

In 2008, TV chef Hugh Fearnley-Whittingstall bought shares in Tesco. This enabled him to force shareholders to vote on the factory farming of chickens. Only 10 per cent of the shareholders supported him, but the publicity pushed Tesco to improve its policy on chicken welfare.

The Fairtrade movement

When products display the **FAIRTRADE** Mark it means that it meets international Fairtrade standards and disadvantaged producers in the developing world are getting a better deal. These include farmers receiving a minimum price that covers the cost of sustainable production, and fair working conditions for estate workers. Producers also receive the Fairtrade premium, an additional sum to invest in social, environmental or economic development projects.

What this means is that when you buy a jar of Fairtrade coffee the farmer who has grown the coffee has been paid fairly for his coffee beans and the additional money has been invested in community projects such as education.

In 1994, when the **FAIRTRADE** Mark was first placed on products in the UK, a total of £2.7 million was spent by consumers on Fairtrade products throughout the year. In 2007, over £493 million was spent on Fairtrade products and in Europe the UK sells the largest number of Fairtrade items.

While most of us would agree that Fairtrade is a good thing, have you actually bought Fairtrade items and do you continue to buy them on a regular basis? Many people support the idea but are unwilling to pay the higher prices for Fairtrade products. In September 2008, with a worsening economy, a survey of shoppers showed that whereas 60 per cent thought price was crucial in their weekly shop, only 3 per cent were concerned about social factors such as fair trade. As the industry develops, however, Fairtrade products are becoming more competitively priced and large retailers have begun to switch ranges such as bananas and their own tea, coffee and chocolate, to Fairtrade. This may make it easier to support Fairtrade products.

Revision Essentials

Ethics – a set of moral principles.

Ethical – doing things because you think they are morally right, e.g. refusing a bribe.

Legislation – laws passed by Parliament, e.g. The Sale of Goods Act, which says that goods sold must be fit to be used, or you can get your money back.

Socially responsible – acting in ways that show care and concern for all members of society, e.g. recycling waste materials.

Social enterprise – a business that trades in goods and services but is associated with a social cause, e.g. Traidcraft.

Pressure group – a group with a common interest/goal who work collectively to further that cause, e.g. a trade union.

Fairtrade movement – a group that support standards for importing goods from developing countries; they aim to ensure a fair deal for farmers and workers.

Exercises

(30 marks; 30 minutes)

A Read the unit, then ask yourself:

1 Explain in your own words what is meant by a firm being 'ethical'. (3)

2 Briefly explain the possible impact on its profit if:

a A supermarket started charging 5p per plastic carrier bag (to cut down usage). (3)

b A car manufacturer stopped producing 4x4 (petrol-hungry) cars. (3)

3 Google one of the pressure groups mentioned in the text. Outline two activities it has recently been involved in. (4)

4 Explain two potential benefits to a retailer of selling only Fairtrade items. (4)

B The Co-op stores are built on a foundation of social responsibility, having developed from the co-operative movement started by the Rochdale Pioneers. In 1992 it became the first UK stockist of Cafe Direct products; in 1999 it made the decision to stock Fairtrade tea and coffee in all its stores; by 2005 it stocked over 100 Fairtrade products. Later that year the company won a prize for corporate social responsibility in the Annual Effectiveness awards. In 2008, the Co-op's 'Fairtrade Fortnight' featured 180 Fairtrade products.

The Co-op stocks Fairtrade products

1 Give two possible reasons for the Co-op making the decision to sell such a large range of Fairtrade products. (2)

2 How might achieving such an award help the Co-op achieve its aims and objectives? (5)

3 Should Tesco follow the Co-op's example? Explain your reasoning. (6)

Practice Questions

Electronics – the downside

From the newest mobile phone and MP3 player to the most innovative laptop, there is no doubting the benefits of technology. But the environmental and safety aspects of an electronic product are often forgotten.

Health hazards

Ted Smith, founder of the Silicon Valley Toxics Coalition (SVTC) warned in October 2008 that poor working conditions in the manufacturing and disposal of electronic equipment pose a danger to health. Those who suffer these consequences are largely 'the poor, female, immigrant, and minority'.

Smith says semiconductor workers in Silicon Valley in California in the USA experience illness rates three times higher than manufacturing workers in other industries. These health hazards are not limited to the USA alone. Due to cheap labour costs and weak health safeguards in the workplace, developing countries such as the Philippines are used for work such as the assembling of computer and other electronic parts.

The main concern here, Smith explained, is that some of the 1000 chemicals used in computer production are toxic. Among these chemicals include:

- lead and cadmium in circuit boards
- lead and barium in monitors
- poly-vinyl chloride (PVC) casings
- mercury switches and flat screens.

'E-waste'

Potential hazards in the electronic industry are not just confined within factories. They extend to the recycling and disposal of products.

As mobile phones have an average lifespan of just 18 months there are as many as 1 billion phones a year being scrapped. The immense quantities of electronic waste (e-waste), make it the fastest growing component of the waste stream. Ted Smith says that much of the e-waste is exported to less developed countries. The USA is said to export 50 to 80 per cent of its e-waste to Asian countries, namely, China, Thailand, Singapore, India and Pakistan. According to environmental groups, some e-waste is shipped as 'working equipment'. But that is just a smokescreen: when it arrives it is treated as e-waste.

Smith says that in any one year around 300 million computers become obsolete. These computers are made up of 4 million pounds of plastic, 1 million pounds of lead, 1.9 million pounds of cadmium, 1.2 million pounds of chromium and 400,000 pounds of mercury. A study conducted by Greenpeace Southeast Asia warned that a host of toxic substances are released into the environment whenever e-waste end up in landfills and dirty recycling operations. This is said to create 'a nightmare of pollution and grave worker and community exposure'.

Questions

(25 marks; 30 minutes)

1   The electronics companies are not operating illegally in the Philippines because the working practices described above are not protected by law. Explain how they arc bchaving uncthically. (7)

2   Creating safe working conditions can lead to a trade-off between ethics and profit.

a What does this mean? (4)

b Explain why managers at a US electronics company might choose ethics before profit when making decisions about factory working conditions. (6)

3   Should the US government ban the export of its e-waste? Outline two reasons for and two reasons against this idea. (8)

Unit 63

Environment

In July 2007 towns in many parts of Britain were under water. In Hull a man died when his trapped foot caused him to drown. Thousands escaped unharmed, but with wrecked houses and wrecked lives. Meanwhile South and Western Australia was entering its sixth year of drought. Many farmers were forced to sell up, with their business plans ruined. Whether or not these incidents were an effect of global warming, there is no doubt that the environment matters to businesses.

How do environmental issues affect business?

Environmental issues can have both short-term and long-term effects on a firm.

In the short term, the environment can be an important stakeholder issue. In the developed world few staff are willing to work in unpleasant or dangerous conditions. Local residents are also stakeholders, and they may have a chance to have their say. For example, in October 2008 Parliament was brought to a stop by protesters from near Stansted, complaining about the planned expansion of the airport. Noise pollution cannot kill, but it can cut property values and make life very unpleasant.

In the longer term, firms need to help to overcome the challenge of global warming.

> 'The devastation sweeping America's southern coast is a "wake-up call" to the world about the dangers of global warming.'
> **Jan Egeland: United Nations Under-Secretary General for Humanitarian Affairs and Emergency Relief Co-ordinator**

The threat of global warming is changing many businesses. The Kyoto Agreement means countries have pledged to reduce their CO_2 emissions. This can only happen if industry can reduce their emissions; but this could damage the economy.

Some British companies are taking steps to cut their carbon emissions. This is partly

Protesters complaining about the planned expansion of Stansted airport brought Parliament to a stop

to help the government meet its international target of CO_2 reduction. Companies also need to be seen to be responsible. This can help when recruiting young, bright staff and can be important to a company's public image. In the first few months of 2008, Tesco, Sainsbury's and Marks & Spencer were each trying to adopt the position as Britain's most environmentally friendly supermarket chain. If one started a scheme to remove plastic shopping bags from checkouts, another would build a wind-powered Green Store.

Far more often, though, UK businesses adopt a route that means not doing anything. They pay for others to act on their behalf. This is done by 'carbon trading'. This is the case with a company that produces toilet paper in Kent. It pays towards a chemical company in China bringing in a new production method that reduces the amount of CFCs it releases into the atmosphere. Then the UK toilet paper company claims that it has reduced its CO_2 emissions.

> 'Global warming is too serious for the world any longer to ignore its danger or split into opposing factions on it.'
> **Tony Blair, British Prime Minister 1997–2007**

Natural energy sources such as coal and gas are being used up and energy companies have to look at alternative fuels for the future. Electricity companies are anticipating growing markets for wind power and for more energy-efficient appliances. The bar chart below shows the big increase in 'alternative energy' supply in Britain between 2003 and 2007. Unfortunately, even in 2007 these natural, renewable sources of clean energy were tiny compared with nuclear power or coal.

Global warming could change other industries, too. Many environmental scientists believe that even if we do reduce emissions the earth will still warm several more degrees in the next few decades. That could cut agricultural harvests, raise sea levels, and bring more extreme weather.

> 'We make the world we live in and shape our own environment.'
> **Orison Swett Marden, founder of Success magazine (1850–1924)**

For businesses, this presents threats – and opportunities. Insurers may face more floods, storms and other disasters. Farmers must

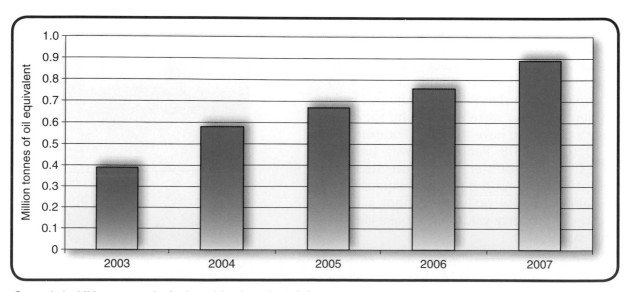

Growth in UK output of wind and hydro electricity

adjust crops to changing climates. In the south of England, wine producers are having more success since their crop is now rarely affected by frost. Some experts believe that the south of England could increase in temperature by five degrees. This would make it more suitable for wine than for wheat or apples.

Resource depletion

All manufacturing requires resources. Plastics, paints and detergents are made from oil, steel requires iron ore and coal, and paper is made from wood. Note the difference. Wood is renewable, in other words, as you chop down a tree you can plant another.

Issue	Effect	Possible business response
Traffic congestion	Heavy traffic may mean customers won't make the trip to the business during certain times of day	The business could open earlier and stay open longer, e.g. Manchester's Trafford Centre is open from 10 a.m. until 10 p.m. It is also working with public transport providers to make it easier to access without a car. More shops operate internet shopping sites so people don't have to travel to stores
Noise pollution	Businesses found guilty of noise pollution receive heavy fines	Manchester Airport has paid for triple glazing for residents who live near the airport. It also has a system for checking noise levels of aircraft taking off. Airlines are fined if they break agreed noise levels
Air pollution	Many businesses pollute the air, e.g. lorries, power stations. The law sets strict limits about how much air pollution companies can emit. Companies that break the law face hefty fines and a poor public image	Following the huge success of the Toyota Prius, all the main car producers are looking at greener fuels – especially electricity. General Motors, Ford and Volkswagen all hope to catch Toyota up by 2010
Water pollution	Companies that pollute water such as rivers and streams are fined. This costs the company both in lost profits and damages their image. It can kill fish and other river dwellers and if it enters our drinking water can cause illness and death	Many businesses have reduced the use of chemicals. Organic farming, i.e. without the use of chemical pesticides or fertilisers, has increased. Waste chemicals from industry have to be disposed of properly
Recycling	The European Directive on waste means that the UK (and all other EU countries) must recover 60 per cent of all packaging waste by 31 December 2008. Composting and recycling are encouraged; landfill is not	More offices need to use recycling facilities for printer cartridges and paper and cut down on power usage by turning off lights, etc. Factories need to find ways to recycle waste materials safely

The world need never run out of trees→wood→paper.

Every gallon of petrol used today is irreplaceable

However, oil, iron ore and coal are very different. The oil used today has been formed underground over the last 10–160 million years. So every gallon of petrol used today is, in effect, irreplaceable. Oil is a youngster compared with coal, which was formed 300 million years ago! Minerals such as iron ore (or copper or lead) are even more irreplaceable, as the earth cannot remake them.

The point is, then, that the 'depletion' (using up) of certain resources is a once-only exercise. If we run out of oil or copper, that's that. For businesses that depend on these items, careful use is essential. A plumber should never want old copper pipe to end up in landfill, because it could and should be recycled. That would prevent depletion of the limited amounts of new copper in the world. The reality, though, is that most people today ignore the risks of depletion that might not cause a serious problem for 10, 20 or 100 years.

Conclusion

Companies that launch low-emission cars, use clean coal-burning technology, or find cheap ways to reduce emissions, will take over from those that don't move as quickly. Every business should always be trying to be as efficient as possible. So recycling waste should be normal practice, as should making sure that energy in the workplace is used as efficiently as possible.

Exercises

(20 marks; 25 minutes)

1   Polluting the environment doesn't just cost the earth – it can also hit your pocket. That's something Anglian Water knows to its cost. In February 2008 it was fined £190,000 after sludge from one of its sewage plants got into a river. It's one of the largest ever fines against a company.

   Explain why Anglian Water received such a high fine. (3)

2   This case was brought about by The Environment Agency, a government body that checks that firms stick to environmental laws. Why do you think it is necessary to have this agency? Explain your answer. (5)

3   Outline how two different UK businesses might benefit from warmer temperatures in Britain. (6)

4   Explain how your school can change to become more environmentally friendly. (6)

Practice Questions

Your Christmas dinner probably travelled 30,000 miles before ending up on your plate.

Your Christmas dinner may have circumnavigated the globe

A European turkey, African vegetables, Australian wine and American cranberry sauce will have notched up enough miles to circumnavigate the globe. Much of this produce could be easily acquired locally.

'There's simply no need to eat mangetout from Zimbabwe,' said Caroline Lucas, MEP for the Green Party. Ms Lucas, a member of the European Parliament's International Trade Committee and an MEP for southeast England, said thoughtless sourcing of produce was contributing significantly to the aviation industry's greenhouse gas emissions and the extension of 'monoculture' farming. She said: 'Ingredients for a traditional Christmas Dinner are in season in the UK right now – that's why they're traditionally eaten at Christmas.'

Author of a European Parliament report called *Stopping the Great Food Swap*, she added: 'African farmers are paying a high social and environmental price for switching traditional production to inappropriate cash crops geared for western markets, but seeing few of the financial benefits. By eating locally grown produce we can enjoy fresher, tastier food, support our local economies – and cut out some of the greenhouse gas emissions produced by the aviation industry as it flies all these vegetables around the world.'

The Green cost of Christmas:

- 200,000 trees are felled to supply 1.7 billion Christmas cards sent in the UK

- 40,000 trees are used to make 8000 tonnes of wrapping paper used for presents

- Nearly 6 million Christmas trees end up in landfill sites every January

Nearly 6 million Christmas trees end up in landfill sites every January

- The UK throws out 3 million tonnes of extra waste over Christmas.

Questions

(25 marks; 25 minutes)

1 Some people argue that by buying our food from other countries we are helping the developing world, while others argue we should eat produce in season from the UK to reduce CO_2 from air traffic. Discuss whether we should only buy seasonal produce from the UK. (9)

2 In 2008, the UK Chancellor planned to increase taxes on airline travel in an attempt to offset the cost to the environment. Discuss the likely affects on:

a the airlines (4)

b supermarkets (4)

c other forms of transport (4)

d a small hotel in the Lake District. (4)

Unit 64

Economic issues affecting trade

If you worked in a factory in the UK, how much do you think you would be paid? Around £8 an hour? It would depend upon the minimum wage, your skills, experience and what hourly rate competitors were offering you. Under EU law you would be entitled to regular breaks and a minimum of ten hours between shifts, and annual holidays. A recent survey by the government found the median weekly wage in the UK to be £447.

However, pay rates vary enormously in Europe and around the world.

Country	Median weekly pay (£)
Brazil	£58
Bulgaria	£25
China	£23
Germany	£392
India	£15
Latvia	£46
Slovakia	£76

Source: www.fedee.com

It is not too surprising, then, that many manufacturers in Britain are struggling to compete with foreign competitors. Not only do UK manufacturers have higher wage bills, but land costs are greater, as are transportation costs. Petrol prices are also much lower in other countries.

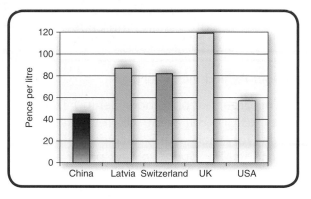

Price of unleaded petrol 2008

It is little wonder that more and more manufacturers are relocating to Eastern Europe and Asia. They are taking advantage of cheaper wages and lower land costs in an attempt to reduce unit costs and remain competitive.

Good business sense or exploitation?

In January 2008 two workers were beaten, one to death, by the security guards at a Bangladeshi clothing factory. The factory accused the workers of loitering with intent to rob the factory because they were washing themselves before leaving. In September 2008 a report from the pressure group Labour Behind the Label concluded that UK fashion brands were doing little to improve the lives of their overseas workers. Many in Bangladesh earn well below the minimum wage of $22 a month (about 20p an hour).

The policy director at the charity War on Want said that: 'The grim reality for garment workers is that no British retailers will yet ensure them a living wage. We cannot rely on companies to clean up their own act.'

Labour Behind the Label logo

The organisation Labour Behind The Label gives just 10 out of 30 UK retailers modest credit for their work, including Gap and Monsoon. *The Guardian* newspaper said that 'the report criticises other traders, including Levi Strauss, Burberry, French Connection and Matalan, for having done "no work to speak of" on living wages.' The report says that no brand surveyed is paying its workers a living wage, even though some are members of the Ethical Trading Initiative.

War on Want logo

The International Textile, Garment and Leather Workers' Federation (a coalition representing trade unions) is clear that the problems need to be solved by union membership. This is largely blocked by the employers and the Bangladesh government. The representative of the British clothing industry, John Wilson, is more comfortable with the situation: 'Clearly the level of wages seems very low to people in this country,' he has said. 'But if it is the minimum wage that is being paid, which I understand is about £20 a month in Bangladesh . . . as long as the audit is taking place at the factories, as long as all of the codes are being followed by all the people concerned – all of which I'm sure is happening in all of these cases – then at the end of the day, these are the circumstances in which these people are operating.'

Talking Point

Should the UK government prevent UK shops from getting clothes made in these circumstances?

Import protection

Many countries try to protect home manufacturers by imposing import **quotas**. These limit the number of imported goods allowed into the country. This is an attempt by the government to protect home industry and employment. However, this reduces competition and gives consumers less choice. It also means the home producers do not have the same incentive to try to reduce costs or improve their products.

> 'The first lesson of economics is scarcity: there is never enough of anything to satisfy all those who want it.'
> **Thomas Sowell, US economist, political writer and commentator**

Farmers in the Isle of Man have had the advantage of import protection and will do so until 2011. The island can currently control meat imports because it is allowed to under special European Commission rules. This gives Manx farmers a much easier life than English farmers, who have to compete with French and other producers. At present, residents on the Isle of Man have a restricted choice of meat. However, the farmers have only until 2011 to prepare for increased competition when the protection stops.

Export subsidy

The EU doesn't just restrict the number of imported goods into the UK but subsidises home producers to export their products. Many EU farmers receive a **subsidy** for their crops, which enables them to compete on price across the EU and around the world.

The EU spends €1.7 billion a year supporting sugar prices. Five million tonnes of European sugar is exported to world markets every year. But under mounting pressure from the World Trade Commission, the EU is promising to reduce export subsidies and prices. This is bad news for sugar farmers who will find that without the EU subsidy they receive much less for their crops and will have to find ways of reducing costs, increasing production or switching to an alternative crop.

Revision Essentials

Economist – someone who studies economics and writes about economic policy.

Scarcity – we have a limited availability of resources so cannot satisfy all of our needs and wants.

Quota – an import quota limits numbers of imports from foreign countries to protect home producers.

Subsidy – paid by the government to home producers to help keep prices competitive compared with foreign imports.

Exercises

(20 marks; 25 minutes)

Read the unit, then ask yourself:

1   Many high street banks have relocated their call centres to India to take advantage of lower wage costs. The NatWest bank however, has kept its centre in the UK. Outline two ways in which NatWest could use this situation to its advantage. (4)

2   Why do you think the World Trade Organisation objects to EU subsidies on farming? (4)

3   Outline two advantages to customers if the EU were to stop import quotas. (4)

4   Outline two advantages to retailers if the EU were to stop import quotas. (4)

5   Outline two disadvantages to UK manufacturers if the EU were to stop import quotas. (4)

Practice Questions

In 2005, more than 75 million garments including jumpers, t-shirts, blouses and bras were held up in European ports. EU officials would not allow them in because China had beaten its quota on clothing imports set by the EU.

Shops throughout Europe warned of stock shortages and higher prices if quotas remained in place. Between 2005 and 2007 Chinese manufacturers used their initiative to get garments out of China. The most popular route was through Hong Kong, which remained quota free.

One clothing manufacturer employed workers in mainland China to cut out shirts, sew the hems, buttons or zips and then send the part-finished goods to Hong Kong. In Hong Kong, workers sewed four seams, connecting all the pieces together before sending it back to China for finishing, washing, ironing and packing. Producing a shirt this way cost between 35 and 40 per cent more than if it was made in China alone.

Consumers had to pay more for some of the best-travelled shirts in the world. A

Made in Hong Kong logo

single garment might travel up to six times across the border before finally being shipped to the USA or Europe. Western customers happily pay more for a shirt 'Made in Hong Kong' than one 'Made in China'.

The process was complicated, time consuming and costly, but remained popular until the quota system was dropped on 1st January 2008. They were abolished under the rules of the World Trade Organisation. This was a bonus for UK customers, able to buy more, cheaper clothes from China. But it was a problem for Italy, with its large number of clothing workers. Jobs have inevitably been lost.

(Source: adapted from BBC News)

Questions

(20 marks; 25 minutes)

1 Explain why the quota system might lead to shops running out of stock. (2)

2 Why do you think British consumers perceive a shirt that is 'made in Hong Kong' to be of better quality than one 'made in China'? (4)

3 The EU uses import quotas to protect EU manufacturers from the market being flooded by cheap imports. Explain how import quotas do this. (4)

4 What evidence is there in the text that import quotas are not working? (4)

5 Should the EU continue with import quotas? Discuss whether import quotas are a good or bad thing and give a recommendation. (6)

The government and the EU

In October 2008 Credit Action announced statistics that the average UK household has credit card and personal loan debts of £9500, with most adults having four credit cards. The average **interest rate** for credit card purchases is 17.54 per cent.

More worryingly, 18,900 families lost their homes when lenders repossessed them during the first half of 2008. This was a 48 per cent increase on 2007, and before the 2008 'credit crunch' took a real grip.

The Citizens Advice Bureau stated that its helpers saw over a million people about their debt problems. On average, its clients owed £13,000 and it would take them 77 years to pay back the debt in full.

If you needed £350 to pay for a new central heating boiler but had been refused a loan by the bank, where would you go? Many people in the UK do not have bank accounts or savings, they have no credit rating and do not own their home. One company which will lend to these people is the doorstep lending company Provident Financial, which charges customers 177 per cent interest, making that £350 loan very expensive (you do the maths). While this rate of interest may seem astronomical, it is legal. Some doorstep lenders charge as much as 800 per cent (borrow £350 today, repay £3150 in a year's time!).

The collapse of Farepak in October 2006 saw more than 100,000 people lose a total of £40 million in Christmas savings. This led to a government review of the collapse and many retailers stepped in to help the families. But the collapse of Farepak was an opportunity for doorstep lenders, some of whom wrote to Farepak customers offering them loans. This caused MPs to demand stricter regulation of the financial industry, including the setting of an interest rate ceiling. This would mean the government would be able to set maximum interest rates. If this regulation was to go ahead, companies like Provident Financial would find their profits badly affected.

This is just one example of how business in the UK is affected by laws. These can be set in the UK or in Europe.

> 'If you have ten thousand regulations, you lose respect for the law.'
> **Winston Churchill**

Why have regulations on business?

There are many laws that govern the way a business behaves. If you and your friends

The average UK household has credit card and personal loan debts of £9500

went to a restaurant for lunch and one of your friends died as a result of food poisoning from their meal, you would expect the restaurant to be prosecuted. But if there were no regulations then standards in food hygiene would not have to be followed.

If you opened a hairdressers 300 yards from another salon you would expect them to compete with you for business, perhaps by starting a loyalty scheme or having some promotional offers. You would not, however, expect them to physically stop clients from visiting your salon, nor would you expect them to stop suppliers from dealing with you. Competition law ensures that competitive practices are fair.

When businesses recruit staff they are not allowed to discriminate on the grounds of gender, age, race, religion or disability.

Competition law ensures that competition is fair

The minimum wage

> 'The precepts of the law are these: to live honestly, to injure no one, and to give every man his due.'
> **Justinian I, Byzantine emperor (483–565)**

What is it?	Benefits to business	Drawbacks
The minimum wage was introduced in the UK in 1999 and guarantees an hourly rate of pay for workers. From October 2008 the minimum wage was £5.73 for adults over 21, while 18–21-year-olds got £4.77 per hour. There are now campaigns for a higher minimum wage to be set for workers in London due to the higher costs of living in the capital	It encourages employers to train and develop staff by developing skills instead of relying on cheap labour. Higher pay reduces staff turnover, which costs employers millions of pounds a year in recruitment and training expenses. Better-paid workers spend their money locally, e.g. buying a sandwich on the way to work and a newspaper on the way home, thereby helping the local economy	Firms which do not pay their workers the minimum would be fined up to £5000. There were some concerns that small firms would not be able to afford to pay their workers the minimum and this would force them to make staff redundant

Health and safety regulation

What is it?	Benefits	Drawbacks
Regulations that exist to protect both the employees and the customers of a business. Some of the obvious things the law covers include providing employees with adequate heating and lighting, ensuring the workplace is ventilated and providing toilets and washing facilities	Many accidents in the workplace can be avoided. This would increase productivity, lower labour turnover (staff will want to stay in an environment where they feel safe and valued) and help the firm gain a good reputation. It will reduce the costs associated with work-related injuries. If the firm fails to follow these regulations it will be prosecuted	Often expensive to implement (special equipment, specialist staff). *Risk assessments* can be time consuming to carry out. Some staff resent the changes in working practices, as they see nothing wrong with how they have always carried out a job

Maternity and paternity rights

To reduce problems of child poverty, the law ensures that parents get financial help when taking time off after having a baby. Women are allowed up to 39 weeks 'maternity leave'. For the first 6 weeks their employer has to pay 90% of the mother's usual earnings. After that, a sum of about £125 a week is paid.

Another key maternity right is that the mother is entitled to get her job back when she returns to work.

For fathers, there are 'paternity rights'. They allow a father to take two weeks paid leave at the time the baby is born. In addition the father can take unpaid leave.

In both these cases, parliament has passed laws to help ordinary people do what's best for their children and families. Some companies complain about the cost and disruption caused by workers who use these rights.

Well-run businesses are more likely to see this help to parents as a thoroughly good thing.

What happens when things go wrong?

A head teacher from Derby was prosecuted for failing to alert his staff that the school had an asbestos problem. The windows were being replaced when the asbestos was discovered and this led to the school becoming contaminated. Asbestos has caused lung problems and cancer, so its discovery should have meant the school was closed.

In August 2007 a Scottish demolition firm was fined £50,000 after one of its workers was crushed to death. A section of the building being demolished fell without warning on excavator driver Gideon Irvine. The company pleaded guilty to breaches of the Health and Safety Act 1974. A Health and Safety inspector said: 'This accident was entirely foreseeable. The demolition company had not carried out a survey . . . in order to identify structural hazards to prevent premature collapse.'

It was not the company's first time in court that month. On 2 August 2007 Central Demolition Ltd was found guilty of causing river pollution. It had wrongly decided that a diesel storage tank was empty after 'tapping' the side of it. The company was fined £7500.

Clearly, a business might decide that the occasional fine is a price worth paying, as long as customers keep giving it more contracts. It is to be hoped that the managers would realise that laws are rightfully there to protect us. Either that, or the penalties must be made tougher.

Taxation

Government decisions about **tax** affect all businesses.

Tax	Explanation	Impact on a business
Corporation tax	A business pays this on its profits (usually around 30 per cent of the firm's profits)	This is deducted from net profit, meaning shareholders will get a lower dividend and the firm will have less to reinvest in the business
VAT (value added tax)	This has to be paid on goods and services at 17.5 per cent. Some items such as children's clothes are exempt	An increase in VAT would affect sales of some items like TVs or PCs
Income tax	A tax paid by employees on their earnings	An increase could lead to people having less money to spend on luxury items like holidays. A decrease in income tax would mean that people could afford more luxuries like holidays or a conservatory

Revision Essentials

Interest rate – the charge for borrowing money and the reward for saving. High interest rates mean consumers will have less disposable income because their mortgages and car loans etc. will cost them more so they will have less to spend on other goods and services.

Discrimination – where one person/group of people is unfairly treated. People can be discriminated against because of their gender, age, religion, race, disability, weight, height, sexual orientation, etc.

Risk assessment – a process of identifying potential risks and steps that will be taken to minimise them. For example, on a school trip a possible risk could be a coach crash. Schools will attempt to minimise the risk by using a reputable coach company and ensuring all students wear seat belts.

Tax – a financial charge set by the government. Taxes are used to finance public services such as schools.

Exercises

(20 marks; 25 minutes)

1   Have you broken the law? In each case you must decide whether a law has been broken and explain your decision.

  a   You run a trendy hairdressers in Covent Garden and are interviewing for a stylist. One candidate is an orthodox Jew who wears unusual clothes and has the typical hairstyle of his community. He has five years' experience at Vidal Sassoon but you worry he is not projecting the right image for your salon. Instead you give the job to a girl who has just finished college. (3)

  b   A light bulb needs replacing in the coffee shop where you work. It is five minutes until opening time and while your manager has said that you must use a step ladder to replace the bulb, you climb on to a table instead so the job is quicker. (3)

  c   John is a mechanic in your garage. After a holiday he returns to work dressed in women's clothing and asks everyone to call him Christine. He wants to use the ladies' toilet but your female staff object and you insist he continues to use the men's toilet. (3)

  d   You are employing a new admin assistant who is Polish. As she is not British you pay her less than the minimum wage. It applies only to British people, doesn't it? (3)

2   You run a building company. How will an increase in income tax affect your sales? (2)

3   A leisure centre in Widnes had to be closed after it was found to have the bacteria that cause Legionnaires' disease in its water system. In this case no one contracted the disease. Thanks to health and safety guidelines, regular checks at the leisure centre had identified the bacteria and swift action by the council protected the public and the workforce. How did health and safety regulation prevent a crisis at this leisure centre? (3)

4   If the minimum wage is increased to £7, how is this likely to affect a small coffee shop? (3)

Practice Questions

Andrea Winders and Tina Dutton from Warrington came up with a unique business idea back in 2005. Concerned with safety and the rising numbers of complaints from young women who did not feel safe travelling home alone after a night out, they saw a gap in the market for a taxi service that was available only for women – with only women drivers. However, due to the rules and regulations surrounding the taxi industry, the women soon realised they would be unable to go ahead with their original plan.

Pink Ladies taxi service

Pink Ladies, which has a women-only policy on drivers and passengers, is run on a members' only basis to avoid sex discrimination laws. Women who would like to use the service have to first become members (at a cost of £1). Because the cars (pink Renault Kangoos with luxury pink leather interiors) do not carry cash, members pay by using their account cards. They can top these up through the website or by telephoning head office. This means if a woman's handbag is stolen she can still get home safely. All drivers are trained in first aid and self-defence.

The service has been hugely popular and is already franchised in Carlisle and St Helens, with plans to open a further 30 franchises. But the expansion plans have been halted due to a new government road safety law, which means the company cannot operate its service without a licence. The Pink Ladies claim they do not need the licence because they are a members-only service, not a taxi firm. Becoming a taxi firm would mean it would have to employ male drivers under sex discrimination law.

Tina and Andrea are determined they will not be beaten and are taking their fight to Parliament.

> *'Bad laws were made to be broken.'*
> **Doctor Who**

Questions

(20 marks; 25 minutes)

1 Explain how Andrea and Tina could be breaking the law. (4)

2 Why may the government be right to be concerned about the safety of their service? (4)

3 Warrington taxi firms have welcomed the new legislation. How would they benefit from the forced closure of the Pink Ladies service? (4)

4 Should the service be allowed to continue or should the Pink Ladies be closed down? Justify your decision. (8)

Exam-style Questions

DON'T RUSH; check answers carefully

1a. Which of these factors is a long-term environmental worry? (1)

a) Resource depletion

b) Noise pollution

c) Traffic congestion

d) Air pollution

1b. i. What is meant by 'global warming'? (1)

ii. Explain how business activity might affect global warming. (3)

1c. Explain why a business might take care to avoid creating pollution. (3)

2a. Why may the Coop Bank have decided not to deal with companies such as manufacturers of cigarettes and weapons? Choose one reason. (1)

a) To concentrate on other types of customer

b) To please the shareholders of the business

c) Because of ethical concerns

d) Because the Coop Bank sees other customers as more profitable

2b. i. Explain the meaning of the phrase 'ethics in business'. (3)

ii. Why may big firms with many shareholders find it hard to act ethically? (3)

2c. Explain why a firm producing fur coats might try to avoid being targeted by pressure groups. (3)

3a. Which one of these factors is *not* likely to help a poor country become richer? (1)

a) Investment in water projects to help irrigate the land

b) Improving the education system so that more people learn to read

c) Providing aid to help build up the country's military strength

d) Making it quicker and easier for people to start businesses

3b. i. Outline the meaning of the term 'income distribution'?   (2)

    ii. Explain one problem a country might have if there is an extreme wealth gap between the rich and poor.   (3)

3c. Explain one possible reason the people of some developing countries have average incomes of as low as $2 a week.   (4)

4a. Which is the correct meaning of the term 'export subsidy'?   (1)

a)   A way for a government to raise taxes from its successful exporters

b)   A way for a government to give an unfair advantage to its exporters

c)   A way for a business to encourage foreign firms to buy its products

d)   A way for a business to prevent imported goods from being too competitive

4b. i. What is meant by the term 'import protection'.   (1)

    ii. Outline two types of import protection measures that a government can use.   (4)

4c. Examine why a government might choose to use import protection measures during a recession.   (6)

Index

Note: Page numbers in **bold** refer to keyword definitions.